K

Eric Rofes

Reviving the Tribe: Regenerating Gay Men's Sexuality and Culture in the Ongoing Epidemic

Pre-publication
REVIEWS,
COMMENTARIES,
EVALUATIONS . . .

"**T**his clear-headed and brave book is the most important book yet written about the ongoing AIDS epidemic. With sharp insight and riveting honesty, Rofes suggests new paradigms for AIDS activism in the critical areas of education, prevention, and community survival."

Urvashi Vaid
Author, *Virtual Equality: The Mainstreaming of Gay Liberation*

More pre-publication
REVIEWS, COMMENTARIES, EVALUATIONS . . .

"**E**ric Rofes brings a personal and social perspective to the important question of how we can live authentically in an enduring epidemic. His insights and clarifications should be considered by all gay men, and particularly those who feel that they are 'coping well' and their human features are secure."

Walt Odets, PhD
Clinical Psychologist,
Berkeley, California

"**R**ofes brings his powerful intellect and twenty years of grassroots activism to bear on the cutting edge issues of our time: contentious sexual politics, our revolving struggle between hope and despair, and the frayed social fabric of epidemic life. Riveting, passionate, and unorthodox, *Reviving the Tribe* is a brilliant and courageous work that will challenge readers and provoke intense thought, emotion, and discussion. The book provides an eloquent and critically needed voice for the regeneration of gay male identity and culture."

Benjamin Schatz, JD
Executive Director,
Gay and Lesbian Medical Association

"**R**equired reading for policymakers searching for fresh vision for the new millennium. *Reviving the Tribe* asks the right questions about why so-called educated gay men continue to become infected with HIV. We could debate Rofes' ambitious plan of action for years, but we take great risk if we ignore his keen observations and original insights."

Harvey J. Makadon, MD
Harvard Medical School

"**A**s *Tales of the City* was to the 70s and *And the Band Played On* was to the 80s, so *Reviving the Tribe* will be to the 90s: a lens through which we fearlessly scrutinize our communal culture, come to a new understanding of our generation, reorder our priorities, and redirect our activism. Through searching self-examination and a searing critique of sex politics, Rofes creates a rich portrait of contemporary urban gay lives and a manifesto for community-building which should be universally embraced."

Reverend Jim Mitulski
Pastor, MCC San Francisco

"**I**n this frank and caring book, Rofes focuses directly on gay men–on our needs, hopes, fears, and sexual practices during the long trauma of the AIDS epidemic. He writes with a true appreciation of gay men's cultures and communities and with a strong commitment to democratic principle."

Henry Abelove
Professor of English,
Wesleyan University

"**E**ric Rofes' *Reviving the Tribe* is clearly the most significant gay reflection on sexuality during the decade of AIDS/HIV. I would make *Reviving the Tribe* required reading for all those doing HIV preventive education to gay male communities. The most provocative and thus insightful contribution is Eric's discussion of an unspoken topic with gay males: What does it mean to be HIV-negative at a time when lovers and friends seroconvert and die from the ravages of HIV? We will continue to see the seroconversion of gay men until we probe the depths of this question and understand the experience of the grief and loss of gay men. Rofes has taken seriously the fact that gay men are survivors comparable to Holocaust and Hiroshima survivors. I lost my brother and my long-time companion of sixteen years on the same day. The numbness and grief was so intense that I was most at risk of seroconversion. I found Eric's path to sexual recovery and healing a credible means to healthy grieving and recovery of a sexuality. It paralleled my own healing and continued work as an AIDS activist."

Dr. Robert Goss
Author, *Jesus ACTED UP;*
Associate Professor,
Comparative Religion,
Webster University

Harrington Park Press
An Imprint of The Haworth Press, Inc.

NOTES FOR PROFESSIONAL LIBRARIANS AND LIBRARY USERS

This is an original book title published by Harrington Park Press, an imprint of The Haworth Press, Inc. Unless otherwise noted in specific chapters with attribution, materials in this book have not been previously published elsewhere in any format or language.

CONSERVATION AND PRESERVATION NOTES

All books published by The Haworth Press, Inc. and its imprints are printed on certified ph neutral, acid free book grade paper. This paper meets the minimum requirements of American National Standard for Information Sciences–Permanence of Paper for Printed Material, ANSI Z39.48-1984.

Reviving the Tribe
Regenerating Gay Men's Sexuality and Culture in the Ongoing Epidemic

HAWORTH Gay & Lesbian Studies
John P. De Cecco, PhD
Editor in Chief

New, Recent, and Forthcoming Titles:

Perverts by Official Order: The Campaign Against Homosexuals by the United States Navy by Lawrence R. Murphy

Bad Boys and Tough Tattoos: A Social History of the Tattoo with Gangs, Sailors, and Street-Corner Punks by Samuel M. Steward

Growing Up Gay in the South: Race, Gender, and Journeys of the Spirit by James T. Sears

Homosexuality and Sexuality: Dialogues of the Sexual Revolution, Volume I by Lawrence D. Mass

Homosexuality as Behavior and Identity: Dialogues of the Sexual Revolution, Volume II by Lawrence D. Mass

Sexuality and Eroticism Among Males in Moslem Societies edited by Arno Schmitt and Jehoeda Sofer

Understanding the Male Hustler by Samuel M. Steward

Men Who Beat the Men Who Love Them: Battered Gay Men and Domestic Violence by David Island and Patrick Letellier

The Golden Boy by James Melson

The Second Plague of Europe: AIDS Prevention and Sexual Transmission Among Men in Western Europe by Michael Pollak

Barrack Buddies and Soldier Lovers: Dialogues with Gay Young Men in the U.S. Military by Steven Zeeland

Outing: Shattering the Conspiracy of Silence by Warren Johansson and William A. Percy

The Bisexual Option, Second Edition by Fritz Klein

And the Flag Was Still There: Straight People, Gay People, and Sexuality in the U.S. Military by Lois Shawver

One-Handed Histories: The Eroto-Politics of Gay Male Video Pornography by John R. Burger

Sailors and Sexual Identity: Crossing the Line Between "Straight" and "Gay" in the U.S. Navy by Steven Zeeland

The Gay Male's Odyssey in the Corporate World: From Disempowerment to Empowerment by Gerald V. Miller

Bisexual Politics: Theories, Queries, and Visions edited by Naomi Tucker

Gay and Gray: The Older Homosexual Man, Second Edition by Raymond M. Berger

Reviving the Tribe: Regenerating Gay Men's Sexuality and Culture in the Ongoing Epidemic by Eric Rofes

Reviving the Tribe
Regenerating Gay Men's Sexuality and Culture in the Ongoing Epidemic

Eric Rofes

Harrington Park Press
An Imprint of The Haworth Press, Inc.
New York • London

Harrington Park Press, an imprint of The Haworth Press, Inc., 10 Alice Street, Binghamton, NY 13904-1580

The Haworth Press, Inc., 10 Alice Street, Binghamton, NY 13904-1580

Cover photo © Rink Foto. Used with permission.

Library of Congress Cataloging-in-Publication Data

Rofes, Eric E., 1954-

Reviving the tribe : regenerating gay men's sexuality and culture in the ongoing epidemic / Eric Rofes.
    p.   cm.
Includes bibliographical references and index.
ISBN 1-56023-876-3 (alk. paper).
    1. Gay men–United States–Sexual behavior. 2. Gay men–Mental health–United States. 3. AIDS (Disease)–United States. I. Title.
HQ76.2.U5R63 1995
306.76'62–dc20   95-35017
                                                                                                            CIP

FOR CRISPIN

ABOUT THE AUTHOR

Eric Rofes is a doctoral student in Social and Cultural Studies at the University of California Berkeley's Graduate School of Education. A longtime activist, he is the founder of the Boston Lesbian and Gay Political Alliance and served as Executive Director of the Los Angeles Gay and Lesbian Community Services Center and San Francisco's Shanti Project. He was part of the *Gay Community News* collective and has been the author and editor of seven books.

CONTENTS

Quotes introducing individual chapters originate from the following sources:

Reinaldo Arena, *Before Night Falls* (New York: Viking, 1993), translated by Dolores, M. Koch, p. 258.

Dori Laub, "Truth and Testimony: The Process and the Struggle," *American Imago* 48(1):80-81 (Spring 1991).

Robert De Andreis, "Restoring a Subculture of Desire," *San Francisco Sentinel* (February 16, 1994).

Pat Califia, "Feminism and Sadomasochism," *Heresies #12: Sex Issue* 3(4), 1981, p. 33.

Bill T. Jones, quoted at AIDS Project Los Angeles' Commitment to Live VII, January 27, 1994. See Karen Ocamb, "APLA's 'Commitment to Live' Entertains as it Raises AIDS $$$," *Bay Area Reporter*, February 17, 1994, 24.

Albert Camus, from "Summer," in *Lyrical and Critical Essays* (New York: Alfred A. Knopf, 1969), translated by Ellen Conroy Kennedy; Philip Thody (Ed.), 169.

The author gratefully acknowledges permission to reprint the following material:

Dwight Okita, "Where the Boys Were," from *Crossing with the Light* (Chicago: Tia Chucha Press, 1992), 48. Used by permission of author.

Audre Lorde, "Uses of the Erotic: The Erotic as Power," from *Sister Outsider,* copyright ©1984 by Audre Lorde, The Crossing Press, Freedom, CA.

Excerpts from the introduction of *Hot Living: Erotic Stories about Safer Sex,* edited by John Preston, copyright ©1985 by John Preston. Used by permission of Alyson Publications, Inc., Boston.

From *Lying: Moral Choice in Public and Private Life* by Sissela Bok. Copyright ©1978 by Sisella Bok. Reprinted by permission of Pantheon Books, a division of Random House, Inc.

Amy Tan, *The Joy Luck Club* (New York: Putnam, 1989). Reprinted by permission of G. P. Putnam's Sons from *The Joy Luck Club* by Amy Tan. Copyright ©1989 by Amy Tan.

Excerpts as submitted from *Death in Life: The Survivors of Hiroshima* by Robert J. Lifton. Copyright ©1967 by Robert J. Lifton. Updated edition

Acknowledgments

Friends and colleagues assisted me in many ways with the creation of this book. Walt Odets, Tom Moon, Ben Schatz, Will I. Johnston, and Jonathan Silin provided a foundation of collegial support as well as critical feedback at various presentations of portions of this work during the past three years. Walt served as a generous mentor to me by sharing his pioneering thinking about issues facing HIV-negative gay men. Tom provided consistent personal support and insightful critiques, and Ben urged my writing forward during dry spells. I am grateful for a particularly detailed reading of the manuscript that Will offered. For years Jonathan has gently prodded me to move into new and challenging bodies of discourse; this book represents an initial and small step in directions influenced by postmodern and feminist theory.

A number of people read sections or drafts of the manuscript and provided helpful suggestions. I especially want to thank Will Seng, Sara Miles, Harvey Makadon, Richard Burns, Cliff White, David Nimmons, Jim Mitulski, Bob Ostertag, Ron Stall, Frank Browning, Joe Kramer, and Keith Griffith. Paul Zak provided detailed criticism of portions of the text and influenced my understanding of mental health issues. Barbara Englis, Nancy Drooker, Andrea Canaan, Fran Reich, Susan Hurwit, and Margo Okazawa-Rey contributed to my understanding of psychological issues and trauma recovery through conversation and/or criticism of specific manuscript sections. I credit Betsy Smith with the initial insights which linked my free-ranging thinking about gay men's emotional experiences of the epidemic with the literature on trauma.

My thinking about sex has evolved in part through discussions with Amber Hollibaugh, Frank Kenealy, Jeff Morey, Jane Rosett, Amy Hoffman, Roberta Stone, Martin McCombs and Ivo Dominguez, Jr. I appreciate feedback I received on my thinking in the sexuality section of the book from various individuals after presentations at the National Lesbian and Gay Health Conference (1993 and 1995), the AAPHR Prevention Summit (1994), the National Gay and Lesbian Task Force's Creating Change Conference (1993, 1994), USC's Queer Frontiers Conference (1995), and the American Educational Research Association Annual Meeting (1995). I am particularly grateful to the New York Lesbian and Gay Community Service Center and Boston's Fenway Community Health Center for organizing public forums at which I could share my work on gay men's sexuality.

The San Francisco Sex/Politics Study Group has had a powerful influence on my thinking about queer issues over the past two years. I thank those who have participated in various stages of the group, including Will Seng, Martha Baer, Larry Rinder, Mimi McGurl, Linnea Due, David Conner, Robin Stevens, Gayle Rubin, Jewelle Gomez, Lisa Hall, Matt Wray, and Allan Bérubé. Colleagues at U.C. Berkeley's School of Education's Social and Cultural Studies program have contributed to my thinking, particularly concerning democratic education and popular culture. Lawrence Cohen's class "Sexuality, Culture, and Colonialism" and Gayle Rubin's class, "From Perversity to Diversity: Social Science Models for Sexual Variety" have influenced my thinking about sexual meanings.

Informal discussions with others altered my thinking about the issues of this book and I am grateful to Tim Teeter, Dana Van Gorder, Kevin Cathcart, Kate Clinton, Robert Bray, Mark Cloutier, Dan Wohlfeiler, Torie Osborn, Jeff Perotti, Alix Sabin, Tom Huth, Diane Sabin, Rose Walton, Marj Sherwin, Bob Hawkins, Tim McFeeley, Victor D'Lugin, George Bellinger, Robert Nankin, Colin Robinson, Melinda Paras, Dennis Nix, Larry Bye, Daniel Brooks, Stuart Fleming, Mark Sponseller, Joe Brewer, Mark Behar, Ken Mayer, Jay Paul, Marj Plumb, David Tuller, Tina Valinsky, Shirley Craig, Vivian Jackson, Janet Ferone, and Sarah Strong. Tom Hehir and Jim Rann are friends who shared with me key turning points discussed in this book.

Daniel Warner's encouragement and commitment to community regeneration provided the impetus to begin this project before his death. Urvashi Vaid was a fellow member of a two-person long-distance support group which guided me through book-writing mood swings. The intellectual exchange and activist fellowship offered by

Suzanne Pharr provided a framework for understanding linkages between sex, mental health, and politics.

I am grateful to my agent, Victoria Sanders, for handling the placement of this book and for Bill Palmer and his many coworkers at The Haworth Press for all their suggestions, support, and enthusiasm for this project.

I greatly appreciate those who provided emotional support for me during the difficult time recounted in the first section of this book. Finally, I thank my own tribe–the Provincetown summer encampment crew–my parents, and Crispin.

Eric Rofes
San Francisco

Introduction: Life Interrupted

People were unprepared for the atomic bomb on many psychological dimensions: the immediate relaxation induced by the all-clear signal, the feeling of being in some way specially protected, the general sense of invulnerability which all people in some measure possess even (or especially) in the face of danger, and the *total inability to conceive of the unprecedented dimensions of the weapon about to strike them.* As one man put it: "We thought something would happen, but we never imagined anything like the atomic bomb."

> –Robert J. Lifton,
> *Death in Life:*
> *Survivors of Hiroshima*

At first I was afraid, I was petrified.

> –Gloria Gaynor, "I Will Survive"

Imagine a world without homosexual men. Consider the landscape of life in America without our participation and talents. Conjure a mental image of our nation, our cities, our neighborhoods devoid of the activity of gay men and the influence of gay male culture.

These possibilities darted through many gay men's minds in 1981 and some of us are imagining them again today. As we grapple with an ever-changing terrain on which we struggle to erect edifices of hope, we find ourselves facing the same painful conundrums we had hoped to resolve a decade ago. If AIDS is a sexually transmitted disease, why don't gay men always practice safe sex? If billions of dollars fund medical research each year in America, why

1

isn't a cure for HIV infection just around the corner? What forms of life can gay men anticipate over the next few decades?

When initial reports of gay cancer confronted us a dozen years ago, many of us were shocked into considering the worst. We huddled over after-dinner coffee quietly tossing out gruesome guesses of how many would fall in the epidemic. Would it be one out of six or one out of three? Glazed-over eyes flashed about the room, each of us pondering who among us would be walking the earth in ten years. Serious discussions ensued about whether the gay male population was doomed for extinction.

After a period of time, we stopped articulating these fears. Our focus shifted from shock into action. We spread the word about sexual transmission, and began formal prevention campaigns. We rolled up our sleeves and set up community-based caregiving networks. We began learning about the health care system and federal research bureaucracy and suddenly knew more about our bodies and our immune systems than we'd ever imagined.[1]

By 1985, despite the tidal wave of death which was beginning to overwhelm us, we found solace in two oft-repeated beliefs: (1) A treatment which would save our lives would be found soon; (2) Gay men in urban centers had implemented safe sex practices and halted sexual transmission in our population. These beliefs became the theoretical and spiritual foundation of our collective lives in the health crisis. They were sources of hope and we constructed elaborate campaigns of optimism upon them, as well as public relations campaigns repeatedly reminding the world that gay men had responded "responsibly" to a burgeoning epidemic.

The gay community's mass reaction to the epidemic has approximated Elisabeth Kübler-Ross's stages of coming to terms with death, described in her landmark book, *On Death and Dying,* published a decade before the advent of AIDS.[2] These phases, while described as distinct entities, are often neither discrete nor sequential and frequently overlap. This is also true of our community's response to AIDS. While some individuals responded immediately to the first reports of GRID (Gay-Related Immune Deficiency) and gay cancer, 1981-1984 were years of denial, shock, and fear throughout much of the gay population; 1985-1989 was a period of agitation and anger. We then shifted briefly into the third stage, bargaining, and made conscious and unconscious pacts (with fate? ourselves? God?) to ensure our individual or collective survival: If we were HIV positive and volunteered in AIDS service organizations, we wouldn't be allowed to become sick. If we were uninfected and donated a lot of money, we would be spared the plague. As a community, we told ourselves that if we were the best little boys in the world, this nightmare would end swiftly. Like a holy prayer, we chanted over and over that HIV is a chronic and manageable illness, hoping no one else would have to die. We repeatedly proclaimed to the world that gay men had halted transmission of the virus, praying no one else would become infected.

Time magazine described similar phases in 1992:

> The first wave of gay response to AIDS was fear, mixed alternately with denial and paranoia. The second wave, the past few years, has been a therapeutic anger, an opportunity for the grief-stricken to vent their pain and for the dying to give meaning to their premature passing. The third and current wave of gay response to AIDS is once again dominated by fear, this time based on a sense of grim inevitability.[3]

In 1993 two events jolted us collectively into Kübler-Ross's stage four–depression. Our creeping recognition that we had not found treatment solutions broke into public consciousness. At the International AIDS Conference in Berlin, the treatment that claimed much of the AIDS establishment's largess of hope–AZT–was repeatedly and publicly undermined. At the same time, multi-city epidemiological evidence and anecdotal reporting began to confirm what many had suspected: new infections among gay and bisexual men were again on the upswing; significant numbers of men were engaging in anal intercourse without a condom.[4] Thus the dual foundation of our collective hope–no new infections and the imminent development of a cure–eroded from under our feet, and a thick veil of depression, which for years had hovered just overhead, dropped over the community.

Some have observed a diminution of public interest in AIDS. San Francisco gay writer Bruce Mirken captured the sentiment of many in an essay titled "Reasons to Riot," in which he wrote:

It's almost as if we've gotten used to this. It's as if we've come to feel that having our friends and lovers die every day is normal. It's as if we believe it inevitable that profit-obsessed drug companies and scientific turf battles will continue to distort the research agenda and the things that could save lives in the short term–like needle exchange and education programs that actually give young people honest information–will never happen on a large enough scale to do any good.

It's as if we've given up.[5]

In a posthumously published cover story in *The New York Times Magazine,* Jeffrey Schmalz wrote:

Once AIDS was a hot topic in America–promising treatments on the horizon, intense media interest, a political battlefield. Now, 12 years after it was first recognized as a new disease, AIDS has become normalized, part of the landscape .... The world is moving on, uncaring, frustrated and bored, leaving by the roadside those of us who are infected and who can't help but wonder: Whatever happened to AIDS?[6]

But has AIDS been normalized? Or is something else going on? Certainly a shift in thinking about the epidemic has occurred. Rather than being a temporary incident necessitating temporary responses, AIDS has become seen as a characteristic feature of contemporary urban life. Accepting that no magic bullet is in sight that will cure the infected or prevent further cases is different from seeing AIDS as the "normal" or "usual" state of being.

Something complex and difficult to quantify is transpiring that is especially evident in the gay community. Schmalz wrote, "Now even the gay movement has pushed AIDS to the sidelines." He cites the 1993 March on Washington as indicative of this shift:

Six years earlier, in 1987, a similar gay march had one overriding theme: AIDS. If there was a dominant theme last April, it was homosexuals in the military. To be sure, AIDS was an element of the march, but *just* an element. Speaker after speaker ignored it. (p. 60)

Schmalz highlights remarks by Torie Osborn, former executive director of the National Gay and Lesbian Task Force, who states,

"There is a deep yearning to broaden the agenda beyond AIDS. There's a natural need for human beings who are in deep grieving to reach for a future beyond their grieving" (p. 60).

The historical response to AIDS by the gay, lesbian, and bisexual communities has been complicated since the start of the epidemic; they have *never* embraced a single-issue agenda with a focus on AIDS— even in the heyday years of AIDS activism. Individuals whose sole political focus is AIDS might feel that the gay community is leaving them behind, but something else is occurring here, different even from a reshuffling of political priorities. Osborn's statement about the need for vision and hope amidst deep grieving provides a clue to what is really going on, but not in her intended way.

The experience of deep grieving does *not* allow for "reaching towards the future." On the contrary, individuals who are in the midst of bereavement experience a heightened sense of focus on the past and profound barriers to looking forward. Only when mourning approaches completion does the human spirit begin to dwell again in the present and reestablish a connection with the future. Deep loss intrudes on life at every turn; "normalizing" cannot occur under these circumstance because suffering people are obsessively revisited by their loss. Yet activism in the gay community has seen a resurgence of energy and resources since 1992. Increasing demands for vision, long-range planning, and concrete achievements have been issued. How is it possible for the community to be "reaching for the future" if such activity is oppositional to a state of deep grieving?

The answer to this question is speculative but my thesis is that many of us have entered a stage of the epidemic where we have reached the limitation of our ability to mourn. This is a concept some of us would have challenged as impossible just a few years ago. When I talk with other gay men who have been greatly affected by the epidemic—some of us HIV positive and some of us HIV negative—and when I look honestly into myself, I find evidence that normal cycles of grief are not occurring. Close friends and lovers die and we feel nothing. Masses of gay men vow to avoid attending memorial services whenever possible. The sight of formerly handsome faces now narrowed and scarred with lesions no longer evokes an emotional response.

Studies of survivors of the Holocaust noted a parallel disruption in the ability to mourn:

> There seems to be an absolute limit to how much an individual is able to give up through grieving. The limitation is a double one–first there is only so much a person can grieve over *at one time*. . . . Secondly, there is an absolute or lifetime limit to what a given person can absorb in terms of either loss or accepting negative qualities of one's self. There are both qualitative and quantitative factors in the limitations on what can be dealt with through mourning. The quantity or quality of losses may be beyond one's capacity to integrate, e.g., when in the case of the Holocaust one's entire people and civilization perished.[7]

The mass psychic numbing occurring in large pockets of the gay community might easily be mistaken for disinterest or a return to other matters because the affect is similar. We accept such an assessment at our own peril. Rather than normalizing the epidemic and accepting its impact in our day-to-day lives, some of us who inhabited the gay community before the arrival of AIDS have been traumatized by it. Frozen feelings are quite different from psychological adjustment; they indicate neither engagement nor adaptation. The dissociation we experience as a lack of feeling, numbness, or ennui is familiar to many clinicians as a common response to mass catastrophes such as earthquakes, trainwrecks, or extreme historical events. Referred to as the "disaster syndrome," this pattern of behavior is a "psychologically determined response that defends the individual against being overwhelmed by traumatic experience. The person appears dazed, stunned, apathetic, and passive."[8]

When visions of cultural extinction again intrude upon the thoughts of many gay men, we are experiencing deepening psychological impact caused by relentless, progressive devastation of our identity and community. Rather than passively becoming bored and losing interest in AIDS, our shell-shocked conditions are caused by deep bruises on our psyches that become more severe as they continue to be unidentified and untreated.

This same phenomenon may be observed in segments of the community that exhibit a contrasting demeanor. Some rail against any change in our assessment of progress against the epidemic, believing the maintenance of hope is possible only if we steadfastly cling to our original sources of hope and assume a studied optimism: a cure is on the horizon and gay men are no longer becoming infected. We repeat these tenets over and over to ourselves, like a mantra. The vast system of AIDS service providers and activists, attempting to fulfill their critical role as the source of collective hope, urges us to "be here for the cure" and insists that "hot gay men practice safe sex 100 percent of the time." Historian Allan Bérubé identified the impact of this kind of incessant optimism early in the epidemic:

> These attempts to protect us from our pain usually go un-challenged because they are often camouflaged with good intentions. They can lie hidden within consolations; they can be disguised by a well-meaning but patronizing desire to give us short-cuts to hope.[9]

Can we acknowledge a profound depression that has settled over a large portion of the community without losing the ability to forge collective response and fight for survival? If we opened our eyes and told the truth about the horrors that we endure, would we fall over the edge of the abyss?

I believe that any hope for collective survival is rooted in the realities of our lives, however harsh and seemingly unacceptable. Our inability to continue confronting the ever-intensifying man-ifestations of AIDS has brought us to the point of paralysis. As long as we continue on a path where our primary strategy for survival ricochets between total shutdown and a mass pep rally cheering on denial, we ensure our doom. Tactics of moralizing, distortion, and outright mendacity must be replaced by facing the realities of con-temporary gay men's lives, however complex and severe. We need to take a hard look at Elisabeth Kübler-Ross's fifth stage: accep-tance. Rather than leaving us on a barren desert of despair, an acknowledgment of what we endure may lead us to a blueprint for the regeneration of social order.

Our ability to pass through the deformed landscape of contempo-rary gay male life without engagement or emotion draws on a skill gay men develop early in life. Many of us have kept information about key aspects of our lives tucked discretely in the closet; this is the "don't ask, don't tell" treaty which has long governed interactions between American gay men and the broader society. Feminist writer Susan Griffin believes this state of emotional shutdown is a common feature of contemporary life:

> There are many ways we have of standing outside ourselves in ignorance. Those who have learned as children to become strangers to themselves do not find this a difficult task. Habit has made it natural not to feel. . . . But this ignorance is not entirely passive. For some, blindness becomes a kind of refuge, a way of life that is chosen, even with stubborn volition, and does not yield easily even to visible evidence.[10]

Living at a step removed from ourselves creates a bizarre state of consciousness. Each day three paradoxical strains weave through many gay men's lives: (1) We witness significant amounts of death and disfigurement which cause us to feel profound threats to our individual and collective survival; (2) We pretend that this is not happening; (3) We analyze, understand, and articulate our situation using metaphors and theories that minimize our circumstances.

Initial work on the psychosocial impact of AIDS during 1981-1983 arose out of the need to cope with the sudden death of individuals. Our great challenge was to support each other through the shocking early death of a close friend or lover. We were informed by various theories of grieving, each constructed around a single, discrete death. The popular discourse on death and dying suited our situation and provided a conceptual framework for understanding AIDS.

Yet by 1985, the weight of death and infirmity had increased exponentially in epicenters of the epidemic. We found ourselves at the limit of the death and dying discourse's application to our situation, and sought new knowledge in theories which attempted to explain human response to a *series* of deaths. Thus "cumulative grief" and "multiple loss" became paradigms through which we understood what was happening to us. An extension of theories of death and dying, the literature of cumulative grief focuses on permutations of the process of mourning resulting from an accumulated overload of loss.[11] Theories of cumulative grief helped explain why we shut down for short periods of time, how our psyches integrated several deaths that occurred in the same period of time, and what effects repeated loss had on the grieving process.

Once again, by 1989, the impact of the epidemic had moved to another level for many gay men and discussions of multiple loss no longer seemed to fit the circumstances. One group of researchers, studying AIDS-related bereavement among New York City gay men, summarized the complexity of their losses:

> In 1981 the annual incidence of AIDS-related bereavement was less than 2%. By 1985 the noncumulative annual incidence had reached 18%. That figure continued to increase to 23% in 1987. These rates do not reflect the fact that of those who are bereaved, over one third have lost two or more close individuals within the same year. Some men have reported as many as six close losses in 1 year . . . whereas others have been chronically bereaved of close loved ones for 3 or more consecutive years of the epidemic.[12]

By the late 1980s, it seemed inappropriate to discuss the "stress" of the epidemic, or to talk about uninfected gay men as simply the "worried well." We realized we weren't affected simply by the fact that people had died, but the manner in which they had died. This was understood also among A-bomb survivors in Hiroshima:

> Survivors were thus affected not only by the fact of people dying around them but by the way in which they died: a gruesome form of rapid bodily deterioration which seemed unrelated to more usual and "decent" forms of death.[13]

The corpses had mounted beyond our most extreme nightmares, but what was worse was the dawning realization that the human death toll was only a portion of the loss we were suffering. Our intimate relationships, erotic response, and sexual subcultures were becoming freakishly deformed by the epidemic. We were pulled in many directions, weighing dead bodies against dead dreams. As one gay man said:

> I've been feeling the loss of unprotected sex for years. It's like mourning: it's a fact of life. Maybe at this point I'm so used to loss, having lost so many friends, that losing forms of sexual expression is just another loss. It's certainly nothing

compared to having lost friends, so I feel I don't really deserve to mourn it too much.[14]

Because the epidemic seemed initially to have a slow, personal, and private impact, we have failed to consider seriously its parallels with earthquakes and other mass community disasters. The vast social science literature of disaster has a great deal to offer our understanding of current response to AIDS. Like a trainwreck occurring in slow motion, or a tidal wave hitting over a period of a dozen years, the epidemic has confronted survivors with an overwhelming volume of death and mutilation, and undermined the fragile social order. We stand now in the path of a tornado, our worldview alternately confused, overwhelmed, and fragmented, wondering whether we are on the brink of destruction or the brink of redemption.

One man summarized the conflict in this way:

> HIV is all around me: in my life, and in my community. I talk about it, I think about it, it's everywhere. Sometimes I walk in a foggy state, not really in touch with my feelings. Sometimes I feel it will overwhelm me, and I need to get away. But I can never really get away from it. Sometimes I feel if I tilt my head it'll come pouring out my ears.[15]

Many of the surviving population of gay men of all antibody statuses who comprised community before AIDS are in a stage of coping with the epidemic fraught with intensifying contradiction. We want to survive and we want to die. We want to comfort and we want to blame. We seek answers and we do not care anymore. While a careful analysis of the situation can promise neither to stop our suffering nor to end the current acceleration of new infections, it may provide an understanding of what is happening to us and some clues to what the future will bring. We may find a foothold of relief in circumspection, but no miracle cure for the malaise.

NOTES

1. Edward King, *Safety in Numbers: Safer Sex and Gay Men* (New York: Routledge, 1993), 170-172 discusses various other periodizations of the epidemic.

2. Elisabeth Kübler-Ross, *On Death and Dying* (New York: The Macmillan Company, 1969).

3. William A. Henry III, "An Identity Forged in Flames," *Time*, August 3, 1992, 37.

4. Jeffrey A. Kelly, et al., "Acquired Immunodeficiency Syndrome/Human Immunodeficiency Virus Risk Behavior Among Gay Men in Small Cities," *Archives of Internal Medicine*, 152:2293-2297 (1992).

5. Bruce Mirken, "Reasons to Riot," *Bay Windows*, June 2, 1994, 12.

6. Jeffrey Schmalz, "Whatever Happened to AIDS," *The New York Times Magazine*, November 18, 1993, 58.

7. Henry Krystal, "Integration and Self-Healing in Post-Traumatic States: A Ten-Year Retrospective," *American Imago* 48(1):104 (Spring 1991).

8. Beverley Raphael, *When Disaster Strikes*, (New York: Basic Books, 1986), 64.

9. Allan Bérubé, "Caught in the Storm: AIDS and the Meaning of Natural Disaster," *Out/look* (Fall 1988):9.

10. Susan Griffin, *A Chorus of Stones* (New York: Anchor Books, 1992), 153.

11. Tom Grothe and Leon McKusick, "Coping with Multiple Loss," *Focus: A Guide to AIDS Research and Counseling* 7(7):5-6 (June 1992). See also Ray Biller and Susan Rice, "Experiencing Multiple Loss of Persons with AIDS: Grief and Bereavement Issues," *Health and Social Work* 15(4):283-290 (1990).

12. John Martin, Laura Dean, Marc Garcia, and William Hall, "The Impact of AIDS on a Gay Community: Changes in Sexual Behavior, Substance Use, and Mental Health," *American Journal of Community Psychology* 17(3):269-293 (1989).

13. Robert J. Lifton, *Death in Life: Survivors of Hiroshima* (New York: Random House, 1967), 59.

14. "Aaron" quoted in Will I. Johnston, *HIV-Negative: How the Uninfected Are Affected by AIDS* (New York: Insight Books-Plenum Press, 1995), 179.

15. From an unpublished interview by William I. Johnston, December 1, 1993.

SECTION I:
RESTORING MENTAL HEALTH

Chapter 1

In the Center of the Cyclone

For the first time in history, it's gonna start raining men.

—The Weather Girls, "It's Raining Men"

It's the nightmare
I keep remembering
of boys falling from trees,
from the sky.
Boys landing in construction sites,
quarries, on top of buses, at intersections
where the lights go green all at once.

Turn your head to cough
and 5,000 boys fall from the sky.
It's frightening. Light candles
in Central Park to their shadows
falling all night. Push them back
into heaven with our little flames.

—Dwight Okita, "Where the Boys Were"

Like many surviving gay men, I distinctly remember when I first heard about the plague. I was living in a small house in Province-town for the summer, along with two friends from Boston. It was a warm, July morning, and we were gathered in the kitchen, making breakfast and chatting about plans for the day. The Cape Cod fog

15

had cleared earlier in the morning, and I had trekked down to the corner market to pick up orange juice, pop-tarts, and *The New York Times*. Now I found myself caught up in what had become a customary ritual of reading headlines to my roommate Kevin.

We all need to tell our version of this story and, to this day, I believe I recall what the room looked like, what we were wearing, and who said what when I came upon that initial article buried deep in the paper. The moment is frozen in time as if someone had taken an instamatic photograph of the scene and branded it onto my memory. This is unusual because I am a man who cannot remember his mother's birthday, or the first date with my lover, or, at times, my phone number. Yet I can recall specific details of the scene in our kitchen during that sunny July breakfast in 1981.

I read the story out loud, slowly and methodically, as it described a strange, new cancer targeting gay men. What did we think about the article? Did we imagine that the handful of gay men with cancer who were referenced in the article had anything to do with us? How did we take in and hold this information and what meaning did we confer on it?

I remember one of my roommates scoffing at the article, dismissing it as "homophobic bullshit"; the other considered the piece in his usual good-natured and measured manner, ruminating over it for the rest of the day. Their reactions sharply contrasted with my own. I'd like to be able to say that the moment was meaningless for me and quickly forgotten, but it wasn't. I'd also like to be able to say that that breakfast scene became meaningful only in retrospect, as the significance became apparent and the cases mounted. This also feels untrue.

The article in the *Times* shot through me like a bullet to the heart. The announcement of gay-related illness and death somehow wasn't new or surprising to me. It was as if I'd finally come across the article that I'd been expecting to read for years.

I can remember standing around sex clubs and leather bars during the 1970s, marveling at the men and the energy while nagging doubts tugged at the back of my mind. I was haunted by a persistent, low-level sense of doom, as if I were watching the orgies I'd imagined preceded the fall of Rome. Where did my penchant for doom come from? I was a twenty-six-year-old gay kid, with my whole life in front of me. I'd come out to my parents, held a job as an openly gay schoolteacher, and had emerged from years of counseling with a modicum of self-esteem. Sometimes I believed my tendency to anticipate a daily apocalypse was part of growing up Jewish in America in the decades following the Holocaust. At other times, I imagined that I was cursed with a flair for the dramatic and would be eternally pessimistic in a grandiose and stylish manner. I can recall as a child looking out the window during blizzards or hurricanes and feeling a thrilling sensation—almost erotic—as I imagined vast destruction.

On that July morning, I began an elaborate dance of denial, hoping that my long-expected cataclysm hadn't arrived. As small articles began to appear monthly, then weekly, in the gay press, I attempted to stave off what I viscerally knew to be true. I went about the routines of daily life, oblivious to the slowly expanding epidemic. I thought of myself as young, gifted, and gay, and I wasn't about to allow a new disease to rain on my parade.

Denial among gay men took various forms during these early years. Some men couldn't allow themselves to believe that gay cancer even existed. A long relationship of doubt and mistrust existed between gay men and both the medical establishment and the mainstream media fed this particular brand of denial. Others could believe that the new disease existed, but couldn't accept sexual transmission as its origin. Recalling Legionnaires' Disease, they imagined that a grand, gay party had been held in a hall which had a toxic ventilation system. My own denial was unabashedly self-centered: if a devastating new disease was dropping on us, it wouldn't get near me or my friends. I needed to think of it as a disease of three cities: New York, Los Angeles, and San Francisco. We happened to be ensconced luckily in cozy old New England.

AIDS did not suddenly shatter the world like an earthquake striking a major urban center in the early morning hours, or instantaneously transform the world from routine to disaster like the Atom bomb falling on Hiroshima. It wasn't like a tornado, suddenly swooping down on a village, ripping the roofs off buildings, uprooting trees, and flipping automobiles onto their hoods. Because it came on gradually, stealing into our world like an intruder creeping up the stairway, step by step, we had a few years to dart back and forth between ignorance, denial, and terror. I have wondered what my reaction would have been like that morning at breakfast if the *Times* had been able to predict what the next dozen years would be like for gay men:

By 1995, half of the men you've loved, hugged, talked, danced, cruised, and had sex with, will be dead or dying. You will feel like a time-traveling dinosaur before you reach middle age. The clubs you've inhabited will be gone, the music will be trashed and disappear, the history will evaporate into a vacuum. You will rip cards out of your Rolodex like pages on a calendar. You will experience so much death that you will forget who died and who is still alive. You will run into men on the street whom you'd thought were long dead. You will send out Christmas cards each year and receive a half dozen back stamped "deceased."

Would I have adjusted more quickly to the scythe sweeping through our bright green field? How would the years from 1981-1985 have been different for me? What precautions would I have taken that I didn't take? Could I have done anything to keep my heart from shattering?

My journal from that summer of 1981 records the names of twenty-one men with whom I had sex. Nine were one-night stands: tourists spending a few days on the beaches of Cape Cod. I don't know what happened to them. Twelve were men I knew for various periods of time and I can tell you what happened to them. Eleven of these men are now dead. I remain uninfected.

Except for rare moments of panic, I have always expected to survive AIDS. I do not say this to brag or to position myself in a place of moral superiority to other gay men. Many of us who are still walking the earth feel this way. While I have had moments of terror when receiving HIV test results, and occasionally found purple marks on my body which I was sure were lesions, most of the time I have not felt like I would get infected. Part of this might come from an inbred cultural sense, as a Jew, that survival is everything. At times I've felt that my sense of invulnerability came from a certain self-appointed role for which I imagined I had been chosen: I was to witness the horrors of the plague and to speak about them ad nauseum.

Most of my intuitive sense of survival comes from one specific and serendipitous fact: I have rarely had much desire for anal sex. During the heyday of gay liberation, I often felt different from many friends because I didn't often allow myself to get fucked, nor did I fuck men. At times I felt that I was missing out on a key aspect of gay male identity because of my lack of interest in this specific erotic activity. I was inspired by men who articulated the transformative powers of anal sex and the way it forever altered one's conception of masculinity. Yet my few ventures into anal intercourse left me uninterested in more. I can count on my hands the number of times I've been fucked, and at best I found it unpleasant—at worst I found it excruciatingly painful.

When I was twenty-three years old, I made a goal for myself that, by the time I was thirty years old, I would learn how to get fucked and enjoy it. It seems funny to say this now, but I felt that I was missing out on a key ingredient in the gay experience and I was determined to be a total gay man. Just a few years later, when it became popularly known that receptive anal sex was the primary transmission route for what was called "the AIDS virus," I was grateful that I'd never developed a taste for the act.

I have often searched for an explanation for my lack of interest in anal sex, especially after it became evident that my preference for other acts was the primary reason I was still alive. At times I've guessed that the anus' role in excretion was the source of my aversion. I wondered if the messages I received from my parents during toilet training made me nervous about having anything up my butt. Sometimes I've felt that the revulsion isn't so much about my anus, but about penetration of any kind. I cannot imagine getting pierced in any part of my body, including the earlobe. I respond to vaccinations and blood tests by fainting. In a contemporary world of pierced noses and lips and nipples, the closest to penetration that I come is a weekly cotton swab in my ears.

The conscious terror that mounted in me during the first few years of the epidemic wasn't so much about my own health but about the effect gay cancer (then GRID, then AIDS) would have on a community I loved. This was not altruism. My daily life had been spent in a whirl of gay activism since I'd gotten out of college: intensive volunteer work at *Gay Community News*, Boston's Gay Men's Center, the 1979 March on Washington for Lesbian and Gay Rights, Boston Area Gay and Lesbian Schoolworkers, Men's Childcare Collective, the White House Conference on the Family, Committee for Gay Youth, Boston Lesbian and Gay Pride Committee. My energy and identity were merged with the post-Stonewall gay community in Boston. The arrival of AIDS felt to me like a confirmation of the punitive predictions of Anita Bryant and Jerry Falwell. The dreams I had for my life and for the gay nation were starting to unravel.

During the early years of the epidemic, I was aware that I most feared a loss of community. I knew few people who were diagnosed or dead: a gentle teacher with whom I'd done schoolworker organizing, the pastry chef at my favorite restaurant, an athlete prominent in the gay hiking club. Their deaths touched me and scared me, but the fear and sadness which began to surround me was as much about the loss of individuals as it was about the loss of certain intangibles–things like innocence, abandon, and unfettered joy. I watched a community I loved greatly inch into the mid-1980s wracked by cataclysmic changes.

Certain powerful scenes stand out in my memory and take on a special importance as I think back to these early years of the epidemic. The first mass AIDS rally and candlelight vigil in Boston filled historic Faneuil Hall with 800 people in June 1983. I organized and served as emcee for the event in my role as Chair of Boston Lesbian and Gay Political Alliance, and I recall looking out from the stage at the crowd and seeing terror and shock in the wide eyes of men and women alike. The evening was a weird mixture of education and politics, but what haunts me most from that evening was the silent, somber march through the streets of Boston, as a horrible new threat to our existence seeped into the souls of hundreds of lesbians and gay men.

During that same summer, a physician friend and I crafted an AIDS education brochure targeting men visiting Provincetown during the summer months. After printing several thousand brochures, we naively went door-to-door to the guest house owners and merchants of this seaside resort. A few eagerly accepted the brochures, but most met us with denial, anger, and ambivalence. One gay man insisted that any connection between AIDS and Provincetown would kill tourism in the town for a hundred years. A lesbian restauranteur chased us out, insisting that the only thing that would stop AIDS would be gay men giving up their "disgusting" and "sick" sexual habits.

On the dance floor at Chaps, a Copley Square clone disco where my friend Tom and I would dance for hours on Sunday afternoons, I noticed a subtle but pronounced shift in the energy of the men I had danced with for years. While the dancing had previously reflected a collective expression of freedom, desire, and celebration, it slowly became manic, intense, even desperate. As a weekly community of dancers, we were shifting gears, and the dance floor was one of the last venues where we could assume masks of denial and pretend the catastrophic world hadn't overtaken us. By 1984, it was impossible to disavow the rising tide of death, although, for the sake of preserving sacred dance rituals, we'd certainly try. Ironic lyrics crept out of our lips. Whether we were mouthing "I will survive," or "So many men, so little time," it became impossible to pretend that we weren't all thinking the same hideous thoughts. One Sunday evening, as the powerful sound system throbbed with Irene Cara singing "What a Feeling" from *Flashdance*, I looked from face to face of my fellow tea-dancers, and a knot of raw emotion tore at my gut as my eyes dampened. In my AIDS story, that was the day the music died.

By 1985, my whole life had changed. Was it turning thirty, or finally facing the awful truth of the epidemic? In one year, I left my career, my lover, and my home. I had fallen in love with a handsome man from San Francisco and, with him, moved to Provincetown to live year-round. The relationship was intense, passionate, and unpredictable and I rode a roller coaster of emotions, fueled by an eroding denial of the scope of a burgeoning epidemic. I finally crashed in a cyclone of clinical depression, endless despair, and twisted thoughts of suicide. On the surface this was about ambivalent love and conflicted relationships and an inability to forge commitment. I was unaware of any ways in which the psychological fallout of the epidemic might be fueling my declining condition. I watched myself turn from an energetic and functional person into a

lethargic couch potato who spent most of one season indoors watching soap operas, eating entire Entemann's cakes in a single sitting,
and crying without a discernable reason. With neither awareness
nor the words to articulate my situation, the stormy waves of the
epidemic washed over me, and left me struggling to tread water,
desperately gasping for air.

THE SECRET LIFE OF GAY MEN

Few of us want to face that our ordinary lives have been twisted
beyond recognition over the past fifteen years. Listening to my own
social banter over the past month, I am struck by its inanity. On the
telephone, I answer my mother's usual question with "Everything's
fine." My physician wonders if there are specific incidents of stress
in my life and, without noting the irony of my statement, I say, "No,
things are no different than usual." A walk through the Castro racks
up a dozen exchanges of denial between men: "How are you,
George?" "I'm fine, and you?" "Couldn't be better!" "Have a nice
day!"

During this particular month, seven friends and colleagues died,
four in San Francisco and three in other locations. I supported one
friend with the planning of his suicide. I attended three memorial
services. I clipped another six obituaries of casual friends out of
newspapers; some of the deceased I hadn't known were ill. I stood
by as my HIV-infected lover developed a series of upper respiratory
infections. I observed my best friend's HIV-infected lymph nodes
swell as his T-cell count dropped dramatically. Although uninfected
with HIV, I spent the month with constant diarrhea and frequent
migraines.

I describe my life not to earn sympathy but as a checkpoint
indicating how I've shut down. The only way I manage to integrate
infirmity and death into my definition of "normal" and "fine" is to
stop feeling. I'm not proud of it, although I know I'm not alone in
living in a state of psychic numbness.

Gay men in America today lead lives which most of us keep
hidden from our families, friends, even ourselves. Because of powerful social and informational divisions between classes of people
in contemporary American life, our heterosexual families, friends,

and neighbors have no idea what our experience of the epidemic is like. Heterosexual social critics, attempting to analyze current gay social trends, haven't a clue about what's going on with us. Because their own losses tally to one friend, a distant relative, and several colleagues, they assume that their experience is the quintessential AIDS experience. They watch the film *Philadelphia* or read *And the Band Played On,* and believe they comprehend what their gay friends have been going through.

Hence we have reached this stage of the epidemic with few people aware of anything beyond broad brush strokes of contemporary reality for gay men who have lived with AIDS since its inception. It is as if the epidemic of AIDS is an event without a witness. A parallel analysis of Holocaust survivors explains the challenge of witnessing extreme atrocities:

> As the event of the Jewish Genocide unfolded, however, most actual or potential witnesses failed one-by-one to occupy their position as a witness, and at a certain point it seemed as if there was no one left to witness what was taking place. . . . It was not only the reality of the situation and the lack of responsiveness of bystanders or the world that accounts for the fact that history was taking place with no witness: it was also the very circumstance of being inside the event that made unthinkable the very notion that a witness could exist, that is, someone who could step outside of the coercively totalitarian and dehumanizing frame of reference in which the event was taking place, and provide an independent frame of reference through which the event could be observed.[1]

The inability of gay men to provide a certain kind of testimony about our current circumstances may be rooted not in individual cowardice or personal failure, but in the limitations that extreme historical events impose on the human psyche:

> The historical imperative to bear witness could essentially not be met during the actual occurrence. The degree to which bearing witness was required, entailed such an outstanding measure of awareness and of comprehension of the event–of its dimensions, consequences, and above all, of its radical

otherness to all known frames of reference–that it was beyond the limits of human ability (and willingness) to grasp, to transmit, or to imagine. . . . What was ultimately missing, not in the courage of the witnesses, not in the depth of their emotional responses, but in the human cognitive capacity to perceive and to assimilate the totality of what was really happening at the time.[2]

There are vast historical differences between the war against the Jews and the AIDS epidemic's impact on gay men. These make it unclear whether the scope of the epidemic is such that witnessing becomes impossible. Analyzing the impact of war, Susan Griffin suggests another explanation: "There are events in our lives that we cannot understand because we keep a part of what we know away from understanding."[3]

Many of our fears and nightmares are kept locked tightly in the closets of our private lives. This makes it difficult for anyone, including ourselves, to gather accurate information on the vast and complex impact of the epidemic on gay men as a class (as if America's mainstream research establishment is trying). How many of us numb out for long periods of time and feel nothing at all? How many of us, infected or uninfected, are on antidepressants and anti-anxiety medication? How common is it for men who have been clean and sober for a dozen years to relapse? How many suicides are occurring among both HIV-positive and HIV-negative gay men?

Instead, our public line continues to be "We're doing fine. We've faced the challenge of HIV in our community by organizing support systems and educating ourselves, and we've halted man-to-man transmission. We're doing fine." As if a population suffering amid a catastrophe should be doing fine! Psychologist Walt Odets has written:

I would place in the area of homophobia the entire idea, promoted in so many subtle forms, that the gay community "is doing well in the epidemic." Why should we do "well" in this situation, and what could that mean? What would we be doing by pretending that we are not distressed and angry about what has happened to our friends, our lives and our sexuality?

Do homosexuals have a special responsibility to prove their strength and endurance?[4]

Only in the recesses of our psyches and behind the closed doors of therapists' offices do the truths of our lives occasionally reverberate. Why didn't I cry as my closest friend died? Why didn't I feel anything? When was the last time I felt a "normal" feeling stir inside of me? Why do I experience long periods of no feelings at all and then a few days of uncontrollable hysteria? Why has my sex life become so crazy? When the human system is overwhelmed beyond capacity, it simply shuts down. Our immersion in an environment of sickness and morbidity fractures our thinking and obscures our vision. Many gay men, during a constant barrage of death and mutilation, are shell-shocked for protracted periods of time, experiencing a syndrome similar to that noted after the bombing of Hiroshima:

> Psychic numbing . . . has to do with the diminished capacity or inclination to feel. It can take the form of a blocking of feelings or images, or both. People in Hiroshima could say to me: "You know, I could see what was going on around me, I could see people dead or dying, but suddenly I felt nothing."[5]

When this occurs in the AIDS epidemic, many of us try to fake it, but it doesn't work. Psychic numbing paradoxically precludes self-conscious awareness at the time that numbing is occurring. Not only do our emotional response systems grind to a halt, but our conscious minds refuse to acknowledge the deep freeze. As isolated individuals, we believe that we alone no longer experience a range of feelings; we are embarrassed to be warped in this way. We feel shame at being shut down. Like the abused child, we heap guilt onto ourselves for our human system's organic response to the supernatural catastrophe we are suffering.

And who is helping us face the horror? Not those who make the common mistake of confusing numbing with normalizing. The structures of our community and culture, with few exceptions, seem hell-bent on avoiding the depth of the impact of the epidemic. Sometimes we think everyone *is* coping just fine except us. Speaking our truths brings on reprimands: we're told that we're exaggerating the situation, indulging the queen's dramatic flair. The mental health establishment underplays the severity of our circumstances by continuing to speak of the "walking wounded" and "caregiver stress" and use models of "multiple loss" to understand highly impacted gay men. Terms such as "cumulative grief" and "caring for the caregiver" may have been meaningful in the mid-1980s, but these seem to many of us today like depoliticized understatements of our experience. Many of our mental states have become more complex, yet clinicians continue to minimize our conditions and refuse to move beyond the concept of multiple loss in considering what has occurred:

> In some cases, psychological flooding of emotion incapacitates rather than heals, and to defend against this flooding, some people become emotionally numb. These alternatives to coping with massive loss have been identified before as the two phases of post-traumatic stress syndrome: intrusive-repetitive and denial-numbing. While in most cases multiple loss does not cause post-traumatic stress syndrome, the similarities of these phases can offer ways to work with the multiply bereaved.[6]

Certainly post-traumatic stress disorder can "offer ways to work with the multiply bereaved." But what keeps us from admitting that numbers of gay men might qualify for clinical diagnoses of post-traumatic stress disorder?[7] Many gay men throughout America are suffering a wide range of psychological responses that extend beyond bereavement and grief. Some may be at the stage of simple grief or multiple loss, but many others are experiencing severe depression, mood disorders, trauma, chronic trauma, and post-traumatic stress disorder. While I do not seek to pathologize gay men, neither do I want critical psychological reactions to AIDS to go unidentified and untreated. As the epidemic engulfs entire networks of friends, cases of multiple loss frequently are transformed into different clinical phenomena. Would "cumulative grief" be used to describe the experience of returning Vietnam Veterans who had witnessed countless and unrelenting incidents of terror and annihilation? Do clinicians discussing the way Nazi death camps impacted Holocaust survivors utilize a term like "multiple loss?" Are gay men overreacting when we make these comparisons?

My analysis of AIDS and trauma has been formed through observations, interviews, self-examination, and an extensive review of existing research. My efforts focused upon a specific gay male population of which I am a member (middle-class, educated, urban men ranging in age from thirty-five to fifty who are mostly white). These men had comprised what was popularly referred to as "the gay community" prior to the epidemic. When I first began presenting my ideas at professional and community conferences, I was careful to begin by explaining that my observations had relevance only to this narrowly focused population. I listened to queers of color in the movement who asserted that they experienced the epidemic in a manner distinct from white gay men and could not relate to my internal wrestling with despair and hope.

More recently, as AIDS continues to march relentlessly forward, destroying a vast portion of the leadership of gay men of color, debates have occurred about this assertion among lesbians and gay men of color. An account of a recent forum about new infections at New York's Lesbian and Gay Community Services Center captures two perspectives:

> Activist Carmen Vasquez tried to counter the tendency to despair by drawing on the traditions of ethnic identity—in her case, Puerto Rican. "I know something about survival," she said at the close of her remarks, to great applause; "ask me." Despair, she pointed out, may be more keenly felt by the privileged, who had higher expectations for their lives.
> But for gay men living in the context of AIDS, ethnic identity may not be solace enough. "I'm torn between Carmen's vision of struggle and survival, and white gay men's experience of despair," says Colin Robinson of Gay Men of African Descent. "To be honest, I find the despair easier to understand. You have to have a cohort that you're surviving with."[8]

African-American gay men from various class backgrounds were the first to challenge me and assert that my analysis might be useful to a broader range of gay men. They felt that the situations described and the psychological manifestations recounted came close to paralleling their own situations. Then gay and bisexual men from small cities and rural areas spoke up and described their lives and emotional conditions in terms similar to my own. In Boston, lesbian health care workers who were closely connected to gay men heard many of their own experiences in the stories I'd told of San Francisco gay men. The issues I describe reverberate for many people of varying ages, sexual orientations, ethnicities, and genders. I am most deeply conflicted about the ways gay men of my generation may experience the epidemic based on antibody status. I am not infected with HIV and the thinking which provided the foundation of this book initially took place among HIV-negative gay men. I believed that working on questions of individual and community survival and regeneration might be frowned upon by HIV-positive men and men with AIDS.

Instead I have learned that–while HIV's presence or absence in one's bloodstream results in profound differences in experiencing the epidemic–there are many issues and concerns where infected and uninfected men may find common ground. Caring about long-range community survival and well-being occurs across antibody status. Concerns about men's mental health and sexuality sometimes may be manifested differently between seropositives and seronegatives, but there is much common ground to explore. I have always believed the uninfected have much to learn from those who are HIV positive and have AIDS; now I believe HIV-negative men may offer a great deal beyond caregiving to HIV-positive men. I will not compare or equate the confusion or pain that has dominated my life these past dozen years to that of men with HIV or AIDS, but my own well-being is now the center-stage concern in my life. I believe it is worth thinking about, talking about, and collectively working to mitigate.

Young gay men who have lived their entire sexually active lives after the onset of AIDS are seroconverting at alarming rates.[9] While there are parallels between their situation and that of gay men over thirty-five, there are many important distinctions. Generational divides may be more pronounced when a mass catastophe intervenes. This book might prove useful to young gay men, but its focus is on the community of men who participated in the collective construction of the nascent gay male culture of the 1970s and early 1980s.

Men who were part of the spirit of gay liberation and broke new ground in our understanding of gender, sexuality, and identity have a shared experience of the epidemic. We were part of the development of cultures that have been mangled over the past dozen years, and we have witnessed the gruesome deaths of many of our comrades from that era. There is something about having been a part of the creation and expansion of gay male identity and culture during the hopeful pre-AIDS years that makes one vulnerable to what feels like a specific syndrome of complex and occasionally overwhelming loss.

Questions of identity and community have arisen for me throughout writing this book. At first I thought that I was attempting to avoid making some of the same errors many have made when writing about "the gay community" or "the gay tribe": conflating many populations into a single, artificial community, universalizing or essentializing gay male identity, making broad generalities that ignore the rich texture of community discourse. I felt the limitations of my skills as a writer, and often the limitations of language itself to capture social manifestations of complex issues. Soon, however, I realized that just under the surface, something else was going on for me.

My own experience of gay identity and community were shifting dramatically during the writing of the book. I watched myself change from someone with an identity constructed most powerfully around gayness and a life and career focused on lesbian and gay issues to a person whose sexual orientation held roughly equal weight with other identities (Jew, man, graduate student). At different times I felt a love for lesbians and gay men which I have long felt; at other times, I experienced alienation, disinterest, even hostility. These shifts–sometimes subtle and sometimes profound–are reflected on various pages of this book.

DEATH-SATURATED CULTURE TAKES HOLD

Matching our individual refusal to acknowledge and name what is occurring in our daily lives is a mass refusal to look at the impact of this decimation at the community level. Analysis of the effect of AIDS on gay movement organizing efforts is usually limited to two cursory conclusions: (1) AIDS has "drained money" from gay organizing efforts; (2) male leaders have been dying and women are replacing them. The pep rally in this arena takes the form of a marketing campaign declaring our current era "the Gay 90s" and insisting that this is our moment in the limelight. We tell each other that our movement is functioning at the peak of its strength. We trick ourselves into believing that the successful achievement of our agenda is simply a matter of media exposure and access to powerful individuals. How demeaning to watch an acceptance-starved community grovel at the media's fifteen seconds of attention, and hail cover stories on "Lesbian Chic" as evidence that our community has "come of age." We embrace the particularly American penchant for making serious political movements into nothing more than momentary trends; we confuse increased visibility and public discourse with impactful social change.

The hidden life of our movement is quite different from our tendency to drone on about the Gay 1990s. Our political position in the nation is as precarious as our mental health. Citizens throughout the nation carry bigotry into the voting booth. Token progress made by limited liberal institutions over the recent past is mistaken for widespread cultural shifts. Even more dangerous is our avoidance of looking clear-eyed at the religious, informational, and funding mega-structures that our enemies have spent two decades constructing and institutionalizing. Instead of using anti-gay initiative campaigns to build oppositional structures (e.g., a movement), our short-sighted aim often is simply to win the vote on Election Day. We close our eyes to the unspoken agenda of the Right–to seize control of the nation by limiting freedom and undermining democracy. Instead of naming the parallels of our current era with historical precedents of the rise of fascism, we cheer on and on about the Gay 1990s.

Likewise, we have pretended that the impact of AIDS on the social order of gay community life has been limited to the discrete deaths of individuals and otherwise has not undermined our communal life. Yet events of such magnitude by nature have major social effects. Catastrophe brings on "the destruction of the human matrix, the group ties and coordinated patterns of existence which constitute what we usually speak of as the social fabric or social structure."[10] This is readily observed after natural disasters:

The study of Mount St. Helen's ashfall showed increased episodes of family violence, increased legal convictions, and some increase in violence and aggression compared to pre-disaster levels. Follow-up studies a year after the Ash Wednesday fires showed an increase in family and marital problems and problems with children, and similar findings appeared following the Darwin [Australia] cyclone. Increased family tensions associated with the disaster experience, its effects, and the added stress of dislocation have already been noted.[11]

An observer of the survivors of a flood disaster that wiped away entire Appalachian villages, concluded that a "loss of communality" followed the disaster.[12] In any disaster, death is only a single, quantifiable component embedded in a broader matrix of devastation. When asked about the impact of the epidemic on their lives, many gay men answer by counting the number of friends and lovers who have died. These losses are tangible and harder to deny than other effects of the epidemic. Yet for many gay men, the epidemic has mutilated our identities, profoundly warped sexuality and intimate relations, and reaffirmed bigoted subconscious linkages between homosexuality and contagion. It has resulted in bizarre patterns of social dislocation, the debasement and destruction of specific social and sexual institutions, and radically transformed gay male cultural life as we had known it.

The replacement of pre-epidemic gay life by a death-saturated culture has caused a profound alteration of the social fabric and the reorganization of communal life. The spoken and unspoken traditions, rituals, and rules that comprise the social order of a community have been seriously disrupted. We have become as familiar with Prozac, Xanax, and Zoloft as we are with AZT, ddi, Bactrim, and pentamidine. The expectations on individual gay men have altered dramatically; the people on whom we counted for lasting friendship and support often are gone. Voluntary networks of altruistic strangers respond to the needs of isolated men in final stages of their lives because entire peer groups of lovers, ex-lovers, and friends have already died.

As we witness extreme behaviors within the gay community, our rush to judgment feels intense and urgent. This is especially true concerning judgments about the conduct of activists in the fight against AIDS. We sometimes feel that the community has gone mad. We sometimes feel that we've gone mad. Robert J. Lifton observed surprisingly intense conflict and political controversy in Hiroshima, years after the bombing:

> There is no proper way to behave for an individual or city that has felt the effects of an atomic bomb. This has to do with the destruction of the social fabric; even though the city of Hiroshima has been rebuilt, the social fabric of that community of survivors has not. A single small weapon has created a totality of destruction. There is unending lethal influence, a sense of being a victim of a force that threatens the species, that reverberates psychologically on those same people.[13]

Until recently, I believed that the epidemic's impact on gay male culture had been limited to our intimate, interpersonal, and communal relations–as well as hundreds of thousands of lives. Unlike what occurs after floods, earthquakes, and bombings, I argued that gay men hadn't lost physical structures, neighborhoods, and landmarks. But I have come to believe that we have our own "corpses of history" as poignant and meaningful to us as the specific burned-out shells of landmarks were to residents of cities that experienced mass bombing during World War II.[14] As one A-bomb survivor wrote:

> I reached a bridge and saw that the Hiroshima Castle had been completely leveled to the ground, and my heart shook like a great wave. . . . This destruction of the castle gave me a thought. Even if a new city should be built on this land, the castle would never be built and added to that city. The city of Hiroshima, entirely on flat land, was made three-dimensional by the existence of the white castle, and because of this it could retain a classical flavor. Hiroshima had a history of its own. And when I thought about these things, the grief of stepping over the corpses of history pressed upon my heart.[15]

During a recent visit to New York City, I found myself in sub-freezing temperature detouring a dozen blocks out of my way to walk through the meat-packing district of the West Village. Without consciousness or planning, I needed to stroll by what had been the Mineshaft, the quintessential gay male sex club of the 1970s. As I stood and stared at the door, tears flowed as I remembered both individual men and the spirit of optimism of the times.

More than any other aspect of gay life, the A-bomb of AIDS exploded directly on gay men's sex culture. We have lost an entire series of gay male venues that held an extraordinary symbolic power in our pre-epidemic sexuality and communal culture. This is especially true in epicenter cities which themselves held incredible meaning for gay men in the 1970s. We've lost dance clubs such as the Saint (New York City) and Trocadero (San Francisco), sex clubs such as the Cauldron and Handball Express (San Francisco), and Mineshaft (New York City), and bathhouses, such as 8709 (Los Angeles), the Saint Mark's Baths (New York City), the Ritch Street Baths, and the Club Baths (San Francisco). We've lost specific backroom bookstores, sex movie houses, leather bars, and sex culture icons as diverse as Sylvester, John Preston, and Al Parker. In fact, entire neighborhoods that were central sites for men's commercial sex establishments (San Francisco's South of Market, New York's West Village, Boston's Combat Zone) have been transformed. Some may argue that other forces such as gentrification, rezoning, or the usual ebb and flow of commercial turnover were the source of these changes. Certainly urban change is multi-factored, yet a combination of death (of owners, staff, and patrons) and repression (of desire as well as licenses) are primary factors creating the "corpses of history" of this disaster.

The impact of the epidemic on gay male geography, in addition to the elimination of key cultural landmarks, involves a mass confrontation with dislocation, displacement, exile, and repossession. Middle class gay men, traditionally a mobile population, face new questions when considering relocating to a new city: Can I keep my insurance and disability plan if I move? Can I leave behind sick or infected friends? Could I let go of my physician? If I get sick, can I get better treatment in another city? Do I want to be closer to or farther from my family of origin?[16]

The geographic repercussions of the epidemic have ranged from lovers abandoning sick lovers, to "AIDS widows" being dispossessed of their homes because the deceased left no will, to men who felt it necessary after friends died to move to a new part of the country and "start a new life." As someone who left his home in Boston in 1985 to move first to Los Angeles and then to San Francisco, I have wondered whether a part of me couldn't bear to stay in Boston and watch up close as a community I had been a part of creating suffered and died. How much of what feels like my manic mobility of the past decade has been the playing out of unconscious issues of self-imposed exile as a mechanism of coping?

The spatial transformation has been accompanied by a distortion and, at times, obliteration of history. These days we've become accustomed to hearing that gay male culture of the 1970s was hedonistic, apolitical, and compulsive. Until the epidemic surfaced to "humanize" us, the thinking goes, our relationship to other gay men was alternately exploitative, disposable, and superficial. An entire generation of new activists makes declarations about earlier gay organizing that display ignorance and disdain. A sort of "history-began-with-me" mentality reigns.

The expunging of history is never without ramification. As Native American lesbian author Paula Gunn Allen has written, "The roots of oppression are to be found in the loss of tradition and memory because that loss is always accompanied by a loss of a positive sense of self."[17] Pre-AIDS gay life has undergone such extreme historical revision that the work of social historians who attempt to write about the period will be unusually challenging, especially since men who could offer an alternative view of the period are often prematurely dead.

All around us we witness strange and desperate behavior; "a catastrophic universe has come into being."[18] A look at local gay newspapers provides extensive evidence of the altered atmosphere in the community. We discuss the gay community as "united," "loving," and "committed to caring for its own," when we are just as often intolerant, fractured, and overwhelmed with self-condemnation. Decimation intrudes profoundly into all aspects of life—our intimate relations, community organizations, social traditions, and interpersonal ethics—and we find ourselves living lives unimaginable a decade ago. As occurs in other disasters, we have witnessed nothing less than "the replacement of the natural order of living and dying with an unnatural order of death-dominated life."[19]

HIV AS MASS CATASTROPHE

The AIDS epidemic is a mass community disaster, striking different parts of the world and different populations with different impact. AIDS activists have used the idea of disaster to move a hostile federal government into funding AIDS services. The Ryan White Comprehensive AIDS Relief Effort Act, the first mass infusion of federal dollars, was modeled on and promoted as emergency disaster relief funding. Why haven't we looked at psychosocial issues through this same lens?

Sociological definitions of disasters speak to the daily lives of gay men in America:

The term "disaster" is used to denote usually overwhelming events and circumstances that test the adaptional responses of community or individual beyond their capability, and lead, at least temporarily, to massive disruption of function for community or individual. We generally think in terms of sudden and dramatic events, but disasters may also be gradual and prolonged, creeping on almost insignificantly, as in the case of drought and famine.[20]

Another definition reads:

Disasters are part of the larger category of *collective stress situations*. A collective stress occurs when *many members of a social system fail to receive expected conditions of life from the system*. These conditions of life include the safety of the physical environment, protection from attack, provision of food, shelter, and income, and guidance and information necessary to carry on normal activities.[21]

Few laypeople are familiar with research attempting to predict the stages of impact and response to disasters. Each new cataclysm is experienced without context, void of any sense of predictable ramifications. Beverley Raphael explicates disasters' after-effects:

There are many costs involved in the various stages of disaster response: the preparatory and preventative, counter-disaster, rescue and recovery operations. Yet most people recognize that one of the greatest human costs is the enormity of the psychological experience–the impact and its residuum–the personal suffering and the "scars on the mind." For those who go through the horrifying threat to life or the loss of loved ones, home and possessions, community, or livelihood, the emotional pain is great. And those who are involved in rescue and recovery operations may themselves confront massive death, threat, and loss, and share it empathically with others, becoming themselves indirect victims of the disaster.[22]

When the "multiple loss" literature stopped speaking to the full condition of my life, I searched for alternatives that could help me understand the shattering which was occurring inside. New Age gurus of the 1980s offered a kind of hope that feels empty these days: so many of my friends who "healed their lives" and "took back the power" from the virus were dead by 1990. Twelve-step dogma presupposes a faith in a higher power that seems excruciatingly difficult to attain in the midst of an ever-escalating epidemic. Yet so many of us force the contemporary horror show of our lives into one of these tight envelopes of worldview. We press our fists firmly around crystals and find the way to keep going.

There is something to be said these days for simply finding a way to keep going on individually and communally. Functionality at any level is an impressive achievement amidst the reality of some of our lives. I marvel at the man who has been twice widowed and is entering another relationship. The ability to become engaged with the world and have a range of emotional response is constricted; some of us walk through years like zombies. Can we understand the perils of a zombie existence? Has a discussion of "quality of life" been stamped frivolous and declared off-limits as the battle rages above our trenches?

The literature that speaks to me these days is the literature of natural disasters and human atrocities. I find myself drawn to stories of individuals and communities who have experienced deep and sustained wounding and abuse. I noticed this a few years ago when I developed a powerful interest in the Donner Party, the pioneer families in the mid-1800s who took a wrong turn on the Oregon Trail and found themselves in the Sierra Nevada under two dozen feet of snow, slowly starving to death as they sat out the worst winter in California history.[23] My lover indulged me by spending a weekend visiting the historical sites off the highway near Tahoe. We sat through nature center filmstrips, wandered into museum exhibits, and tramped through snowy fields to find the exact location of their makeshift huts.

Next I found myself reading the daily newspaper with different eyes. Stories of human tragedies that I always glossed over, deriding them as the "National Enquirization" of American journalism, now grabbed my attention and wouldn't let go. A young married couple whose car ran out of gas in an isolated rural area were sheltered in a cave for five snowy days along with their month-old infant; they became my nightly news fix. An eleven-year-old girl abducted from her parents' home in the middle of the night would frequently intrude into my waking thoughts. I would buy half a dozen daily papers to read, clip, and file stories of volcanic eruptions, earthquakes, train derailments, prisoners of war, and inner-city infernos.

I finally had to ask myself what internal changes had brought on this new fascination? Slowly it became apparent that I had been seeking comfort and validation for the pain currently suffered by the gay community. The mythic scope of disasters spoke to the depth of tragedy in my own life. And as I talked with other gay men, I came across others who shared my penchant for disaster stories. One HIV-positive man was deeply involved in a study of his family's experience in the Holocaust. An uninfected black gay man was reading everything he could get his hands on about slavery in America.

While acknowledging the political minefield one enters on considering parallels between atrocities, I believe it is useful to seek out historical and contemporary precedents for gay men's current plight. We are not the first or only community who has suffered greatly; we are not the only ones in our cities today whose lives have been bizarrely interrupted and damaged. Reading the essays of death-camp survivors informs our lives amidst this current epidemic. Parts of ourselves may be gleaned in the stories of battered women and abused children. Middle-class gay men may find more in common with those living amidst the twin epidemics of poverty and addiction, enduring nightly drive-by shootings, gang warfare, and drug-related murders, than we find in the lives we lived prior to the onslaught of AIDS. While acknowledging distinctions among populations that have sustained repeat trauma, torturous abuse, and cultural genocide, I believe an examination of the cycle of community-wide trauma and recovery, more than the paradigms currently utilized to grapple with our experience, can provide assistance in gay men's coping.

Gay men are handicapped by a determination to prove that we are "good boys" and can handle all situations placed before us. As gay activist Ben Schatz has said, "Straight people think we're all best friends with Elizabeth Taylor. Of course they don't think we need public health services."[24] This has made it difficult for many to admit—even under the weight of a dozen years of the epidemic— that our personal systems that interface with the world and ordinarily provide a sense of order, relationship, and significance to our lives, have been overwhelmed. Because many people view the gay male population (particularly white, middle-class gay men) as privileged, some of us are shamed into silence about the terrors we suffer—as if catastrophes that befall privileged populations are less worthy of societal empathy.[25]

We act as if the deaths of over 200,000 men with whom we share a highly politically charged identity should leave us unscarred or at most, mildly affected. The Earthquake of 1906 in San Francisco killed approximately 700 people out of a population of 340,000 and burned down four square miles of city.[26] Historians attribute mass social, economic, and cultural changes in twentieth century San Francisco to this event. Yet the first decade of AIDS, while not destroying buildings and neighborhoods (at least not literally), killed 10,000 citizens out of a population of 700,000. The story of the mass changes wrought by *this* disaster has yet to be written.

Likewise, the bombing of Hiroshima resulted in massive death within the city's population:

> The number of deaths, immediately and over a period of time, will probably never be fully known. Variously estimated from 63,000 to 240,000 or more, the official figure is usually

given as 78,000, but the city of Hiroshima estimates 200,000–the total encompassing between 25 and 50 percent of the city's then daytime population (also a disputed figure, varying from 227,000 to over 400,000).[27]

Observers have noted the huge effect of the bubonic plague on Asia, Africa, and Europe in the fourteenth century and its ability to dramatically alter the course of economic, political, and social trends:

> Civilization both in the East and West was visited by a destructive plague which devastated nations and caused populations to vanish. It swallowed up many of the good things of civilization and wiped them out. It overtook the dynasties at the time of their senility, when they had reached the limit of their duration. It lessened their power and curtailed their influence. It weakened their authority. Their situation approached the point of annihilation and dissolution. Civilization decreased with the decrease of mankind. Cities and buildings were laid waste, roads and way signs were obliterated, settlements and mansions became empty, and dynasties and tribes grew weak. The entire inhabited world changed.[28]

The bubonic plague is estimated to have killed one-third of the population of Europe. I believe more than one-third of the men who comprised gay male cultural and political life in the 1970s are dead or infected and this figure may exceed 75 percent in epicenter cities. Is it unrealistic to expect that our own social order could avoid severe alterations amidst such intense stress? Historians have documented the far-reaching impact of the plague on European society; is it "extreme thinking" to posit that a parallel impact is being felt among gay men?

Writing in 1986, before the vast international impact of the epidemic was understood, Beverley Raphael believed that the effects of the AIDS epidemic would be significantly smaller than that of the plague:

> Many other endemic and sporadic infectious diseases have caused disastrous mortality through the ages. . . . But they did not have the awe of terror evoked by the Black Death, and

even now by the very word "plague." Even today we are afflicted by viral epidemics such as AIDS. But, although dangerous and frightening, none of these recent epidemics carries the same emotional impact, the same sense of disaster, as is conjured up by the Black Death, the plague.[29]

As the epidemic continues to widen and deepen, it is difficult to judge whether Raphael's assessment is accurate if one considers the gulf between the impact of the bubonic plague on Europe and Asia and the specific effects of AIDS on North American gay and bisexual men. The social conditions of the fourteenth century and ease of transmission of plague allowed for relatively equal levels of impact throughout most sectors of the population. This was *truly* a plague that did not discriminate. Unlike HIV, its effects did not disproportionately target specific communities. While the impact of AIDS on American society-at-large may be less pronounced than the plague's on Europe, the impact within specific American populations–including gay men–has been as complex and extensive. Perhaps because the ramifications of the epidemic occurred gradually, they do not seem as shocking or as far reaching as those occurring after a sudden catastrophe. Yet descriptions of the bombing of Hiroshima could be read like metaphors for the decimation of AIDS:

> Those closest to the hypocenter could usually recall a sudden flash, an intense sensation of heat, being knocked down or thrown some distance, and finding themselves pinned under debris or simply awakening from an indeterminate period of unconsciousness. *The most striking psychological feature of this immediate experience was the sense of a sudden and absolute shift from normal existence to an overwhelming encounter with death.*[30]

This mirrors what occurred to gay men over a period of a few years: our ordinary lives and social networks shifted into a constant confrontation with infirmity and death.

NOTES

1. Dori Laub, "Truth and Testimony: The Process and the Struggle," *American Imago* 48(1):80-81 (Spring, 1991).

2. *Ibid.*, 84.

3. Susan Griffin, *A Chorus of Stones* (New York: Anchor Books, 1992), 32.

4. Walt Odets, "AIDS Education and Prevention: Why It Has Gone Almost Completely Wrong and Some Things We Can Do About It" (paper presented at the National Lesbian and Gay Health Conference, Houston, TX, July 23, 1993), 9. Used by permission of Walt Odets.

5. Robert J. Lifton, "In A Dark Time . . . ," in *The Final Epidemic: Physicians and Scientists on Nuclear War*, ed. Ruth Adams and Susan Cullen (Chicago: Educational Foundation for Nuclear Science, 1981), 18.

6. Tom Grothe and Leon McKusick, "Coping with Multiple Loss," *Focus: A Guide to AIDS Research and Counseling* 7(7):5 (June 1992).

7. Post-traumatic Stress Disorder is diagnosed when the following are present: "The person has experienced an event that is outside the range of usual human experience and that would be markedly distressing to almost anyone," "the traumatic event is persistently reexperienced," "persistent avoidance of stimuli associated with the trauma or numbing of general responsiveness," and "persistent symptoms of increased arousal." See *Diagnostic and Statistical Manual of Mental Disorders*, 3rd ed., revised (Washington, DC: American Psychiatric Association, 1987), 146-148.

8. Michael Warner, "Unsafe: Why Gay Men Are Having Risky Sex," *Village Voice*, January 31, 1995, 36.

9. Ron Stall, Don Barrett, Larry Bye, Joe Catania, Chuck Frutchey, Jeff Henne, George Lemp, and Jay Paul, "A Comparison of Younger and Older Gay Men's HIV Risk-Taking Behaviors: The Communications Technologies 1992 Cross-Sectional Survey," *Journal of Acquired Immune Deficiency Syndrome* 5:682-687.

10. Robert J. Lifton, *Death in Life: Survivors of Hiroshima* (New York: Random House, 1967), 83.

11. Beverley Raphael, *When Disaster Strikes* (New York: Basic Books, 1986), 105.

12. Kai T. Erickson, "Loss of Communality at Buffalo Creek," *American Journal of Psychiatry* 133:302-304 (March 1976). This special journal section on "Disaster at Buffalo Creek" includes additional papers that inform my thinking about AIDS and natural disasters. See Gerald M. Stern, "From Chaos to Responsibility," 300-301; Leo Rangell, "Discussion of the Buffalo Creek Disaster: The Course of Psychic Trauma," 313-316; James L. Titchener and Frederic T. Kapp, "Family and Character Change at Buffalo Creek," 295-301.

13. Lifton, "In a Dark Time . . . ," 12.

14. *Ibid.*, 86.

15. Yoko Ōta, quoted in Lifton, *Death in Life*, 86.

16. Two recent accounts of gay people and geography surprisingly appear to downplay the impact of AIDS. See Sidney Brinkley, "Studies Find Gays Moving Out," *Washington Blade*, May 13, 1994, 25; Also, Heath Row, "Gays Moving Out of the 'Hood,'" *San Francisco Examiner*, April 20, 1994, A-7.

17. Paula Gunn Allen, "Who Is Your Mother? Red Roots of White Feminism," in *The Graywolf Annual Five: Multicultural Literacy,* ed. Rick Simonson and Scott Walker (St. Paul: Graywolf Press, 1988), 14-15.

18. Martha Wolfenstein, *Disaster: A Psychological Essay* (Glencoe, IL: The Free Press, 1957), 153.

19. Lifton, *Death in Life,* 30.

20. Raphael, *When Disaster Strikes,* 65.

21. Allen H. Barton, *Communities in Disaster: A Sociological Analysis of Collective Stress Situations* (Garden City, NY: Doubleday & Company, 1969), 38.

22. Raphael, *When Disaster Strikes,* 4.

23. See C.F. McGlashan, *History of the Donner Party: A Tragedy of the Sierra* (Stanford, 1947); Walter M. Stookey, *Fatal Decision: The Tragic Story of the Donner Party* (Salt Lake City: Deseret Book Company, 1950); Joseph A. King, *Winter of Entrapment: A New Look at the Donner Party* (Toronto: P.D. Meany Publishers, 1992).

24. Personal conversation with author, Pajaro Dunes, CA, March 12, 1994.

25. For one perspective on cultural differences in response to disaster see Ruben Martinez, "1 Quake, 2 Worlds," *The New York Times,* January 20, 1994, A19.

26. Gladys Hansen, *San Francisco Almanac* (San Francisco: Chronicle Books, 1980), 195. See also Charles Morris, *The San Francisco Calamity by Earthquake and Fire* (Secaucus, NJ: Citadel Press, 1986), 5.

27. Lifton, *Death in Life,* 20.

28. Ibn Khaldūn, quoted in Michael Dols, *The Black Death in the Middle East* (Princeton: Princeton University Press, 1967), 67.

29. Raphael, *When Disaster Strikes,* 13.

30. Lifton, *Death in Life,* 21.

Chapter 2

Out of the Frying Pan

In a way insane people are angels who, unable to bear the
realities around them, must somehow take refuge in another
world.

—Reinaldo Arena,
Before Night Falls, p. 258

I think you're heading for a breakdown;
Oh be careful not to show it.

—Laura Branigan, "Gloria"

In 1985, I picked myself up from my year of depression and
despair, only to step onto the frontline of the epidemic. I accepted a
job as the executive director of the Los Angeles Gay and Lesbian
Community Services Center, the largest gay-focused nonprofit organization in the world. With a 1985 budget of $2.5 million, twenty-
one government grants, and fifty-eight employees, the Center was a
large multi-purpose agency providing a wide range of social services. Among the projects under its direction at the time were a
shelter for runaway youth, a sexually transmitted disease clinic, an
active counseling center, and a job training program for youth.

At the time, I believed that I uprooted myself from Massachusetts
and took the job in Hollywood because I wanted to work full-time
for the gay and lesbian community. As the epidemic mounted, and
gay community concerns became more visible, I was motivated to
leave my career as a schoolteacher and apply my skills to my own
community. My reasons for accepting the position included elements of ego gratification, increased salary, and expanded authority,

but I had wanted to leap into "professional" community work for some time and this position was a prize.

So I thought. The Center had been through a difficult eighteen months, with several "acting" directors, much internal controversy, and a major staff unionization drive. Morale was low, money was tight, conflict between men and women was intense. With little awareness of what I was getting into, I drove cross-country in early autumn, so that I could begin my job in October. The weeks preceding my arrival brought a sea-change in public awareness of AIDS: Rock Hudson succumbed to AIDS in a highly visible drama observed step-by-step by mainstream America. Just two weeks later, I took over the helm of the Center, one of the key vessels trying to steer through the AIDS storm in Rock Hudson's home town.

When I had accepted the position, I was aware that the Center provided an enormous quantity of AIDS services and public policy expertise. Educational programs targeting the gay community of Los Angeles had originated at the organization, including the nationally acclaimed "L.A. CARES" marketing campaign, featuring diminutive actress Zelda Rubenstein as every gay boy's mother. The agency's legal department handled a huge volume of AIDS discrimination cases, and its mental health services included a number of support groups for HIV-infected individuals. The month I arrived saw the opening of the Center's HIV-testing clinic, which quickly became the highest volume test site in the nation.

Despite the impressive services provided by the organization, the Board and management had failed to articulate clearly the Center's role in the health crisis. It was unclear what turf we occupied and what belonged to AIDS Project Los Angeles, the massive HIV focused agency which began as a phone line in the Center's medical clinic. I discovered deep ambivalence in the organization about the epidemic and, while this conflict first appeared to take the form of debates about balancing AIDS services with gay/lesbian services, once I settled into the job I realized something even deeper was going on.

The Center, like many gay and AIDS organizations throughout the nation in 1985, was at the center of a cyclone. As death and disfigurement became commonplace in the gay community, it grew increasingly difficult for individuals to maintain a state of denial. Gay newspapers inaugurated special obituary sections to document the mounting death toll. It became common to see men at gay restaurants and community events whose faces were scarred with lesions or who appeared as gaunt figures walking with the assistance of a cane. While 10,000 people had been diagnosed with AIDS between 1981-1985, in the three years between 1986 and 1988, *72,000* people were diagnosed, over 70 percent of them gay men.[1]

My job directing the Center always seemed a bit unreal to me. Our day-to-day work focused on the mundane tasks all human service agency staff undertake–fundraising, phone referral, direct service provision, building security, budget preparation–but the culture of the organization was becoming increasingly suffused with death. How did a Board of Directors continue functioning when half its members had recently learned they were HIV positive or had been diagnosed with AIDS? What was it like to try to put personnel policies in place that covered health benefits, sick leave, disability insurance, and bereavement leave, when a large portion of the gay men on staff were infected and several were rapidly becoming ill? As the demands for AIDS information, HIV testing, legal assistance, and mental health services rapidly overwhelmed our systems and long waiting lists for services began, how did each of us on staff find ways to adjust to the individual and agency-wide limitations?

I have never ceased to be amazed that throughout America, gay men, lesbians, and bisexuals continued to provide services, pioneer new treatments, and deal with vast non-AIDS social service needs of the community during these years when the tidal waves began to crash relentlessly against the shore. Serving the gay community has never been easy, but the terror and shock that struck after 1985 brought along new challenges that no one had time to identify, articulate, and troubleshoot. Rage began to sweep over the tribe during these years–directed as much against the federal government and medical bureaucracy as against our own community. The "horizontal hostility," prevalent in gay organizing since early efforts, took on a level of viciousness and insatiability as well as new names such as "oppression sickness" and "community cannibalism." Terrorized populations seek relief and escape in any possible way and many gay men retreated into drug and alcohol abuse. Bizarre personnel situations arose as addiction took its toll on Center staff members. I remember seeing erratic changes in my colleagues–one day hyperactive, the next day sullen. Sometimes it seemed like our biggest challenge was keeping some semblance of sanity among the agency's Board, staff, and volunteers. We were the service providers, the AIDS "experts," the infrastructure of the community; there was no way we could let ourselves fall apart when the rest of the community needed us.

I did everything I was told to do in order to maintain mental health during these years. I went to the gym daily before work, releasing tension through aerobics classes and weightlifting. I began psychotherapy with a prominent West Hollywood psychologist who had pioneered gay mental health treatment. I told myself that my job had unique stressors and tried to take vacations regularly and get out of town. Yet I was unaware that I was dealing with a situation that vastly outpaced my coping capacity. It was as if the Center was a massive dam attempting to hold back the mounting floodwaters inundating the community. As the epidemic's toll increased, as it became harder and harder to look toward the future, the waters began breaking through the dam and relentlessly surged forward.

It was not unusual for any of us at the Center to work sixty to eighty hours, week after week. We would sit through workshops on "Caring for the Caregiver" and then go out and stuff ourselves with fried foods before returning to work into the late hours of the night. I started receiving regular massages, but the strong hands of the masseur couldn't stop my shoulders and back from twisting into a contorted mass. On top of the death and the demand for services, Right-wing extremists successfully placed measures on the California state ballot to quarantine HIV-infected persons and the community had to mount expensive and energy-draining efforts to defeat these initiatives.

My daily schedule was a melange of frantic activity. I ran between my office at the Center, press conferences at City Hall, and late-night organizing meetings against Lyndon LaRouche's AIDS quarantine initiative. I worked with an intensity of which I never imagined I was capable. Somewhere in the back of my head I would tell myself that something was very wrong but, in my conscious mind, I believed I was managing a normal amount of stress and simply playing hardball in the big leagues of nonprofit life. I would get home at midnight, listen to my answering machine, and find a dozen messages that invariably included news of friends who had been diagnosed or died, calls from colleagues who were flipping out under the pressure of the epidemic, and abusive messages from anonymous fanatics who had seen me quoted in the newspapers, looked me up in the phone book, and spewed obscenities into my message machine.

Until recently, I believed my years in Los Angeles were intense, productive, and relatively happy. I feel fortunate to have been part of a team that revived a critical community institution against great odds and made it viable once again. I was proud of the increased fundraising, expanded services, and enhanced public image that we brought to the Center. Yet I was unable to see the toll that life at the center of the cyclone was taking on me. Perhaps because the epidemic was new and striking us in different ways at the same time, it was hard to sort out exactly how it affected the staff and Board of the Center.

In a three-month period, a relationship ended, my best friend and mentor died a demented death from AIDS, and my sister died of complications from diabetes. Like the Energizer rabbit, I kept going forward, not stopping a minute to let myself feel a thing. Jim was diagnosed, then Riff, then Julio, then Fred, and Tony. The range of feelings within me became more and more constricted; I felt anger, fear, or nothing at all. Bob died, then Shelly, then Steve and Ramon. Aspects of myself that I once considered vital were shed without awareness. I had always found comfort in books, but I lost all relationship to literature during these years. I stopped exercising, taking aerobics classes, going for bicycle rides. I went for months without having sex, then would spend a weekend compulsively searching for sex partners. My life and identity had slowly been buried under a vast avalanche called AIDS.

AIDS AND TRAUMA

Disasters of all kinds have powerful psychological effects on survivors. In a landmark study of chronic trauma, Dr. Judith Herman succinctly summarizes the effect of trauma on the human psyche:

At the moment of trauma, the victim is rendered helpless by overwhelming force. When the force is that of nature, we speak of disasters. When the force is that of other human beings, we speak of atrocities. Traumatic events overwhelm the ordinary systems of care that give people a sense of control, connection and meaning. . . . Traumatic events are extraordinary, not because they occur rarely, but rather because they overwhelm the ordinary human adaptations to life. Unlike commonplace misfortunes, traumatic events generally involve threats to life or bodily integrity, or a close personal encounter with violence and death. They confront human beings with the extremities of helplessness and terror, and evoke the responses of catastrophe. According to the *Comprehensive Textbook of Psychiatry*, the common denominator of psychological trauma is a feeling of "intense fear, helplessness, loss of control, and threat of annihilation."[2]

Trauma victims commonly understate or deny the depth and impact of the traumatizing incident. This feature of the trauma syndrome encourages victims to avoid comparison with other disasters. Thus a coping mechanism allows for low-level but continued functioning, as psychic numbing takes hold:

> It is possible for this process to stay at the point where a degree of "psychic closing off" has been accomplished which permits a certain automaton-like behavior which is necessary for survival in situations of subjugation such as prison and concentration camps.[3]

Acknowledging that one has been overtaken by something powerful, and that one's emotional and psychological systems have been overwhelmed is more than most people can handle. For some, a system of denial may be needed for continued functioning, albeit at a low level. Traumatic shutdown in gay men may reflect a psychic inability to master and integrate the epidemic.

Human beings respond to disaster with a range of behavior. One researcher who studied the impact of an explosion and fire in a Norwegian paint factory classified the responses of survivors as "optimal (29.8 percent), adaptive (49.6 percent) and maladaptive (20.7 percent)."[4] Another disaster researcher divided post-disaster behavior into three general categories:

> A group of 12-25 percent was characterized as "cool and collected," able to formulate appropriate plans of action and carry them through. A group of 50-75 percent showed the "normal" response of being stunned and bewildered, as well as a

restricted field of attention, lack of awareness of any subjective feeling or emotion, but behaved reflexively nonetheless. A group of 10-25 percent evidenced obviously inappropriate responses, including panic, paralyzing anxiety, and hysterical behavior.[5]

We can expect gay men's behavioral and psychic responses to AIDS to vary greatly. As the epidemic rages, it is difficult to maintain a continual assessment of the range of impact on individuals and the percentage of the population occupying specific categories of impact. This further encourages social observers to minimize the effects of HIV on the gay community and resist acknowledging the severity of trauma bearing down on us.

Psychologist Walt Odets has documented the multilayered psychological impact on uninfected gay men in his book *In the Shadow of the Epidemic: Being HIV-Negative in the Age of AIDS*. Much of his analysis of psychosocial issues facing HIV-negative gay men may apply to HIV-positive men as well. In an early draft of the book, Odets summarized the psychic landscape of gay men:

> Much of the distress of gay men living in the AIDS epidemic is like that of other individuals and groups–though rarely seen in such large numbers within discrete, isolated communities to mental health care providers. Among the familiar elements are depression, anxiety, isolation and sexual, social and occupational "dysfunction." Such responses must *be expected* in reaction to an event like the AIDS epidemic, but our denial of both the predictability and *fact* of these responses is a measure of how little psychological resilience the epidemic has left us.[6]

Odets presents case histories of psychotherapy clients who manifest depression, hyperactivity, hypomania, mania, anxiety, hypochondriasis, sexual dysfunctions, and survivor guilt. Psychologist Jay Paul and his colleagues summarize parallel psychological fallout among both HIV-positive and HIV-negative gay men, including depression, anxiety, confusion, anger, and suicidal tendencies.[7]

Individual and community-wide trauma are not newly discovered phenomena; they have been probed and analyzed for over a century. By synthesizing the experiences of disparate populations and linking the social science of public trauma (e.g., war or earthquakes) with private trauma (e.g., rape or child abuse), researchers have developed an understanding of the range of effects of trauma as well as specific methods of treatment. Key to an understanding of trauma is a range of subconscious guilt reactions on the part of victims:

> Traumatic events, by definition, thwart initiative and overwhelm individual competence. No matter how brave and resourceful the victim may have been, her actions were insufficient to ward off disaster. In the aftermath of traumatic events, as survivors review and judge their own conduct, feelings of guilt and inferiority are practically universal. Robert Jay Lifton found "survivor guilt" to be a common experience in people who had lived through war, natural disaster, or nuclear holocaust. Rape produces essentially the same effect: it is the victims, not the perpetrators, who feel guilty.[8]

Tom Moon, a psychotherapist working with gay men in San Francisco's Castro district, has described survivor guilt and its many manifestations in gay men who have tested negative for HIV antibodies. Moon catalogues specific symptoms manifested in the population: "paradoxical reactions to learning one's HIV status," "inability to believe one is really negative," "hypochondria," "relapses into unsafe sex," "immobilization," and "self-destructive behavior." He concludes:

> My own work with gay men as well as reports from other clinicians have convinced me that very few HIV negative gay men are not dealing with at least some of the effect of survivor guilt. . . . The continued survival of the gay male community depends, in part, on as many of us as possible achieving an unambivalent commitment to survival.[9]

Dan Wohlfeiler, of San Francisco's Stop AIDS project, in explaining the reasons gay men have unprotected sex, said,

> I think the most powerful factor is the whole question of survival. The rational decision is: I want to survive, therefore I'm going to have safe sex and put the rubber on. But what happens when survival becomes a very iffy concept? When five

of your boyfriends have died? When 50 of your closest friends have died? When people you used to see walk down the street– the baker, the banker, the people you do business with every day, the people you dance with, all the people you wanted to survive with–aren't there anymore?[10]

Is an "unambivalent commitment to survival" possible in the face of a continuing cycle of infection, illness, deformity, and death? Do men with AIDS who are long-term survivors and long-term asymptomic HIV-positive men share survivor guilt with HIV-negative gay men? Is it desirable for gay men facing a future filled with suffering and loss to embrace survival above all else? Would dedication to community continuance be easier to rouse if a cure or a vaccine were in sight?

A single traumatic event is different from an unceasing series of traumatic incidents. Likewise, post-traumatic reactions are distinct from the clinical condition known as "post-traumatic stress disorder." Common reactions to trauma include recurrent flashbacks to the incident, intense anxiety, and avoidance of memories. Post-traumatic stress disorder is a severe, protracted, and intensely disruptive condition:

> People subjected to prolonged, repeated trauma develop an insidious, progressive form of post-traumatic stress disorder that invades and erodes the personality. While the victim of a single acute trauma may feel after the event that she is "not herself," the victim of chronic trauma may feel herself to be changed irrevocably, or she may lose the sense that she has any self at all.
>
> The worst fear of any traumatized person is that the moment of horror will recur, and this fear is realized in victims of chronic abuse. . . . Chronically traumatized people are continually hypervigilant, anxious, and agitated . . . [they] no longer have any baseline state of physical calm or comfort. Over time, they perceive their bodies as having turned against them. They begin to complain, not only of insomnia and agitation, but also of numerous types of somatic symptoms. Tension headaches, gastrointestinal disturbances, and abdominal, back, or pelvic pain are extremely common. Survivors may complain of tremors, choking sensation, or rapid heartbeat. . . .[11]

A wide range of symptoms common to victims of post-traumatic stress disorder increasingly have been observed in diverse populations of gay men: anxiety, agitation, insomnia, depression, panic attacks, hypochondria, back pain, tension headaches, stomachaches, rapid heartbeat, nervous tremors, forgetfulness, loss of memory. Many gay men manifest these symptoms and simultaneously discount their presence or their seriousness. Do we believe the symptoms will abate with our continuing denial of their core etiology? Will we wait until these symptoms become more intense or our overall condition moves to the next level of seriousness before we seek treatment? How long must we deny our psychic condition before facing its severity?

A TIDAL WAVE HITS THE SHORE

I waited until my psyche was overwhelmed with grief, terror, and guilt before I did anything about it. I learned the hard way what dancing between denial, fear, numbness, and exhaustion can do to the human spirit. When I crashed, I crashed big time–personally, professionally, and on the front page of newspapers.

I remember hearing from colleagues that the occupational lifespan of an executive director of an AIDS organization was two years. We would all express surprise and alarm at this rumored statistic. Stable leadership is highly desired in the non-profit sector because it offers an anchor amid rapidly shifting organizational dynamics. Yet during an era of diminishing government support for human services and escalating client need, only a rare individual can survive the extraordinary pressures focused on the leadership of community-based service organizations. Although AIDS service programs received increasing public and private funding after 1985, executive directors of AIDS groups faced overwhelming challenges and were confronted with unresolvable contradictions in our work roles and community politics. We were expected to be grassroots activists and mainstream lobbyists, thrive in the world of affluent donors as well as the shooting galleries and homeless shelters of the inner city, meticulously manage rapidly growing institutions and attend countless out-of-town conferences and political demonstrations. The greatest challenge for gay men leading AIDS organizations has been finding ourselves boxed into tighter and tighter spaces by mounting piles of corpses.

I didn't crash in Los Angeles. After almost three years leading the Center, I ran out of steam. At the time, I told myself I was homesick for Boston, wanted time to write, and missed old friends. Now I believe that a quiet voice within was urging me to get out before I lost my mind. While some felt I left my job too soon, I was satisfied that I had accomplished precisely what I was hired to do: facilitate an agency turn-around, restore public confidence, and begin the process of diversifying the staff, Board, and programs of the agency.

I exited Los Angeles in May 1988 and drove in record time to Provincetown to spend the summer on the beach. While this Cape Cod resort provided me with a place to rest and regain some sanity, even away from full-time AIDS work, my mental state continued to deteriorate. I found it impossible to get away from the epidemic anywhere. Whether one was in Southern California or New England, by 1988, the death toll approached unforeseen heights. This was exacerbated by the dawning awareness throughout epicenter cities that a large chunk of the gay male population was infected already. I spent a total of nine months on the East Coast, shuttling between Boston, Provincetown, and New York City, before I found myself following moving vans once again to the West Coast. I had accepted a position as executive director of Shanti Project, the leading provider of AIDS services in San Francisco, the city of greatest per capita impact of HIV in the nation.*

What was I thinking? Shanti Project had just been dragged through a wrenching year and a half with much-publicized warfare within the organization, a departing executive director, the staff

---

*What follows is a sketch of a protracted and complicated controversy. If my account seems to gloss over details it is because my intent here is not to reveal my perceptions of the complex series of events that resulted in organizational crisis, nor is it to attribute responsibility, distribute blame, or be vengeful. Since my resignation from Shanti Project in 1993, I have refused to comment in the press about specific incidents which occurred inside the agency or the health department, believing it to be unprofessional and unethical to do so and not in the best interest of any of us involved or the organization itself. I have never corrected facts, attributed actions or motives to others, or defended myself. Because this incident is a critical part of my experience of the gay community and the epidemic, I must sketch it out here, but the focus is on me and my emotional state, rather than on a detailing of key incidents.

split into factions, and a Board of Directors that appeared to be doing its best to handle a situation beyond its expertise. There were lawsuits, front-page stories, threats of governmental funding withdrawal, and a community battle for ownership of the organization. Services continued steady and strong, thanks to the powerful commitment of a huge cadre of volunteers, supported by staff members who were understandably running on empty.

Why I thought I could make a contribution to the situation is beyond me. I look back and marvel at my ingenuousness. My experience at the Los Angeles Center had given me some confidence in handling organizational turn-arounds, but I think I was attracted by what I imagined was the glitz of being a leader in San Francisco's gay community and led astray by a combination of naivete and ego. In the midst of the AIDS crisis, I dragged a martyr complex into the work. I imagined I would find my new job demanding and exhausting, but satisfying. Several friends encouraged me to reconsider, warning me of San Francisco's reputation for devouring gay leaders, but I wasn't listening. I had found my calling and there was no turning back.

For three years, I succeeded. Working in partnership with a skilled and talented team of managers, we restored the agency's public image, doubled–then tripled–the agency's service capacity, and began to introduce sound management systems into what seemed like chaos. These were the years of geometric increases in diagnoses (1989-1993) and our top commitment was to try to meet client demand although funds were not increasing at a comparable rate. The Board of Directors adopted an historic, far-reaching plan to transform Shanti into a multicultural organization which brought on enormous political and programmatic ramifications. On the surface, I felt I was in my element, mastering the demands of the job, and believing that my skills and experience were put to good use ensuring services to the burgeoning numbers of people with AIDS in the city by the Bay.

Inside, however, I was dying. By 1990, I had collected obituaries for over 300 friends, colleagues, boyfriends, and dance pals. Because I was new to San Francisco, the deaths of local individuals didn't hit me with the intensity experienced by coworkers within the organization who had lived in the city for years. Yet deaths in

Boston and Los Angeles–while kept at a distance–began to smother me. I felt as if the three cities where I had participated in community-building were being bombed daily, like London during the Blitz. My attitudes about everything changed rapidly, as if someone else occupied my skin. While once I had loved community events and the spirit of the gay ghetto, I now found the Castro, the neighborhood in which I lived, depressed and run down. I began maneuvering my way out of attending key community events and avoiding gay social functions. Even though I held a position of leadership, I began to feel like an outsider within my own organization and estranged from the gay community.

I had been surrounded on all sides by the epidemic and the walls were closing in. My best friend had been diagnosed. I had moved in with a lover who was HIV positive. I wore AIDS t-shirts, hung AIDS posters on my walls, played AIDS-benefit albums on my stereo. I went to safe sex education parties, bought holiday gifts at the AIDS benefit store, and attended AIDS bike-a-thons, dance-a-thons, walk-a-thons, and aerob-a-thons. I rushed from a theatre opening benefitting AIDS service groups, to a press conference about new AIDS statistical trends, to a planning meeting on funding for AIDS services. My mission in life was focused on providing increased services for people with AIDS in San Francisco; beyond that, I didn't have a life.

During this time, I again told myself and other people that I was doing fine. On the surface, I was still functioning–performing my job, going to the gym, starting to build a new relationship. Yet on a deeper level, I was ripped apart inside. If I had been honest with myself, I would have recognized that my feelings had become incredibly constricted. Often I felt nothing at all–not joy, or sadness, or fear, or happiness. I found myself writing postcards to dead people and seeing on a crowded subway car friends who had died several years ago. I developed a range of somatic illnesses–severe back pain, insomnia, memory loss, asthma, and twitches. Death seemed to intrude on my life every moment of every day as I moved through a surreal landscape of illness and deformity.

It takes a person with a strong psyche to survive intact in the middle of disaster. I was a gay man living in the neighborhood of greatest impact in the city of greatest per-capita AIDS cases, directing the largest provider of AIDS services. I worked all day with HIV, then it followed me into bed at night. But I was doing fine, I told myself. I didn't need therapy, and I didn't need a vacation. I'm just fine, thank you.

I continued to persevere, arranging for weekly massages, going to bed earlier, and trying to eat a healthier diet. Yet my attempts at self-care couldn't compensate for the inhuman demands I placed on myself in the workplace, and couldn't reverse the damage being done to my mental health by a spiraling epidemic. I only went to "required" funerals, stopped reading *The New York Times*' obituaries, and refused to attend movies or plays that dealt with AIDS. I rushed from work to the chiropractor then to a support group, then to dinner with a friend. Like a salmon fighting its way upstream, I forced myself forward, even though I was constantly close to exhaustion.

After three years on the job, as power shifts took hold within the organization, pressures began to mount. A few volunteers railed against changes made in the organization's system for training counselors. Some white men rebelled when they were passed over for promotion and vowed to take revenge on women-of-color managers who had begun to accrue some degree of organizational power. Typical crises of AIDS organizations—a Board member losing his temper and screaming abusively at staff, reporters sniping at our heels twenty-four hours a day, escalating culture wars between all races, classes, and genders—began to get to me. As I felt the tension mount and my own psyche wear thin, I began to consider that it might be time for me to step out of the storm.

When I met with key Board members to confess that I was out of steam, I was urged not to resign and I easily settled for a few weeks' rest. Why didn't I honor the need welling up inside to get out of AIDS work? The spreading psychic numbness within made clearheaded thinking impossible. This time, I would pay for it dearly.

Less than a year later, everything blew up. A personnel matter flared into an all-out war, complete with stormy memos, lists of accusations, and threats of retaliation. Before I knew it, a campaign of revenge had been launched against a senior manager, myself, and the agency, and the press had jumped into the fray. An endless list of supposed management abuses and violations were lodged against the manager and me. I tried to steel myself to this criticism, telling myself it came with the job, but I was close to breaking point, and people could tell.

The organization was under siege for two months and, try as I might to keep the personal and professional attacks from getting to me, my reservoir of emotional reserves rapidly ran dry. I tried to summon up the energy to lead the agency through one final crisis, but I didn't have anything left inside. My mental health was already precarious and the added stress of work controversy made my psyche collapse. At the same time, my lover's health was experiencing a sudden and unexpected decline. I lost sleep, couldn't concentrate, and began to have vision problems. Migraine headaches overtook me daily. A therapist diagnosed severe depression, anxiety, panic attacks, and suicidal ideation.

Maybe I was trying simply to "be a man" about things and keep pushing forward, toughing it out and ignoring the toll that the attacks were taking. As I look back on that period, I am struck by how suddenly I moved myself mentally into a position to be victimized and how swiftly the entire system seemed to comply. I vowed not to jump into the quagmire and correct the lies that rapidly were being written into history as "facts," knowing that my mental state was too tenuous to engage in continued sparring and that I had always believed it unprofessional to play out internal organizational disputes in the public eye. Instead of aggressively defending myself and rising to the occasion of protecting the organization, I allowed myself and the organization to be positioned as sacrificial lambs.

I went to see my physician about what I termed a mild rash and she was shocked to see welts covering my stomach, chest, crotch, and beginning to spread over my arms and legs. She sat me down and confronted me with the serious nature of my situation. "It's time to take care of yourself," I remember her telling me. "I think you should consider leaving your job. At the very least, you should take a few weeks' medical leave."

I chose the medical leave over resignation. Yet I still phoned into the office and even traveled to Florida for a conference. Once I arrived, I called back to the City only to hear the madness escalating in the organization. I could go no further. I called my lawyer, tendered my resignation, then left the conference and retreated to my parents' home nearby.

My departure was widely interpreted as an admission of guilt and some felt betrayed by my sudden resignation. The papers printed that I had been triumphantly ousted and a few Board members, perhaps sensing in this plot twist a public relations strategy that might benefit the agency, provided the media with corroborating quotes. As a community I deeply cared about demonized me, I learned what it was like to become a pariah. I had certainly made mistakes and felt them powerfully, but I was at peace with my conscience and knew that I had conducted myself in an ethical manner. Yet rumors circulated that branded me an embezzler, ogre, and madman. Once it became clear that I was not going to counter the charges, people moved quickly to assume roles in the playing out of a classic scandal. While a few scoundrels were the engine driving the madness, most decent people were as overwhelmed as I and simply tried to protect the agency and its services using whatever tactics necessary. The manager and I became larger-than-life symbols of evil and avarice, inviting the masses to check in weekly with their condemnation in the letters pages of gay newspapers.

For the next three months I sat in my apartment, barely able to function. I couldn't eat, couldn't sleep, and couldn't answer the phone. I cried uncontrollably, vomited frequently, and continued to be covered with rashes. After I was assaulted on the street by a stranger who recognized my face from newspaper photos, I was terrified to leave the apartment. I watched my psyche, once seemingly healthy, strong, and resilient, unravel around me. It felt as if someone had taken off the top of my head and my brain had spilled out like spaghetti strands. At the time, I thought that I simply had been done in by the stresses of my job, another casualty of gay community internecine warfare. Only through months of intensive therapy did I realize that something larger than me, larger than the controversy, was going on. I finally came face to face with the backlog of a dozen years of psychological fallout from the epidemic.

GOING OUT OF OUR MINDS

An understanding of trauma has much to offer gay men of my generation as we attempt to grapple with ourselves and understand our community-wide response to the epidemic beyond surface observations that we are "normalizing AIDS" or minimizing its impact. Perhaps the greatest question facing an application of current trauma paradigms to the impact of AIDS on gay men involves a key distinction between the ongoing epidemic and the experience of victims of rape, combat veterans, Holocaust survivors, and Central American refugees. The groundwork for trauma recovery involves the establishment of safety. Before reparative therapy can take place with a battered woman, she is moved into a shelter and obtains restraining orders against the perpetrator. Combat veterans return home before clinicians begin to work with them, leaving the killing fields thousands of miles away. Attempting intervention with gay men while the death toll continues to mount, seems akin to providing reparative therapy to prisoners of war when they are still locked in underground cages. What kind of recovery is possible in the absence of safety? The challenge we face may be similar to that facing pioneering efforts to examine and mitigate the impact of unsolved child kidnappings on surviving family members after years of roller coaster emotions. How can we alleviate post-traumatic stress disorder when the "post" period has not yet been reached? Much of trauma recovery theory is based on clearly differentiated roles of victim, perpetrator, witness, and helper. How does the complicated overlap of roles and shifting identities of both HIV-positive and HIV-negative gay men confuse our application of these research findings to AIDS? Can a gay man occupy multiple roles? Can recovery occur without a designated perpetrator?

As we project into the future and attempt to anticipate the increasingly severe impact of a deepening epidemic on gay men in need who have failed to initiate any kind of reparative treatment, an ominous question emerges: Beyond the initial impact symptoms, which Judith Herman describes as dominated by "the persistent expectation of danger," "the indelible imprint of the traumatic moment," and "the numbing response of surrender" (or, in clinical terms as "hyperarousal, intrusion, and constriction"[12]), what happens to individuals who continue to experience deepening chronic trauma? If the epidemic's impact intensifies without a significant shift in the community's current self-awareness and methods of coping, what will happen to some of our lives and psyches in the coming years? What awaits us when we move beyond hysteria and depression?

Herman provides some clues as she discusses the responses of individuals who have experienced prolonged captivity and isolation:

> During prolonged confinement and isolation, some prisoners are able to develop trance capabilities ordinarily seen only in extremely hypnotizable people, including the ability to form positive and negative hallucinations and to disassociate parts of the personality . . . prisoners develop the capacity voluntarily to restrict and suppress their thoughts. This practice applies especially to any thoughts of the future. . . . [They] consciously narrow their attention, focusing on extremely limited goals. The future is reduced to a matter of hours or days. Alterations in time sense . . . eventually progress to the obliteration of the past. . . . Thus prisoners are eventually reduced to living in an endless present.[13]

Chronically traumatized people who go without intervention or treatment often experience severe psychiatric upheaval and ongoing major mental illness–thought, mood, and personality disorders. Many adult trauma victims have a childhood history of trauma[14]–battering, incest, sexual exploitation, emotional abuse–and some clinicians believe the process of growing up gay in a culture that hates homosexuals is traumatizing.[15] Such underlying conditions may foment a severe reaction to trauma in adulthood, bringing on major mental illness. Individuals with a history of childhood abuse might experience multiple personality disorder; those manifesting particular biochemical imbalances might begin to exhibit signs of schizophrenia and bipolar conditions.

In its extreme form, chronic trauma may result in the immobilization of its victims, while a psychic paralysis takes hold that is followed by "progressive constriction of cognitive processes including memory, problem solving, until a mere vestige of self-observing ego is preserved. This process may culminate in psychogenic death."[16] While substantial cases of these severe conditions among gay male survivors of the first dozen years of the AIDS epidemic have not been documented yet, anecdotal information has started to appear concerning individuals who, as the inferno blazes around them, are literally going out of their minds.

RESTORING COMMUNITY-WIDE MENTAL HEALTH

Until our understanding of what is happening is broadened, the primary psychosocial coping strategies utilized by gay men will remain rooted in denial and the deliberate adoption of false consciousness. Many men consider this kind of avoidance justifiable, believing that the circumstances we face necessitate continued tactics of cheerleading, forced optimism, and even deception. Yet those who continue down this path risk encountering a fate similar to that facing other sufferers of untreated chronic trauma: a gradual erosion of psychological functioning. The application of treatment strategies utilized with other forms of trauma to the specific circumstances facing large sectors of the gay male population offers a compelling alternative.

In *Trauma and Recovery,* while acknowledging the recovery process as "inherently turbulent and complex," Judith Herman offers three stages that individuals and communities attempting recovery have experienced, although not in a discrete and ordered manner: (1) the establishment of safety; (2) remembrance and mourning; (3) reconnection with ordinary life.[17] The broad mission of this kind of reparative work can be considered the integration of the post-traumatic self with the pre-traumatic self:

> Extreme trauma creates a second self. . . . In extreme involvements, as in extreme trauma, one's sense of self is radically altered. And there is a traumatized self that is created. Of course it's not a totally new self, it's what one brought into the trauma as affected significantly and painfully, confusedly, but in a very primal way, by that trauma. And recovery from post-traumatic effects, or from survivor conflicts, cannot really occur until that traumatized self is reintegrated. It's a form of doubling in the traumatized person. . . . The struggle in the post-traumatic experience is to reconstitute the self into the single self, reintegrate itself.[18]

In the midst of a continuing epidemic, what possibilities exist for the resurrection of gay men's psyches? What resources are available to us and what kinds of programs need to be developed? Does the special nature of the AIDS epidemic introduce unbreachable barriers to psychological stability for highly affected gay men?

A review of services available to gay men in many urban areas uncovers programs that might assist individuals at the three stages of trauma recovery, yet no comprehensive, managed system of treatment supporting a community-wide psychological revival. In order to establish a cohesive model, health systems planners and community-based advocates may need to overcome personal denial about their own precarious mental health conditions, and fill crucial gaps in their understanding of current mental health issues facing gay men.

Why isn't there a strong health care system ready to address the needs of gay men beyond HIV and AIDS? What happened to the pioneering efforts of gay liberation to create systemic approaches to gay health concerns? What are these programs like in the 1990s?

Like so much else, the establishment of a health care system to address the needs of gay men and lesbians was interrupted by an epidemic swooping down onto the community in the early 1980s. No one ever made a system-wide decision to cease development efforts in areas not directly related to AIDS. Instead, community activists, health systems planners, medical personnel, and researchers were drawn to the demands imposed by a new state of emergency. Government funding for HIV-related health projects—however limited and late in arriving—has been vastly greater than resources devoted to other gay and lesbian health concerns such as addiction recovery, rape and anti-gay violence, depression and suicide, smoking cessation, cancer, and adolescent mental health. An embryonic system of health care initiated in the early 1970s experienced major permutations in its developmental process that, by the late 1980s, resulted in leaving it stunted, fractured, and bizarrely chained to the massive and politically driven AIDS care system.

Similarly, the fields of gay-affirmative psychology, social work, psychoanalysis, and counseling, born shortly before the onset of the epidemic, have experienced significant interruptions to their development and expansion. Our current knowledge of these fields is limited; hence many of the constructs we use to understand gay male identity formation, sexuality, and mental health are tentative and undeveloped. Because research has been limited and politically charged, programs designed to serve gay men have been based on assumptions and hypotheses about gay men's lives rather than well-researched, explicated, and proven theories.

How have we managed to create systems of gay male HIV prevention and mental health without strong components designed to support community-wide trauma recovery? Many community advocates who lead the charge for health care funding have no experience or training in these fields and discount the relevance of mental health constructs as "psychobabble." They adopt purely behaviorist approaches to the human service needs of the community, believing that information translates into behavior change and is not mediated by the unconscious mind. The debate over inclusion of mental health concerns in the Clinton Administration's universal health care proposal revealed the limited value many Americans place on psychological matters. An erosion of the infrastructure of public health systems nationwide during the Reagan-Bush-Gingrich years has left mental health advocates without resources for systemic approaches to *any* problem. Hence a system conceived as preventative has become crisis-driven and unable to respond in effective and strategic ways.

At this stage of the epidemic, health systems planners literally cannot afford to acknowledge that their target population is comprised of individuals with mental health conditions all over the map: some gay men continue to process and integrate the grief and losses of the epidemic without becoming overwhelmed, others suffer significant grief overload; some men show symptoms typical of post-traumatic reactions while others appear to be experiencing severe post-traumatic stress disorders. Even though psychological state is a determinant of receptivity to HIV-prevention efforts, we have repeatedly deemphasized mental health issues in the creation of gay male prevention campaigns. People assigned responsibility for educational programs focused on the gay community are often community organizers or public health workers operating out of limited paradigms that minimize the impact of mental health and discount insights of psychologists.

Equally challenging are the entrenched "beliefs" maintained by much of the gay community's vocal leadership. On an almost visceral level many resist acknowledging that we are no longer who we were before the epidemic occurred and that we will never return to our pre-epidemic selves. Collectively we deny that the gay male community has been scarred permanently. We still participate in discussions about the day when "a solution" is found and the community "can return to normal." As activist and author Cindy Patton writes,

> At first, AIDS, our dying friends, our own fears of illness and death seem unreal, and we respond by thinking, "If I can just *get through this part,* life will return to normal." As more friends receive various diagnoses, and we live with new fears and new needs to allocate finite time and energy, it begins to dawn on us that *this is our lives now,* and things will never go back to the normal we once knew. . . .
>
> Underlying the practical aspects of life in this war zone is a sense of living in another reality, a sense of alienation from "ordinary life" that obscures the ways in which complex social and cultural attitudes insistently construct the domain of AIDS as unreal in order to contain the fears about sexuality and about death. Demanding that life near AIDS is an inextricably *other* reality denies our ability to recreate a sustaining culture and social structures, *even as we are daily required to devote much time to the details of the AIDS crisis.*[19]

By telling ourselves that the epidemic is a temporary displacement of resources, pleasure, and people and avoiding accepting it as a permanent feature of our lives, we also are kept from initiating any kind of reparative process. Adaptations and adjustment cannot occur without accepting the cataclysm's ability to bring profound change. Is it possible to consider a return to anything that resembles "normal" life during a disaster that continues unabated? Or should our energies be directed towards the consideration of new forms of life that integrate the reality of AIDS into our communal culture? Does acceptance bring with it an inevitable spiraling into depression?

Acknowledging the ways various aspects of the epidemic have been underestimated is not the same as normalizing AIDS, throwing up our hands, and heading home. Admitting the powerful ways our lives have been permanently changed by great suffering and loss does not mean that we let go of working for treatments and cures or stop caring for sick friends. It seems like heresy to feel that many or all of us won't "be here for the cure," as if acknowledging deep doubts will bring research efforts to a dramatic halt. While the political rationale remains compelling to insist that coordinated research could lead to swift solutions, we have allowed our internal feelings to the contrary to go without expression. This has had catastrophic cost. Because our public posture often stands in direct contrast to our inner thoughts, we stifle ourselves to the point of suffocation. In part, by living at extremes and insisting publicly that a cure is imminent and privately that pathetically little progress has occurred, we fail to recognize that aggressive intervention has been able to mitigate the onset of specific infections and prolong healthy functioning. The increasingly parochial nature of discourse within the formal structures of gay communal life has exacerbated many men's pre-existing alienation from the community. One therapist describes this phenomena:

> Another gay therapist tells me that for many years, when he did an initial interview with a new client, he sometimes wrote a shorthand notation "FOBO"–which meant "Feelings of Being an Outsider." After some years he realized that he made this notation for every gay client he saw. I have had a similar experience. I would be hard pressed to come up with a single example of a gay man or lesbian in my experience who was not deeply acquainted with the feeling of being an outsider.[20]

The AIDS epidemic did not initiate gay men's struggle with "outsider" status in what we ironically consider to be "our" community. Yet at this stage, many men who have long embraced gay identity and communal life are opting out. They feel alienated at gay pride parades, limited patience with community politics, and tremendous despair after skimming the headlines of gay newspapers. For the first time in their adult lives, these men are questioning their connection to core parts of their sexual identity and joining the chorus of voices asking whether "gay community" really exists.[21]

There are many factors that might lead gay men to question community participation these days, but often unacknowledged are the ways in which our individual processes of gay identity formation and development have been derailed by the epidemic. Identity development among marginalized populations in America follows a unique developmental process that includes various phases of grappling with and living out one's ethnic, religious, gender, or sexual orientation-focused identity. The way one experiences being gay at eighteen might be different at twenty-five, still different at forty, and different again at sixty. As an individual man negotiates life tasks such as coming out, entering a social arena, finding work, and coupling, he "holds" gay identity differently–sometimes with greater ease and comfort, at other times with greater conflict and ambivalence. While the many ways AIDS has affected the process of gay identity formation have yet to be documented, I believe the epidemic's introduction of major contortions into an evolutionary process has left many men surprisingly unsettled and dubious about their relationship to gay identity and gay communal life. When gay identity is linked with AIDS, do we de-gay ourselves as a form of self-preservation?

NOTES

1. Centers for Disease Control, *Morbidity and Mortality Weekly Report: Reports on AIDS* (Atlanta: Centers for Disease Control, 1986):91, (June 1981-May 1986); 1990: 15.
2. Judith Lewis Herman, *Trauma and Recovery* (New York: Basic Books, 1992), 33.
3. Henry Krystal, "Integration and Self-Healing in Post-Traumatic States: A Ten-Year Retrospective," *American Imago* 48(1):100 (Spring 1991).
4. L. Weisaeth, *The Study of a Factory Fire* (PhD diss., University of Oslo, 1983), 65, quoted in Beverley Raphael, *When Disaster Strikes* (New York: Basic Books, 1986), 65.
5. J.S. Tyhurst, "Individual Reactions to Community Disaster: The Natural History of Psychiatric Phenomena," *American Journal of Psychiatry* 107:764-769 (1950), quoted in Beverley Raphael, *When Disaster Strikes* (New York: Basic Books, 1986), 65.
6. Walt Odets, *In the Shadow of the Epidemic: Being HIV-Negative in the Age of Aids.* (Durham, NC: Duke University Press, 1995), 23. Used by permission of Walt Odets.
7. Jay P. Paul, Robert B. Hays, and Thomas J. Coates, "The Impact of the HIV Epidemic on U.S. Gay Male Communities," in *Lesbian, Gay, and Bisexual Identities Over the Lifespan: Psychological Perspectives on Personal, Relational and Community Processes,* ed. Anthony R. D'Augelli and Charlotte J. Patterson (Oxford: Oxford University Press, in press).
8. Tom Moon, "Survivor Guilt in HIV Negative Gay Men," unpublished paper.
9. *Ibid.*
10. Michael Munzell, "Dancing With Death," *San Francisco Chronicle and Examiner,* Sunday, August 23, 1992, *Image Magazine,* 24.
11. Herman, *Trauma and Recovery,* 86.
12. *Ibid.,* 35.

13. *Op. Cit.*, 88-89.

14. Beverley Raphael, *When Disaster Strikes* (New York: Basic Books, 1986), 82.

15. Laura S. Brown, "Not Outside the Range: One Feminist Perspective on Psychic Trauma," *American Imago* 48(1):119-133 (Spring, 1991).

16. Krystal, "Integration and Self-Healing in Post-Traumatic States," 99-100.

17. Herman, *Trauma and Recovery,* 155.

18. Cathy Caruth, "Interview with Robert Jay Lifton," *American Imago* 48(1):164 (Spring 1991).

19. Cindy Patton, *Inventing AIDS* (New York and London: Routledge, 1991), 107-108.

20. Tom Moon, "A Community of Outsiders," *San Francisco Sentinel,* March 30, 1994, 22.

21. During the time I was writing this book I attended a special weekend retreat for HIV-negative gay men in San Francisco who shared a long history of community leadership. As we went around the opening circle, man after man expressed feelings of deep ambivalence and alienation from the gay community and the group collectively noted and scrutinized this surprising realization.

Chapter 3

Recovering the Psyche of the Body Politic

It is the realization that the lost ones are not coming back; the realization that what life is all about is precisely living with an unfulfilled hope; only this time with the sense that you are not alone any longer–that someone can be there as your companion–knowing you, living with you through the unfulfilled hope. . . .

–Dori Laub, "Truth and Testimony"

I got all my sisters and me.

–Sister Sledge, "We Are Family"

Experts on trauma insist "no other therapeutic work should even be attempted until a reasonable degree of safety has been achieved."[1] What is required for gay men to feel safe in the contemporary environment? If we are uninfected with HIV, do we need assurance that we will never become infected? If we are HIV positive do we require a guarantee that we will not develop illnesses and die? Or is the safety we seek protection from watching more people become infected, ill, deformed, and dead?

These vexing and unanswered questions require the breaking of new ground in our understanding of trauma recovery. Either we accept that recovery is impossible until the epidemic is "over" or we can attempt a close examination of the components of safety and attempt to redefine the term under continuing catastrophic circumstances. Can one feel anything that approximates safety in one's body, mind, and relations during an ongoing epidemic? And can one do this without running away from the epidemic?

As I began therapeutic work after my psyche crashed, I was forced to confront these questions in partnership with my therapist. Could I pinpoint specific aspects of the epidemic and circumstances in my own life that were key areas of danger? Was my primary terror about becoming infected and dying? Was it about my lover becoming sick or more close friends dying? Perhaps it wasn't about individuals at all and instead focused on a fear that the gay community would cease to exist? Was I trying to be safe from a virus or from death or from another broken heart? From the Radical Right or continuing distortions of sexual desire? From the demonizing I experienced in my professional life or from loss of the history and culture of our pre-epidemic existence?

Individual men will identify different sources for the dangers that preoccupy their psyches. Which fears can be ameliorated and which require acceptance and adjustment? My own therapy allowed me to distinguish between areas primarily under my own aegis and those over which I had only the illusion of control. This allowed me to focus on minimizing my risk for sexual contagion and forging a new relationship to community life that left me less vulnerable to being a lightning rod for accusations, grief, and rage. At the same time, I began to seek ways to adjust to the realities of life that I could not control–friends becoming sick and dying, continuing sudden changes in my sexual response, an acceleration of anti-gay mobilizing nationwide.

SAFETY, DANGER, AND POST-STONEWALL GAY LIFE

By drawing on the vast knowledge and experience of clinicians and community organizers working with survivors of various types of trauma, it may be possible to propose models of safety restoration amid the continuing impact of AIDS. These models will undoubtedly be complex and require protracted analyses, but some kind of safety must be achieved before healing can be initiated. This may require the intellectual deconstruction of "safety," an examination of its core components, and its reconstruction in the contemporary epidemic environment. Feminist analyses of post-trauma survival have faced similar predicaments. Laura S. Brown writes:

How, rather than desensitizing survivors to symptom triggers, a currently fashionable approach to the treatment of posttraumatic symptoms, can we help them to reconstruct their world-views with the knowledge that evil can and does happen? Rather than teaching trauma survivors ways to attain their pre-trauma levels of denial and numbness, how can we facilitate their integration of their painful new knowledge into a new ethic of compassion, feeling with, struggling with the web of life with which they relate?[2]

An additional provocative question emerges. Did gay men as a class ever enjoy lives of safety? While it has become common to nostalgically recall pre-epidemic gay male culture as carefree, breezy, and frivolous, my own life during those years, steeped in emerging gay culture and politics, seemed fraught with hazards. Certainly pre-Stonewall gay life had its dangers: electroshock, mental hospitals, suicide, scandal. The risks involved in coming out as a gay man in the 1970s may have been frequently articulated but post-Stonewall gay life held many other dangers that are often glossed over by memory. Bars, discos, and sex clubs were located in high-crime neighborhoods and were often sites of queerbashings, muggings, and murders. The drug culture of the 1970s, often sentimentalized as ebullient and harmless, was laced with breakdowns from bad acid and deaths from overdoses. Even our sex lives, which held more peril than we often remember, have been romanticized. While some men did attempt to keep syphilis and gonorrhea in check by popping antibiotics, even more dangerous were tenacious intestinal parasites which resisted treatment for years, hepatitis which spread madly and killed many, and sex-related battering and murder.

I was twenty-six when the epidemic first surfaced and I had been involved in gay community life for almost a decade. I was part of the *Gay Community News* collective in Boston and "safety" isn't a word I would use to describe the world we inhabited. Our investigative reporter was found dead under suspicious circumstances. The office manager was killed outside a gay bar. We received daily phone calls threatening violence. Bullets were shot through our front windows. Our offices finally were burned to the ground.

These were not uncommon features of community life in the 1970s (in many parts of the nation they continue to be common). Metropolitan Community Church buildings were torched throughout the nation. Gay porn theatres became infernos and dozens of men died in several different cities. Suicides were alarmingly common. Men arrested in city parks went home and pulled the trigger. Leather-men chatting in front of a bar in New York City were killed by rifle shots. Harvey Milk was assassinated in San Francisco City Hall.

Many of the individuals who have romanticized pre-epidemic gay life are men who maintained a distance from the more perilous sides of community life. Closeted men of the middle class often experienced the safest aspects of gay male culture. The closet shielded them from losing job opportunities, family relations, and access to power. Because they weren't involved in gay politics and community organizations, they often were unaware of the hazard-ous nature of such activity. Even clubs oriented toward these men often were situated in less hazardous neighborhoods and, on the occasions when they ventured to bars in the waterfront, meat-pack-ing districts, and industrial areas, they drove their own cars or could afford cabs. Since their own lives appeared relatively safe during these years, these men may imagine all gay life to have been with-out significant danger.

The myth of the safety of gay life before the epidemic may have taken hold because of a deep need to believe that a golden age existed for gay men at some time in the past. This experience is common among survivors of other extreme historical events:

Both Hiroshima and concentration camp survivors, in dis-cussing their early lives, frequently presented images of a "golden age," of "idyllic childhoods, spent in the bosom of close, harmonious families." While expiatory needs to ideal-ize the dead are important here, this kind of image serves another important function: it is the survivor's effort to reacti-vate within himself old and profound feelings of love, nurtu-rance, and harmony, in order to be able to apply these feelings to his new formulation of life beyond the death immersion. Inevitably these relate to early childhood, a universal "golden age" in which, whatever its pain, one is capable of uncomplicated happiness.[3]

While utopian fantasy might provide comfort for memories, the dangers of pre-epidemic gay life force a consideration of whether current efforts with gay men should aim to *restore* safety or consider AIDS a new trauma visited upon an already traumatized population. Openly gay men in America *have never known safety.* The movement for gay liberation aimed to create a modicum of freedom and protection. The tragedy of the epidemic is that it occurred after only a dozen years of mass effort to bring peace of mind and security to a despised population. Hence the construction of safety must consider and respond to the special questions raised by this epidemic. What do we mean by "safety" when we are talking of gay men?

Evaluating gay men's current obstacles to successful engagement in a therapeutic relationship and the creation of bonds of interpersonal trust also may prove especially useful. Ample justifiable reasons make it difficult for some gay men to be honest and candid with mental health practitioners. Certainly questions of access and cultural appropriateness often limit therapy to the middle class. Likewise, group therapy introduces complex barriers to participation for gay and bisexual men of all classes, including homophobia and biphobia in groups including heterosexuals, and issues of competition, approval, and power between men. Groups designed to create peer support may assist many individuals in achieving some sense of safety in the world but not without a careful assessment of sexual and cultural dynamics between men.

Interventions successfully utilized with victims of other trauma (e.g., earthquakes, trainwrecks, sexual assault, and rape) should be considered for application to contemporary gay men in America. While many of these are already being utilized (stress-reduction techniques, aerobic exercise, meditation), they frequently are applied in haphazard and ill-considered ways and are rarely considered as serious interventions that could mitigate ongoing trauma symptoms. More experimental techniques used with disaster survivors might be considered, including visualization of emergency safety plans, assignments of specific daily, self-care tasks, and journal writing that routinely documents symptoms and describes the effect of specific interventions.

The use of antidepressant and antianxiety medications has become quite common in many segments of the American population and especially among survivors of trauma. Urban gay men appear to make increasing use of such medications: one San Francisco therapist estimated that almost 50 percent of uninfected gay men are on antidepressant or antianxiety medication.[4] While the long-term use of prescription drugs is currently much debated in the mental health and addiction recovery fields, many gay men attribute improved functioning and psychological well-being to medication.

The initial phase of trauma recovery holds at its core the creation of some sense of personal power and control for the traumatized individual. Placing the survivor at the center of decision making about treatments and interventions is key to establishing safety and promoting an improved sense of authority. Gay men attempting trauma recovery will need support and guidance, yet any effort to remove the individual from the locus of control will undermine his critically needed sense of genuine power and responsibility.

REMEMBRANCE AND MOURNING

Judith Herman names the second phase of recovery from trauma "Remembrance and Mourning":

> The ordinary response to atrocities is to banish them from consciousness. Certain violations of the social compact are too terrible to utter aloud: this is the meaning of the word *unspeakable.*
>
> Atrocities, however, refuse to be buried. Equally as powerful as the desire to deny atrocities is the conviction that denial does not work. Folk wisdom is filled with ghosts who refuse to rest in their graves until their stories are told. Murder will out. Remembering and telling the truth about terrible events are prerequisites both for the restoration of the social order and for the healing of individual victims.[5]

Many gay and bisexual men stopped telling our stories after the initial years of the epidemic. We repress specific memories and avoid quantifying our loss. Even among close friends or between lovers many of us have never shared fully our experiences and feelings concerning the epidemic. An explicit recounting of hearty lovers becoming hollow men with sunken eyes or of cleaning shit off the pencil-thin legs of dear friends, seems more than we can bear. Some of us believe we've recited our stories millions of times, like Coleridge's Ancient Mariner forcing wedding guests to hear his gruesome saga. Others think, "Who cares? Every gay man in my city has a painful story to tell. Who would want to be burdened with mine?"

At best, we choose euphemisms over graphic detail, broad generalities over specific description, off-the-cuff remarks and caustic asides over direct and serious testimony. In part, this explains why it appears to some as if we've normalized the epidemic–we have an investment in acting as if the avalanche had never happened. Yet methods of healing from trauma are predicated upon self-examination and revelation. Casual references do not have the healing potential of full disclosure.

This summer on a beach vacation with gay and lesbian friends of many years, we acknowledged that we had never spoken with one another about our concrete experiences in the epidemic. All of us have lived and worked close to the center of the epidemic. What was it like to care for one of our colleagues as he died a slow and demented death? How do those of us with infected lovers manage to look toward the future? How are our organizing efforts undermined when we serve on task forces comprised of people who are either dying, taking care of sick friends, or emotionally shut down? What does it feel like to spend twenty years building community, to watch it crumble under our feet?

Detailing our experiences is the start of a concerted attempt toward restoring sanity. The critically important relationship between testimony and survival is evident from accounts of Holocaust survivors:

Towards the end of her testimony at the Video-Archive for Holocaust Testimonies at Yale, one woman survivor made the statement: "We wanted to survive so as to live one day after Hitler, in order to be able to tell our story." In listening to testimonies, and in working with survivors and their children,

I came to believe the opposite to be equally true. The survivors did not only need to survive so that they could tell their story; they also needed to tell their story in order to survive.[6]

Likewise, I believe many gay men who have survived the first fifteen years of decimation need to tell our lengthy and detailed stories if we are to survive this epidemic. Yet the difficult work of testimony cannot occur in isolation. We need to have one-on-one and small group relationships that permit and support uncompromising truth-telling. If much of our community is not ready to listen, in what spaces can our stories echo? Nonjudgmental peer support groups designed to facilitate honest revelation, however unpredictable or ugly, are vital for affirming the experience and feelings of survivors:

> Relationships with those who shared the death encounter and survival are always considered of particular significance. Those who have "been through the same thing" seem to feel a special understanding and empathy. Whereas others may not understand or even recognize problems that occur in the post-disaster period, these people are often experiencing similar difficulties. There is enormous recognition and mutual support from association with those who do "know just what it was like." Shared feelings, memories, perceptions, and interpretations of the event are all significant in these bonds.[7]

Many existing HIV-related groups maintain a covert agenda that conflicts with authentic disclosure. For example, groups designed to promote community norms of safe sex and "healthy lifestyles" cannot pretend to be sites for an honest and full imparting of stories that include unsafe sex. Ongoing, reliable, and well-facilitated groups free of other agendas are life-saving. Groups targeting gay men of specific ethnicities, races, ages, and HIV-antibody statuses may be necessary for the creation of safety, given highly charged cultural biases and the many men who feel unsafe in heterogenous groupings.

An encounter with a friend who summons up a sense of the pre-AIDS world may bring out conflicted response. Sometimes we avoid these friends, while at other times we seek them out as they offer a unique route into our memories and emotions. Last summer, while on vacation on Cape Cod where I once lived, I ran into a man with whom I'd been close during the late 1970s. We ran with the same beach-cocktails-disco crowd. His lover and almost all members of our circle are dead. My chance encounter with him caught me off-guard: we exchanged cursory greetings and I quickly moved on. I later found myself seated next to him on the beach and we began conversing, cautiously at first, about the "good old days." This evolved into a two-hour discussion interweaving memories and regrets. We laughed, cried, dreamed, and gossiped our way from the first death through the last. I came away lighter, feeling that certain kinks in my psyche had finally been unknotted.

Telling stories is time-consuming. The process involves remembering back and recounting dreams and lives before the epidemic began. Discussion of experiences at the different stages of the epidemic must be detailed and thorough. Recollecting explicit sensations, smells, feelings, and sights associated with key events may help trigger memories. At times it might be appropriate for the survivor to be asked questions that encourage him to delve into particularly painful and frightening incidents.

The difficult process of testimony allows for a courageous confrontation with the pervasive ways extreme historical events transform values and challenge meaning in life. By facing our personal and collective history head-on, we gain the opportunity to integrate it and begin to move forward. As one author wrote about Holocaust testimony:

It is this very commitment to truth, in a dialogic context and with an authentic listener, which allows for a reconciliation with the broken promise, and which makes the resumption of life, in spite of the failed promise, at all possible. The testimony cannot efface the Holocaust. It cannot deny it. It cannot bring back the dead, undo the horror, or reestablish safety, the authenticity and the harmony of what was home. But neither does it succumb to death, nostalgia, memorializing, ongoing repetitious embattlements with the past, or flight to superficiality or to the seductive temptation of the illusion of substitutions. It is a dialogical process of exploration and reconciliation of two worlds–the one that was brutally destroyed and the one that is–that are different and will always remain so.[8]

This precise form of testimony may be particularly challenging to gay men due to the complex role guilt, shame, and responsibility have played in our lives before and after the onset of AIDS. How have we, individually and collectively, acted responsibly? How have we acted irresponsibly? What factors contributed to our becoming the primary initial vectors of HIV transmission in the United States and how did our community become the site of so much suffering? How has our belief in God been altered and our system of values changed? The recounting of our experience in the epidemic, done conscientiously, may allow for the beginning of an integration of the disaster we refer to as "the epidemic" into our psyches.

Beyond individual efforts, community-wide activities that enumerate the collective experience of the epidemic assist in healing the social order. Cultural expressions of remembrance may be the site of communal gay male recollection and primarily occur informally, around dinner tables, after memorial services, and through community-based media. Theatre pieces such as *The Normal Heart* and *Angels in America,* movies such as *And the Band Played On* and *Longtime Companion,* and books such as *Borrowed Time* by Paul Monette and *The Body and Its Dangers* by Allen Barnett become collective rituals for a community deeply ambivalent about facing its past.

The televising of Armistead Maupin's *Tales of the City* initiated one-on-one and group discussions that encouraged gay men throughout the nation to recount our pre-epidemic lives. These informal exchanges, along with prolific media discourse, editorials, and letters to the editor that focused on the series, created a spontaneous, collective ritual that struggled with remembrance and testimony. Was gay life in the 1970s depicted accurately? What do we remember about gay bars and bathhouses before the epidemic? Did drugs occupy a central and positive role in our lives? What kinds of possibilities did we imagine for ourselves during this earlier stage of our lives?

This lengthy process of witnessing, recollection, and testimony must occur before the mourning can begin authentically. While the mourning process is key to healing, hiding from grief has become common practice for gay men. We fear that if we open up, we will never stop crying. Some refuse to read the obituary section of local gay papers. Others have stopped attending funerals. Occasionally we avoid visiting a sick friend months before his death and tell ourselves that we simply can't handle additional corpses. Mourning is shunned by some who feel it makes us compliant with HIV–our grief is evidence that the epidemic has succeeded in robbing us of so much. Just as some trauma victims "refuse to grieve as a way of denying victory to the perpetrator,"[9] many gay men avoid mourning in an attempt to deny the power and the devastation caused by AIDS.[10]

The display of the Names Project's AIDS Memorial Quilt in Washington, DC in October 1992, provided a snapshot of disparate gay male experiences of grief. People traveled from distant parts of the nation to witness the Quilt's display in its entirety and to walk its pathways, locate swatches, and pay homage to deceased friends. Yet for many, the expansive quilt proved more powerful than anticipated and evoked a surprising range of reactions. For some visitors, the Quilt brought out a painful grief they expressed by openly weeping. When individuals cried loudly, "grief monitors" were available to offer comfort. The man who hugged me kept whispering in my ear, "It will be all right." I didn't know what he meant. Would anything ever again be all right?

Some Quilt visitors I observed didn't seem to emote at all; others simply became numb or felt vague, low-level sadness. I was struck by the large number of people who engaged in social banter, flirtation, joking, and laughing during their visit. Often people shifted rapidly from a state of weeping into a state of joking and then into a numbing state. Strong judgmental reactions were triggered by others' responses to the Quilt, as if a single method of reacting was appropriate to all people at the same moment. With each of us sitting on a powderkeg of complex emotions, a bizarre range of reactions from gay men to anything should surprise no one.

RECONNECTION WITH ORDINARY LIFE

Judith Herman writes, "The major work of the second stage is accomplished . . . when the patient reclaims her own history and feels renewed hope and energy for engagement with life. . . . When the 'action of telling a story' has come to its conclusion, the traumatic experience truly belongs to the past."[11]

Is it possible for gay men to feel "renewed hope" and "engagement with life" in the face of a continuing epidemic? What would it look like for us to reclaim our terrible recent history and integrate it into our psyches?

These are open questions that merit exploration by clinicians, social scientists, and community advocates. I believe that such integration of the disaster of AIDS would result in an adjustment to the new conditions of our lives that we have been reluctant to make. While AIDS itself cannot be relegated to the past, its powerful initial impact finally may be taken in and integrated. As this occurs, attention might begin to shift to the third phase of healing, "reconnecting with ordinary life."

Reconnection involves shifting out of a state of intense preoccupation and entering a period where one can choose to recall or not to recall the painful experience without tremendous personal upheaval. This phase focuses on reconstructing routines and being present in daily life. It also allows for a look again into a future—an activity impossible to consider while in the traumatized state.

This reengagement with life beyond the epidemic might be manifested differently for uninfected gay men, HIV-positive men, and people with AIDS. The hope and engagement with life possible for an individual suffering severe illnesses are manifested quite differently in HIV-positive people who have not experienced symptoms. Much progress has occurred through the self-help movement of people with AIDS that has shifted focus from suffering and dying toward pleasure and living. The quality and texture of daily life becomes a thing to treasure. Workshops have assisted with "living in the present" and taking life "one day at a time." Similar attention has been focused on the development of support groups, twelve-step programs, therapy models, and retreats aimed at encouraging hope and vitality among HIV-positive gay men. This same determination to embrace life and actively engage in a range of life-affirming activities must be extended to those uninfected gay men who have endured psychological battering that has left them depressed, despairing, and mired in guilt and fear.

As a survivor reaches the stage of reconnection with life, he emotionally and psychologically begins to accept that the epidemic has occurred and irreversibly altered his life. This can lead to the rebuilding of one's identity and the creation of an identity which acknowledges, yet refuses to merge, with AIDS. The profound ways AIDS has altered our lives are neither ignored nor diminished. Acquisition of special community-sanctioned identities may occur during this phase. HIV-positive gay men or men with AIDS may come to think of themselves as "long-term survivors." Uninfected men may take on an identity of "HIV negative." The increasingly small numbers of gay men who had participated in pre-epidemic gay culture may think of themselves as "war survivors" or "survivors of the 1970s." Like rescued passengers from the Titanic, public attention encourages us to observe cautiously the continuing role the disaster may hold in our lives and identities:

> Sometimes victims develop a special identity based on the circumstances of their victimization. Thus, the survivors of the Holocaust may feel they are forever so labeled and known. Publicity may lead to intense and sometimes distressing interest in the victims, their views, and their outcomes. There may be such public expectancies and interest that the victims' own individual reactions and needs may be submerged. In some instances, the publicity may maintain the victimization, rather than allowing the victims to be perceived in other roles or from other points of view. The identity of "victim" may come to exclude all others.[12]

The psychic work of reconnecting focuses on opening minds again to the future and creating meaning in life which takes account all that has occurred.[13] It is at this stage that survivors seek out participation in collective activity that confronts root causes of the trauma: rape survivors may become volunteers on hot lines; war veterans may become peace activists. This stage provides impetus for some gay men to be active in efforts against HIV. In fact, many gay men may feel renewed interest in such work, without the messianic zeal or the entwining of entire identities with the epidemic, as earlier. Other men may find new interest in gay activism or non-gay political and cultural work that links them to a "survivor mission."[14]

Intimacy provides an important and common route to reconnection with life. Because the trauma no longer saps all one's energy and interest, its impact on one's intimate relations, sexual response, and erotic activity comes into clearer focus. An existing relationship may no longer meet one's current needs. Potential lovers may have different qualities than previous partners. Decisions concerning management of sexual risk may be vastly different now than when submerged in a state of psychic numbness. Major shifts may occur in one's relationship to gay male friends and to the gay community at large.

Political, spiritual, and social pursuits are the laboratory for survivors' experimenting with a new engagement with the world at a heightened level. Life had been bizarrely interrupted but is now permitted to resume. Gay men of both antibody statuses may now be able to invest energy in long-range plans. For many middle-class men, career changes, educational opportunities, and questions of home ownership that had been put off by the psychic strain of the epidemic, may be reconsidered. The idea of parenthood, perhaps abandoned earlier, may arise again. While there may be certain significant discrepancies between HIV-positive and HIV-negative men's attitudes toward the future, both may experience an enhanced sense of personal control and self-determination during this stage.

Unlike less impactful losses, trauma is never fully resolved; the survivor is never "recovered" and never returns to his "old self." With the continuing spread of AIDS and new waves of infection among gay men of all ages and races, the revisiting of traumatic memories may be triggered. Yet for many men, thorough, ongoing work at healing the shattered psyche will allow for participation in life at a level that had seemed impossible. Through the reparative process, the ability to be present within one's own body, to engage fully in relationships with others, and to find a modicum of peace while acknowledging the devastation of the epidemic, are again possible.

ONE PATH TOWARD RECOVERY

All sufferers of overwhelming loss must find their own way back into the land of the living. There is no available road map, no singular prescription for the revival of the human psyche. Each story shares elements of heroism and triumph, progress and relapse, success and failure.

I spent three months sitting on a couch in a shell-shocked state that shifted between terror, exhaustion, depression, and anxiety. My mind could not focus, concentration eluded me, and I frequently lost my train of thought mid-sentence. At times I could not read, write, or watch television. I sat wrapped in a blanket on the couch, sipping tea, staring into space.

It was difficult to maintain the usual routines of my life. When I couldn't bring my feet to step out of the apartment, I gave up daily workouts, trips to corner markets, even visits to the video store. My life became smaller and smaller as phone calls and letters went unreturned and most visitors were kept at a distance. As I had trouble sleeping as well as staying awake, I moved in a perpetual state of listlessness. I would lie awake in bed for seven hours in an intense panic attack, and spend the day sleep-walking zombie-like between the living room couch, bathroom toilet, and my bed.

My recovery process emerged slowly and with neither awareness of my full condition nor an understanding of depression, trauma, or mental health restoration. Three key sources of support nurtured my lackluster efforts to work through my recent crash and the backlog of a dozen years of decimation: the love and care of family and friends; intensive therapeutic work with an astute, knowledgeable counselor; and participation in gay-oriented twelve-step groups. While I do not feel that my efforts to find some kind of psychological adjustment to the epidemic's impact are complete, I feel reinvigorated and have experienced a significant broadening of the spectrum of emotions, and am once again alive in my life.

Of paramount importance to the regaining of my sanity has been the love and support of individuals—my lover, assorted friends and colleagues, key family members. While often omitted from professional analyses of mental health recovery, my own experience places such emotional support and nurturing center stage. Those who held me and loved me, despite their shock at my condition or their fears for my health, stand out powerfully because others seemed to abandon me, perhaps because of the accusations made against me. I received no phone calls or notes from individuals I had considered to be friends on the staff or Board of Shanti Project, and I imagine them caught in their own complex tangle of judgments, legal concerns, and organizational loyalties. Colleagues in the AIDS system–including other executive directors with whom I had been close–kept their distance. I wasn't sure if they were kept away by their judgments of me, discomfort with the psychologically broken, or fear of being tainted by scandal. On occasional excursions to medical appointments, I would run into individuals and feel their awkwardness. Some offered to come by for a visit but invariably would not. Because I looked like the walking dead, I wonder now whether some saw their own insides reflected by my outsides. Numerous social acquaintances and lunch-time companions were never heard from again.

At the same time, a handful of close friends surrounded me and loved me in meaningful ways. My network of old friends on the East Coast–some of whom feared for my life–called daily, leaving warm, even humorous messages when I wasn't taking phone calls. Even through my fog, these calls made me feel valued and kept me connected to life. When I wasn't particularly alert, friends dropped by to force me into social exchange over afternoon tea–sometimes trying to amuse me with stories, at other times simply sitting with me in silence or holding me as I cried. One friend visited for hours at a time, enthusiastically telling me stories of her day-to-day life. I'm not sure she knows how much it helped to become caught up in the dramas of someone else's existence instead of mired in my own psychological swamp.

A loving relationship can offer a great deal during times of crisis. While my lover was enmeshed in difficulties of his own–health concerns, job uncertainty, the fallout of my situation in his life–he was able to reflect to me my own thoughts and feelings, and offer hope, love, and esteem. During my worst days, I imagined him leaving me–either abandoning me as too much trouble, or getting sick and dying. Instead he provided a voice for angry feelings against injustice which I was not able to express, two arms that cradled and comforted me, and a spirit of confidence in my eventual renewal.

I also received several hundred supportive cards and letters from a wide range of people. Many were from volunteers or clients with whom I had worked; others came from total strangers in the local community or from old acquaintances who had read the wire-service story about my supposed firing published in newspapers throughout the nation, or from empathetic donors and foundation executives with whom I'd worked. These communications meant the world to me: at a time when I was feeling like a pariah, they offered broader perspective. People with greater insight than I provided words of wisdom that I could comprehend only months later. They instinctively knew my condition involved much more than job controversy.

I put the cards and letters into a scrapbook and thumbed through it several times a day during my bleakest periods. The restoration of my psyche could not take place in isolation—even when I was feeling incredibly pained around people. What the phone calls, letters, and visitors offered was a safety net of people who let me know I wasn't crazy, I wasn't bad, and I wasn't unimportant. They provided me with what all of us need from the social worlds we create: voices that tell us we matter, our pain is real, and our lives are worth saving.

Therapy was the site where I engaged in active dialogue about the roots of my mental health crisis. This involved not solely a thorough review of the specific circumstances surrounding my crash, but a search for key unresolved issues that may have played a role in my contemporary situation: the disciplinary treatment I experienced as a child, schoolboy harassment because I was dubbed a "sissy," the recent death of my sister, survivor issues related to being Jewish. My therapist suggested readings that illuminated my situation and broadened my narrow perspective. He provided a stable, constant witnessing of my attempt to come to terms with distressing feelings and to begin to forgive myself and others for what had occurred.

A large portion of my work in therapy focused on telling my story of a dozen ugly years of the AIDS epidemic. While at times I thought this might unfold in a planned, orderly fashion, instead I found myself vaulting from year to year, incident to incident, without rigid concern for sequencing. I went back to pre-epidemic life and remembered old hopes and dreams. I dug out journals and calendars to prod my memory. I talked through the deaths of close friends, mentors, tricks, and boyfriends. My therapist encouraged me to recall intangible losses—the loss of innocence, optimism, and hope. I was able to pinpoint the moment when my spiritual faith was first rocked, and incidents that caused me to discount any belief in a god or higher power. Therapy allowed me to pick up the pieces of a scattered psyche and— one by one—slowly put the puzzle of my head back together.

Participation in gay twelve-step meetings was the final crucial element in my psychic restoration. I had been involved in twelve-step groups for almost a decade and had gone through periods of loving "the program" as well as phases when I hated its dogma. While I look at certain aspects of twelve-step recovery with a critical eye, I have always found other parts helpful. Attending meetings usually relieves my internal tensions. The slogans and prayers that I found silly and trite during my early days of involvement now provided me with daily, gentle inspiration.

During the period of my most intense work in therapy, I experienced tremendous difficulty listening to twelve-steppers minimize their own HIV-related losses using program jargon. I would hear people say things like, "My ten best friends are dead, my lover's on his deathbed, and I've just been diagnosed with KS, but I'm doing alright today and my higher power's looking out for me, so everything's going okay. I'm doing fine." I would sit in my seat and become crazy with judgments and agitation. But twelve-step programs were critical to my working through a dozen years of HIV-related issues because they provided rooms of empathetic people who listened to me as I recounted painful memories. At a time when it felt unsafe to be around most gay people, gay twelve-step meetings were always warm and safe spaces for me. I felt understanding and love from countless unnamed sources and, through them, I gained the strength to reenter the world.

Reconstructing my psyche took much time and energy. It didn't occur overnight and progress wasn't made in a constant move forward. I had setbacks and disappointments. When I was assaulted by a stranger, my fears of being in public were heightened and I was drawn back into my apartment for a long period of time. Continuing newspaper coverage hammered at my head and left me heartsick and despondent. But slowly strength returned–not solely physical energy but an emotional vitality determined that I would survive and again participate in the world. By the time spring arrived, exactly a year after I crashed, I was ready to reenter the land of the living. I have reemerged on a heightened level, aware that more difficult experiences and deaths lie in the future and the epidemic isn't over, yet determined to construct a life and a future for myself that is worth living.

RESTORING THE SOCIAL FABRIC OF GAY MALE LIFE

A second disaster follows in the wake of AIDS which, because its symptoms do not scar the face, has been easy to overlook. When an upswing of new infections that could be blamed neither on drugs nor youth became undeniable among gay men, attention became riveted on the previously hidden mental health crisis among survivors. That a vast number of gay men should be suffering enormous psychological consequences after a dozen years of watching the decimation of community and the disfigurement of collective identity now seems logical, even predictable. Yet first-decade priorities for AIDS response focused the surge of communal efforts on treatment and care for infected people and did not allow for secondary focus. Like everything else about the epidemic, we have denied or underestimated its impact on the gay men who are as yet uninfected.

In 1990, when I began speaking publicly about these problems, I experienced great resistance from certain colleagues, especially gay men working in the AIDS service industry. Whether I framed my remarks around gay male mental health or the unaddressed psychosocial needs of HIV-negative gay men, some insisted I was exaggerating the situation. I was called "hysterical." Many considered the topic diversionary, insisting our sole focus remain on meeting the needs of people with AIDS. Because a key impetus for my exploration of these matters came from my own tenuous emotional state, I questioned my objectivity and the validity of my observations. In fits and starts, I somehow managed to keep pursuing the issues.

These charges and others continue to serve as a tactic attempting to silence uninfected men and prevent the shattering of the fragile illusion of community normalcy we're all supposed to maintain at any cost necessary. In a piece called "Negatives Being Negative," one long-respected HIV educator who is HIV positive lashed out at critiques of San Francisco's AIDS prevention efforts apparently offered by Tom Moon and Walt Odets, two leading voices on the psychological needs of the uninfected:

> Chicken Little has returned in the guise of nail-biting therapists. . . . It is insulting and disrespectful to the majority of HIV-negative gay men who are finding ways to cope successfully with the epidemic to insist that those who are having the most

difficulty represent the norm. . . . I think these arguments are nothing but the whinings of some victim wanna-bes. Being a victim has a lot of currency in contemporary culture, and seems to have really taken hold of the lesbian and gay community.[15]

A letter to the editor in a weekly San Francisco gay paper offers a surprisingly personal attack on Walt Odets and misrepresents his work:

I've been hearing about Walt Odets for a while now and have been reading about the theories about HIV negative men and the fact that prevention agencies have failed them and that HIV negative men are the "victim du jour." What crap! Fucking safely is everybody's responsibility. The epidemic has been damn difficult on all of us, positive and negative alike. And the last thing we need is for some self-appointed "community spokesman" like Odets to tell us the real reason for unsafe sex is that all those nasty HIV positive men are hogging the spotlight. Grow up, Mr. Odets, and give us some credit.[16]

For me to discuss my experience of the epidemic in the public sphere, I had to find support. It took time, but I finally identified a handful of men–including Tom Moon and Walt Odets–who shared similar observations and concerns. These HIV-negative men were in their thirties and forties, worked as therapists, researchers, and as staff of AIDS organizations. They had been involved in urban gay life since the mid-1970s and shared concern and commitment to the continuance of gay life. They provided the support I needed to aggressively explore this frightening yet surprisingly familiar territory. As friends seroconverted who did not fit the "young, dumb, or drunk" characterization popularized by prevention experts, my motivation increased. Listening to these friends' stories and the way they explained how they came to engage in unprotected anal sex, convinced me that our collective inability to address the psychological and quality-of-life needs of gay men at the center of the epidemic was taking a toll. I arranged meetings with prevention specialists, but found myself speaking to brick walls. They seemed so invested in public health worldviews which saw prevention efforts divorced from psychological and sociological interventions. Concepts such as unconscious motivation or chronic trauma had no meaning to these men. It was as if Freud had never existed. For more than five years, one-third of gay men had self-disclosed to interviewers in scientific studies and social surveys that they had unprotected anal sex in the recent past.[17] Still, we insisted that gay male infections had ceased. Only when the epidemiological surveys confirmed the anecdotal reports and declared increasing rates of infection among gay men whom we thought we had successfully educated did discussion of these matters move out of the margins. Finally the studies' findings were taken seriously, especially since self-disclosure in sexual matters usually represents only a partial portion of the true population.[18]

The unexplored terrain of contemporary gay men's lives becomes a concern to many health policy planners only when it drives infection rates and undercuts much-touted success in supposedly halting gay infections in the mid-1980s–or when it stands to create an economic cost to society. Yet a growing number of clinicians and advocates are motivated by sincere empathy and compassion. They see a population that is suffering greatly under one of the extreme human crises of our time. They are as committed to keeping people alive as they are to improving the quality of those very lives.

After the first wave of response to a typical disaster, services and succor that had been focused only on the narrowly defined "victims," expand and assist witnesses, survivors, and rescuers (roles that are neither distinct nor rigid in the AIDS epidemic). We are now observing the beginning stages of attempts to conceptualize and create models to assist large numbers of gay men of all classes and races who are suffering cumulative grief, mild to severe depression, trauma, post-traumatic stress disorder, and major mental illness.[19] The burgeoning mental health and quality-of-life needs of this population require not only treatment for the individual but community-wide intervention. As the epidemic once again escalates within the gay male population–an unthinkable possibility just a few years ago–and additional surprising permutations of infection and impact occur, the challenges of keeping gay men alive and regenerating social order will likely increase.

A fresh approach to mending the fabric of gay community life, based in cross-discipline thinking, is needed. I offer three suggestions as components of a systemic attempt to alleviate suffering and improve quality of life for gay men:

1. Our understanding of gay male psychology and sociology must be significantly and swiftly improved.

Research, analysis, and theory about gay men is in its infancy and remains hampered by the cowardice of funders and the entrenched homophobia of academic institutions. The refusal to seek substantive scientific knowledge about the population most impacted by a tremendous new medical epidemic damns politicians, scientists, and researchers alike. As infections spread, our efforts to respond are continually frustrated by a lack of information about gay male psychology, sexuality, and social relations. This is true about gay men as a collective entity, and is particularly true about specific highly impacted gay male populations: men of color, young men, working class and poor men, bisexual men, and old men.

Educators, clinicians, and public health workers responding under the pressure of increasing infection rates may feel pulled toward focusing their energies on finding immediate "solutions" to the myriad problems that confront us. A parallel effort, which expands funding for extensive and systematic research, analysis, and theorizing about gay male lives, must take place.

I do not make this suggestion because I want to turn the gay community into guinea pigs or research subjects; I am aware of the perils of any marginalized population becoming the subject of mass study. Yet we face significant challenges without the most basic information needed to determine a proper course. As two leading prevention researchers wrote in 1994:

> It is appalling that we have been able to locate fewer than 200 published evaluations of HIV preventive interventions. It is appalling that there are so few studies in high risk populations, including homosexually active men, women, commercial sex workers, and STD patients.[20]

Hence we commonly accept research conclusions about gay and bisexual men as fact, despite sample populations of extremely limited size and without race, ethnic, or class diversity. We apply theories of male psychology and social development directly to gay men, despite their origin in studies of entirely heterosexual male populations. We use bad science to create models of service delivery and community-based education and then we wonder why our efforts don't succeed.

2. We must be unafraid to examine the experiences of survivors of a wide range of natural disasters and human atrocities to gain understanding of the human psyche's functioning under extreme conditions.

Since the early days of the epidemic, some gay men have claimed a political parallel between AIDS and modern historical atrocities such as the Holocaust and the bombing of Hiroshima and Nagasaki. Comparisons frequently have been controversial and occasionally the men making the comparisons have been ignorant of historical fact and promoted long-held, insulting views (e.g., Jews walked meekly to their deaths in Nazi Germany). In the highly charged atmosphere of contemporary political life, linkages between genocidal events cannot help igniting a firestorm of reactions. This should not stop gay men from properly and respectfully considering connections between AIDS and other disasters.

Little work has occurred that examines the psychological parallels between survivors of AIDS and survivors of the detonations of atomic bombs or the great earthquakes of our time or years of terrorism in El Salvador. Aggressive research into the extreme historical situations of this century has much to offer our understanding of the complex psychosocial fallout of this epidemic.

Some gay men have the mental health and ego strength to continually process the ongoing horrors of the epidemic and remain psychologically stable and emotionally open. Others may be shielded from severe impact by maintaining identities and social circumstances at a distance from a full immersion in gay culture and community, or because they lack close personal exposure to HIV or individuals infected with HIV. Simple serendipity has protected others. While all gay men will not suffer chronic trauma or manifest signs of mental illness, those who do desperately need to understand that they are no more to blame for their conditions than the survivors of other psychologically overwhelming events. Ironically, our varying responses are neither "normal" nor pathological; they are simply the way that human beings react under extreme conditions.

3. Improving quality of life and alleviating suffering requires diverse strategies that integrate many fields: psychology and social theory, the performing and visual arts, religion and spirituality, popular education and political activism, sexuality and play.

There is no simple route to reestablishing baseline social order and mental health in the gay male population. Individuals who have suffered greatly often spend the rest of their lives coming to terms with their experience and attempting to derive meaning from circumstances that appear unfathomable. At the societal level, what often looks like bizarre response to crisis has understandable roots in the extreme conditions endured.

The task of creating a roadmap toward a future for gay men must be shared across disciplines, subpopulations, and political viewpoints. While prevention specialists, mental health clinicians, and community organizers are likely to be the ones to initiate discussion of these issues, they must invite into the process individuals with a wide-range of expertise in multi-disciplinary organizing. The point here is not merely to spread the responsibility and the work: individual gay men derive succor and meaning from vastly different sources. While therapy speaks to some, theatre, competitive sports, or spirituality work for others. An approach that is unrestricted by narrow disciplines and spans gay male cultures may have the greatest chance of providing relief to the mass of survivors of the epidemic.

Restoring sanity to gay and bisexual men amid the whirlwind of an epidemic is an ambitious challenge. The protracted decimation of AIDS requires a cadre of clear-headed individuals to initiate the progressive changes necessary to mitigate the impact of this scourge on gay men. Nowhere is the social fabric of the gay community put to a greater test and nowhere is thinking more muddled than on issues related to sexuality. Any attempt to improve the mental health of gay men must be accompanied by a similar attempt to unbraid the barbed and twisted wires that have tightly bound our erotic lives over the past dozen years.

NOTES

1. Judith Lewis Herman, *Trauma and Recovery,* (New York: Basic Books, 1992), 159-160.
2. Laura S. Brown, "Not Outside the Range: One Feminist Perspective on Psychic Trauma," *American Imago* 48(1):131 (Spring 1991).
3. Robert J. Lifton, *Death in Life: Survivors of Hiroshima* (New York: Random House, 1967), 524.
4. Tom Moon, conversation with author, San Francisco, CA, February 6, 1995.
5. Herman, *Trauma and Recovery,* 1.
6. Dori Laub, "Truth and Testimony: The Process and the Struggle," *American Imago* 28(1):77 (Spring 1991).
7. Beverley Raphael, *When Disaster Strikes,* (New York: Basic Books, 1986), 92.
8. Laub, "Truth and Testimony," 90.
9. Herman, *Trauma and Recovery,* 188.
10. The complexity of mourning for the lesbian, gay, and bisexual communities amid a continuing epidemic are insightfully discussed in R. Dennis Shelby, "Mourning Within a Culture of Mourning," in *Therapists on the Front Line: Psychotherapy with Gay Men in the Age of AIDS,* eds. Steven A. Cadwell, Robert A. Burnham, Jr., and Marshall Forstein (Washington, DC, American Psychiatric Press, Inc., 1994), 53-79.
11. Herman, *Trauma and Recovery,* 195.
12. Raphael, *When Disaster Strikes,* 229.
13. I was able to locate one important study of the challenge of creating meaning out of the epidemic and it focuses on HIV-positive gay men. See Steven S. Schwartzberg, "Struggling for Meaning: How HIV-Positive Gay Men Make Sense of AIDS," *Professional Psychology: Research and Practice,* 24(4):483-490 (1993). Additional research on uninfected gay men's formulation of the epidemic is needed.
14. Countless articles and editorials have appeared in the gay press that reflect the struggle to find a survivor mission amid an ongoing epidemic. See, for example, "Visiting the Dead," *Frontiers,* May 6, 1994, 12; also, "What We the Living Owe," *Windy City Times,* May 26, 1994, 11.
15. Chuck Frutchey, "Negatives Being Negative," *San Francisco Sentinel,* October 12, 1994, 22.
16. Tony Reynolds, "Botkin: Pro," letter to the editor, *Bay Area Reporter,* March 9, 1995, 8.
17. Jeffrey A. Kelly et al., "Acquired Immunodeficiency Syndrome/Human Immunodeficiency Virus Risk Behavior Among Gay Men in Small Cities," *Archives of Internal Medicine* 152:2293-2297 (1992) focused on men in sixteen small and moderate-size cities and found "nearly one third of all men had engaged in unprotected anal intercourse an average of eight times in the past 2 months, usually outside monogamous relationships." NIAID AIDS Agenda (Summer 1993) reports results of San Francisco's Young Men's Health Study

presented at the IXth International Conference on AIDS held in 1993 in Berlin. The study focused on San Francisco gay and bisexual men and found an annual rate of 2.9 percent new infections among 18-29 year olds. For a report of self-disclosure of unprotected sex see AIDS Action Committee, "A Survey of AIDS-Related Knowledge, Attitudes and Behaviors Among Gay and Bisexual Men in Greater Boston: A Report to Community Educators," (Boston: AIDS Action Committee, 1991). For press coverage of unprotected sex in San Francisco see Jane Gross, "Second Wave of AIDS feared in San Francisco," *The New York Times,* December 11, 1993, A1.

18. Walt Odets, "AIDS Education and Harm Reduction for Gay Men: Psychological Approaches for the 21st Century," *AIDS and Public Policy Journal,* 9(1):2 (Spring 1994).

19. The Boston Division of Public Health and Fenway Community Health Center have produced a manual outlining one model program for HIV-negative men. To obtain "A Short-Term Support and Education Group for HIV-Negative Gay and Bisexual Men" by Douglas Hein, Gail Beverley, and Vincent Longo, contact Gail Beverley at the Fenway, 7 Haviland Street, Boston, MA 02115, (617) 267-0900 x 283 or Douglas Hein at Boston Division of Public Health (AIDS Services), 1010 Massachusetts Avenue (4th floor), Boston, MA 02118, (617) 534-4559.

20. Thomas J. Coates and Jeff Stryker, "HIV Prevention: Looking Back, Looking Ahead," (keynote address presented at the 1994 Charles C. Shepard Award Ceremony, Centers for Disease Control and Prevention, Atlanta: May 5, 1994), 8-9.

SECTION II:
RECLAIMING SEXUALITY

Chapter 4

What We Did and What We've Become

The most taboo subject in the gay world is not greasy fists, slings, little boys or cock piercing. It's the relationship between the past and the present, more significantly, between what we did and what we've become.

–Robert De Andreis
San Francisco Sentinel

Water and winds are gonna drown all your sins. . .
A hurricane's coming and it's looking for you!

–Carol Douglas, "Hurricane's Coming Tonight"

Television and newspaper reporters have become obsessed once again with the sex lives of gay men. Editorial writers marvel at the opening of new sex clubs in cities that are the epicenters of the epidemic. News reports of mounting statistics on HIV infection among gay men under the age of twenty-five leave people shocked and dumbfounded. Middle-age gay men who have remained uninfected for the first dozen years of AIDS and are now having anal sex without condoms are seen as idiots or madmen.

Within communities of gay men throughout America, questions repeatedly surface about our individual and collective erotic lives. In gym locker rooms and around dinner tables, gay men debate a complex range of sex issues. Is it true that so-and-so recently tested positive after years of testing negative? Is phone sex a healthy outlet for desires, or simply a way to avoid intimacy? Should bathhouses be allowed to open while an epidemic continues to rage?[1]

Often anxiety and confusion about our individual sex lives go unstated. Whether HIV positive, HIV negative, or unaware of antibody status, significant numbers of gay men in America appear to be experiencing confusion, dysfunction, impotency, and deep ambivalence about sexuality and intimacy between men.[2] Those who are single increasingly become frustrated with the limited options for meeting appropriate men. Men exchange phone numbers but never call one another. When one man finds the courage to ask out another who has flirted with him for months, he's surprisingly greeted with sudden disinterest. Trust, honesty, and communication–areas which have never seemed easy between men–now seem more difficult than ever.

Male couples also experience rising frustrations.[3] Antibody status wreaks havoc between lovers–even when both share positive or negative serostatus. Sexual issues that had been ironed out years ago may again flare up. Concerns about fidelity, roles, and communication may provoke volatile discussion. Lovers who thought they knew one another very well, now may find themselves looking at each other like sexual strangers.

For many, sexual congresses may have become places of frustration and terror rather than satisfaction and joy. Some gay men find themselves thinking about contagion and death even when masturbating. It isn't unusual for men to commit themselves to avoiding certain sex acts and a few days later to violate the boundaries. Sometimes in the middle of having sex men discover that they are seething with resentment over the ways by which long-held desires have been restricted. Some men find themselves involved in unsafe acts that *they don't even like.*

Long periods of time without interest in sex is no longer unheard of among gay men.[4] One HIV-positive gay man wrote a guest opinion in a local gay newspaper:

> After I tested positive six years ago, my sex drive practically disappeared. . . . I had recurring anxieties about getting sick and dying, about not being able to have any children, and about infecting others.
>
> Afraid that getting into a sexual situation would bring these anxieties to the surface, I stopped having sex completely. At

one point, I felt so depressed I couldn't even masturbate, except maybe once or twice a month. I couldn't disclose my feelings because I feared people would think I was abnormal. It was very embarrassing and frightening to feel I had lost so much of my sexuality that I couldn't even get stimulated.[5]

In a story about uninfected gay men, *The New York Times* featured an interior designer and AIDS volunteer who had been celibate for two years:

The man says AIDS has stirred up deep-seated feelings, like shame over being gay. But he says he is mostly depressed over so many dead friends, so many that he no longer keeps track of them in his journal. "I feel very old," said the man. . . . "I feel this gap between me and the rest of the gay population."[6]

Others find themselves obsessively focused on sex—compulsively tricking or masturbating many times a day. Periods of clinically defined sexual dysfunction are increasingly common, even among men who had never before had such problems. Men can't get hard or consistently ejaculate prematurely or are entirely unable to climax in the company of another man. Is medication causing this problem? Is something physiologically wrong? What's going on?

Little attention has been devoted to the impact of the AIDS epidemic on gay men's sexual functioning. Government funding for HIV-prevention efforts and research into sexuality has consistently bypassed the populations most at risk for contracting HIV: only 10 percent of the prevention dollars in California have targeted gay men, for example, while 80 percent of the diagnosed AIDS cases in the state are among this population.[7] The Gay and Lesbian Medical Association reported that less than 5 percent of education funding in the United States targets gay men.[8] Federal funding has been deliberately withheld from scientific research and social surveys targeting gay men's sexual activities.[9] The richest information we have about gay sexuality is primarily anecdotal and hence subject to the distortions caused by denial, manipulation, and reputation.

Because of confusion and shame surrounding the landscape of contemporary gay romantic and sexual lives, many men have confided frustrations and fears to no one. Gay men trivialize what is happening by telling themselves that sex problems have been caused by drinking too much coffee or by the aging process. Terse excuses are uttered to tricks or lovers. Something precious and affirming to life has become tortured and secretive, yet most discount their feelings and go about business as usual.

Psychologist Walt Odets has described a pervasive sexual dysfunction among gay male clients and articulates a powerful analysis of the tragic effect of the epidemic on homoerotic life:

> The pairing of sex and death in human life is a pairing of intimacy with betrayal, love with violence, and giving of oneself with the taking of life. It is a horribly destructive irony, that a quirk of nature and timing has brought this epidemic to gay communities, which were beginning to clarify and correct a social legacy that for so many centuries brought despair to the lives of homosexual men. This prejudicial legacy paired homosexual intimacy and love with hurt, shame, and guilt. That the AIDS epidemic has appeared to make traditional social representations of homosexuality quite literally the case threatens to reverse much or all of the psychological progress made by gay men over the last decade.[10]

Most clinicians and sexologists who have considered these matters attribute the increasingly complex sexual issues facing gay men to the AIDS epidemic. A lethal, sexually transmitted disease spreading through a community defined by its sexuality surely will wreak havoc on erotic functioning.

While AIDS has enormously affected gay men's sexual response, another factor, rarely acknowledged, has powerfully warped the erotic lives of gay men. Just as a sexually transmitted disease will have a huge effect on a population's sexuality, societal response to disease also will have impact. Under conditions of escalating social stress, deeply embedded attitudes and judgments about sexuality rise to the surface and acquire tremendous power and significance.

If male erotic lives appear as frightening, unmapped terrain, it may be because many surviving members of a generation of gay men have undergone a sea-change and become born-again zealots decrying their wanton youth and proclaiming the saving graces of the intervention of the epidemic. Deep reservoirs of ambivalence and guilt have broken down dams and flooded the erotic landscape. Gay men pretend to be self-actualized when they actually may be self-disgusted. Out of this soil has sprouted a new crop of mangled vegetation, raked over by a decade of safe sex education that has attempted to wean gay men away from authority and responsibility for sexuality. Gay men are not passive victims of a strategy by external anti-gay or anti-sex forces. The agents who have devalued gay men's authentic desires and undermined gay sexual agency often are ourselves. While believing that safe sex efforts respected long-held community tenets and promoted sex-positive attitudes, an often ambivalent community has used them as the primary tool to shift away from pre-AIDS sexual values.

Taking on these issues is difficult. One cannot talk about topics such as new infections, safe sex education, bathhouses and sex clubs, men having unsafe sex, and the sex cultures of the 1970s without igniting a firestorm of response. What we know is that fifteen years into the epidemic, many gay and bisexual men we love are still becoming sick and dying, and others are still becoming infected. It sometimes feels like we could go crazy simply trying to hold this knowledge inside our fragile psyches. We are mad for answers–easy answers, quick answers, complicated answers, long answers–anything that offers flotsam and jetsam of hope to grab onto as we struggle to keep our heads above water rather than sinking into an ocean of despair. And the answers have not been coming.

Jonathan Silin, in an early analysis of AIDS prevention efforts, was among the first to articulate dangerous contradictions contained in gay male safe sex education:

> How is it possible for safer sex programs, so often planned and implemented by gay professionals, to foster desires and behaviors in us that reinforce rather than challenge a sociopolitical system that is so obviously oppressive to us? Can those who are instructing us in survival techniques be allowing their professional commitments to take precedence over their own best political interests? What are the alternative strategies that would not only teach individuals how to protect themselves but also how to strengthen the entire community in the future?[11]

Contrary to popular understanding, prevention efforts targeting urban gay men have not succeeded in halting transmission.[12] They have served to enable most men to feel neither capable of self-determination over sexual conduct nor committed to ensuring behavior change that would keep the majority of at-risk men uninfected. Instead, a conspiracy of forces has converged that has manipulated statistics, denied the realities of contemporary gay lives, and unabashedly tugged at the heartstrings of a desperate community, in order to justify continued support for many of the current ineffectual methods of AIDS prevention among gay men.

However well-intentioned, gay men's HIV-prevention programs have replicated a traditional pattern of interaction between marginalized people and newly formed classes of "professionals" and "experts" who offer assistance. The relationship that has formed between the gay masses and many gay male prevention leaders has "chained the colonizer and the colonized into an implacable dependence."[13] As a community, the perspective of gay men has been so distorted and our desires so contorted that we have lost the ability to distinguish veracity from dissembling, dispossession from restoration, and empowerment from dependency. Perplexed and deeply conflicted, men are left gazing out over a wilderness of lies, secrets, and silence in which we are expected somehow to thrive.

HOMOSEXUAL DESIRE BEFORE AIDS

At a workshop on contemporary gay men's sex culture at a national conference of community activists, a series of twenty-something gay men described their erotic lives and the sexual venues they've constructed in direct opposition to gay men of the 1970s. "For us, sex isn't about anonymity or alienation," one young queer insisted. "It's about connecting and brotherhood." Another proudly declared, "We're the first generation of gay men to see our sexuality as political and to integrate activism into our erotic lives."[14]

I seethed inside. AIDS has encouraged and affirmed deeply homophobic judgments of pre-epidemic gay sexuality. It has created both a generation of young queers that imagines sex in the 1970s as decadent, apolitical, and void of joy, and an older generation of "survivors" who perpetually wrestle with despair and guilt about the sexual worlds we inhabited. Is it possible for any of us to recall gay culture of the 1970s clearly? Or have the events of the past decade so radically altered our vision that the cinema of our memory no longer screens the original black and white movie of the period, and instead presents a newly restored and colorized version?

How quickly post-Stonewall gay life has been distorted! Jonathan Silin summarizes the dangerous myths that have been created about pre-epidemic gay life:

> The history to which we are subscribing tells us that a rebellious state of youth, carefree and uncaring, has been abruptly ended by a disease that has brought us to our senses and taken us out of the disco and bathhouse and into the hospital and funeral home. We have apparently been chastened by a disease that has taught us the limits of sex and drugs. If we did not properly care for ourselves or others in the past, by implication bringing AIDS upon ourselves, now as mature adults we have the chance to redeem the community through personal sacrifice and love.[15]

Cindy Patton also has described the pervasive historical revisionism of this period in the development of gay male cultures:

> It is now commonly believed–among gay men as much as in society at large–that gay male sexual culture before AIDS was chaotic, amoral, and thoughtless. Randy Shilts' epic *And the Band Played On* has been particularly influential in confirming just this view. Shilts argues that gay men used doublespeak to avoid the "truth" of the epidemic, which in Shilts' view is that the community's sexual heyday was over once the epidemic set in, and that it was time to adopt relationships like those of the heterosexual mainstream.[16]

We inhabit social worlds in the 1990s that rarely understand or value sexual expression, so it is difficult to remember an era that attempted to conceptualize and experience sex in new ways. For a brief moment, a class of gay and bisexual men daringly entered a world that explored dynamic erotic questions. We crossed an initial bridge to claim desire for other men, only to find a second span whose crossing offered entry into an unexplored realm of sexuality itself. The body politic of the times urged us forward, supporting us to take risks, make mistakes, make discoveries. Having suffered for years an estrangement from important parts of ourselves, many of us found joy and exhilaration as we sought increased integration of mind, body, and spirit:

> Gay male liberation of the 1970s emphasized the celebration of gay male sexuality, the avoidance of constrictive gender roles, and the exploration of new ways of bonding. Sexual experimentation was a means whereby gay and bisexual men could free themselves of societally-imposed notions of guilt and shame around homoeroticism.[17]

This is not currently how pre-AIDS gay sexual culture and gay men's sexuality commonly are discussed. More common are viewpoints expressed in local gay publications around the country:

> If you are of a certain age, you know what we did because you were there doing it—unsafe sex until the leather-clad cows came home, non-stop as if there were no tomorrow—and now we find out there wasn't was there? . . . Massive sexual hysteria swept through the burgeoning gay community 20 years ago. Whether it started out as a joyous expression of freedom or as the release of generations of pent up sexual oppression, it spun out of control.[18]

Another gay man wrote:

> Men are sexually irresponsible. Our dicks still function one step quicker than our brains can process logic. We want sex wherever, whenever, however, and how often it's available. A bathhouse is still the ultimate sexual smorgasbord of sweaty armpits, steamy crotches, and spontaneous sex scenes.[19]

Author John Rechy has described this period as "the profligate years."[20] A view has been put forward and become dominant that indicts gay male culture for pushing the limits of biology. We are told that the 1970s were a time of selfishness, excesses, decadence, and self-abuse. With perspectives imbibed through recovery movements focused on drug addiction, alcoholism, incest, sexual compulsion, and child abuse, we look back at this period and see only three features: drugs, attitude, and kinky sex. We pathologize the men and the culture of the 1970s from what we consider the superior morality of the 1990s. Huge numbers of men who participated most intensely in gay culture in the 1970s are dead and thus unable to provide voices that would broaden recollections and perspectives on these years. Many men died ugly and painful deaths, yet never stopped valuing the erotic experiences of those years and died with no regrets. But the smugness of these sober times, and the powerful homophobia and sexphobia affirmed by a sex-borne virus, allow many to sit in harsh judgment of others . . . and of themselves.

THE ALIGNMENT OF EROTIC ORBITS

The erotic is a source of tremendous knowledge and power. It is of the mind yet it goes beyond the mind; one with the heart, yet greater than the heart; rooted in the soul, yet branching beyond the soul. Many gay men know that the erotic is a force for metamorphosis; our lives provide indisputable evidence of its transformative powers. Sexual desire springs from deep and complex sources and tapping into it unleashes energy and creativity which makes us stronger, clearer, and more engaged in the richness of life.

In a landmark essay, "Uses of the Erotic: The Erotic as Power," Audre Lorde wrote:

> The erotic is a measure between the beginnings of our sense of self, and the chaos of our strongest feelings. It is an internal sense of satisfaction to which, once we have experienced it, we know we can aspire. For having experienced the fullness of this depth of feeling and recognizing its power, in honor and self-respect we can require no less of ourselves . . . . Once we know the extent to which we are capable of feeling that sense of satisfaction and fullness and completion, we can then observe which of our various life endeavours bring us closest to that fullness.[21]

The suppression of the erotic has been widely and successfully used to dominate people. The mysterious and non-rational nature of desire makes it easily discounted and mistrusted in cultures that prize logic and science over intuition and instinct. The communal life that gay men created in the 1970s tapped into a core eroticism that fueled the mass explosion of gay liberation. Sexual desire was not cut off from deep and genuine feeling, nor was it separate from and unrelated to the political movement. As Lorde writes:

> The dichotomy between the spiritual and the political is also false, resulting from an incomplete attention to our erotic knowledge. For the bridge which connects them is formed by the erotic–the sensual–those physical, emotional, and psychic expressions of what is deepest and strongest and richest within each of us, being shared: the passions of love in its deepest meanings.[22]

While history has rewritten the post-Stonewall years as profligate, abusive, and devoid of spirituality and love, the 1970s provided many gay men with the opportunity to bring the erotic into full realization. My own experience grappling with my sexual orientation as well as my sexuality aligns with Lorde's thesis.

In 1969, I was a fifteen-year-old adolescent living in the suburbs of New York City. The powerful weight of shame that surrounded my dawning awareness of the longings I held for other teenage boys didn't preclude a highly charged fantasy life. Even though I had kissed handsome men only in my dreams and hadn't yet made contact with evolving gay culture, certain physical attributes and specific sexual acts had somehow accrued significance for me. What tools sculpted my adolescent erotic desires? Why did peers with body hair and facial hair elicit excitement from me at an early age? What caused me to be fascinated with some body parts (forearms, chest, neck, calves) and not others (penis, thighs, biceps)? Why did my imagination focus on kissing and body rubbing rather than cocksucking or anal sex? How did ideas such as forced-stripping and bondage find their way into my fantasies?

By the first time I read gay personal ads in the underground press of the 1960s, my sexual desires aimed in very specific directions. Before I had sex with another young man, I had a pretty good idea what I wanted to do. My desires–for specific men and specific acts–had been nurtured in a complex web of interactions within the social worlds I inhabited. As Muriel Dimen has argued:

> Sexuality is simultaneously highly individualized and high-ly socially constructed, subject to will and at the mercy of compulsion. Erotic sensation, like any feeling, is experienced personally. It is as idiosyncratic as any aspect of character, perhaps seeming even more so because spoken language, the means of adult communication, is so poor a vehicle for sharing bodily experience and its meaning. Yet sexuality, like charac-ter, is socially contextualized. The overt rules that shape sexual possibility, form, and feeling are common knowledge, but they are made more compelling by almost invisible, nearly insensible politico-moral judgments.[23]

A variety of incidents and influences–some remembered, others forgotten–inspired the specific features of my adolescent desires. No one ever sat me down and explained how specific sexual acts occurred; no one discussed the range of feelings and the meaning I might find in such acts. Highly charged strains of information and dispositions slowly weaved themselves around my libido: long-for-gotten early childhood experiences, illicit ventures into friends' soft-core porn collections, remarks overheard while eavesdropping on older boys at summer camp, media depictions of male/female dynamics, the sensations I experienced when touching parts of my body, games of power and humiliation acted out among schoolboys.

When I was sixteen, I made my first tentative forays into gay culture: visits to New York's Greenwich Village, bars on Chris-topher Street, the beach at Cherry Grove. I scanned bookstores for reading material with homosexual themes and sneaked paperbacks by Gordon Merrick and John Rechy into the bedroom I shared with my younger brother. I went by myself to to see movies such as *Sunday, Bloody Sunday* and Fellini's *Satyricon*. Finally I met real-live gay men, had fumbling sexual encounters, and kissed mouths crowned by moustaches. Yet I still didn't allow myself to walk upright into an erotic world. It was enough to be placing myself in homosexual settings and relating to other men. My deepest desires remained as stifled fantasies, too scary yet to touch.

For the next five years, I lived a schizophrenic existence. I was the proper Jewish boy in school who kept his homosexual desires and secret life tightly locked away. My family and close friends knew an imposter. At the same time, I kept gay men at a distance. Sex was furtive, surrounded by fear, and always followed by post-orgasm paroxysms of guilt. As I yielded my self-knowledge and self-esteem to others, I entered a dangerous world. Lesbian writer and activist Amber Hollibaugh noted the hazards of such denial:

> It is always dangerous to refuse the knowledge of your own acts and wishes, to create a sexual amnesia, to deny how and who you desire, allowing others the power to name it, be its engine or its brake.[24]

The divisions that ripped through me–straight life/gay desire, good boy/evil man, carnal craving/aesthetic disgust–left me deeply troubled and kept me alienated from important parts of myself. I know what alienation from core desires can do to a person. A key conduit of power is shut tight. Instead of offering an infusion of vitality and strength, repressed desire saps life-affirming energy from the soul. Again, Muriel Dimen wisely writes:

> Constraint of desire leads directly to self-betrayal and social bad faith. We suffer not from too much desire, but from too little. One reason we fail to rebel, or have incomplete revolutions, is because our hopes have been truncated, particularly by sexism whose core is sexual oppression. Sexual oppression resembles other kinds of domination, like class or race. Yet it is different, because it goes for the jugular of all social related-ness and psychological integration–desire.[25]

A vampire was draining my blood nightly. I wore alienation on my face, carried it in my body, held it lodged deep inside my mind. My demeanor, my dress, the way I moved–all reflected inner discord. In the vernacular of the times, I was awkward and nerdy. I experienced life from the neck up. My body was the container of my desires and hence a source of anxiety and terror. I held my physicality at a distance. I was out of touch with sensations and had a distorted relationship to the part of me that longed for erotic fulfillment.

It was only as I finished college and allowed myself to emerge fully into gay community life of the mid-1970s that an integration began to occur. The spirit of gay liberation, and its incessant urge to be true to inner feelings, ignited something inside. Deeply repressed sexual feelings rose to the surface and, with the guidance of new-found friends, I found opportunities to realize them. I began to have the kind of sex I wanted to have with the kind of men I desired.

Lorde articulates the joy and the power that accompanies erotic fulfillment:

> Once we begin to feel deeply all the aspects of our lives, we begin to demand from ourselves and from our life-pursuits that they feel in accordance with that joy which we know ourselves to be capable of. Our erotic knowledge empowers us, becomes a lens through which we scrutinize all aspects of our existence, forcing us to evaluate those aspects honestly in terms of their relative meaning within our lives. And this is a grave responsibility, projected from within each of us, not to settle for the convenient, the shoddy, the conventionally expected, nor the merely safe.[26]

As I broke through my internal resistance, the orbits of my emotions, politics, desire, and spirituality moved into alignment. A surge of energy seemed to lift my entire being and transport me to a new plateau of personal power. I began to care about how I looked and notice the statements given off by my body language. I joined the YMCA, lifted weights, and watched my diet. I began to lose long-standing passive/aggressive tendencies and became more certain of my political vision. I became clear headed and assertive. My confidence increased and I felt my heart open. My life was changed forever.

Gay liberation saved my life by guiding me toward the erotic within. I know that other men shared this experience, just as I know many did not. Some of our lives and sexual explorations during these years were empowered and life affirming, while others' were bifurcated between spirit and sensation. Drug addiction, alcoholism, physical and emotional abuse, nihilism, and spiritual despair actively weaved their way through gay male sexual cultures, but did not diminish the profound experience many had in meeting erotic power head on for the first time. Some were acting out compulsions and unresolved traumas; others were finding fulfillment and connection. Some were doing both. With AIDS as a reference point, it is easy to see only a partial picture. This leaves those who gained vital knowledge during these years shaken and despairing of contemporary discourse on sexual desire between men.

PRE-EPIDEMIC GAY ORGANIZING

I recall the 1970s fondly and am aware some will accuse me of sentimentalizing the nascent gay community. The developing culture we embraced seemed determined to pull away from the legacies of lies we had experienced and to sort out our various muddled truths. Weekly rap groups facilitated by "peers" rather than licensed psychotherapists (the enemy!) were sites of agitated discussions of sex issues of the time: promiscuity versus monogamy, the ethics of sleeping with heterosexual married men, the risks of sex in parks and tearooms. We sat through workshops on loving our anuses, picking through bowls of garden vegetables and tropical fruits to insert inside and then breathing in unison. These years were guided by an impulse to strip away layers of falsehood, invent our gay bodies, and define our identities and sexualities.

Any attempt to understand the evolution of safe-sex organizing in the AIDS era is hampered first and foremost by the moralistic rewrite of post-Stonewall gay male culture. Yet a dearth of historical information and thoughtful analysis of gay political organizing of the period also impedes our vision. In 1981, when we heard the first sporadic reports about gay cancer, "the community" was not the powerful, monolithic force with a shared agenda which many now claim. Historian John D'Emilio has documented deep pre-AIDS divisions between politics and culture:

> Among white middle-class gay men, AIDS has bridged the gulf that divided the movement from the subculture. The epidemic elucidated, in a manner that movement rhetoric could not, the continuing strength of gay oppression. Men with a firm sense of gay identity, but who had eschewed activism, were forced to acknowledge that only a deeply rooted, systemic homophobia could explain the callous, even murderous,

neglect by the government and the mass media of an epidemic that was killing them and their loved ones.[27]

Before the epidemic, gay men were a new and fractured class with divisions reflecting not only racial and class distinctions but profound differences in political vision and principles. The formidable challenge facing gay organizing has been to take men whose values and original identities were formed in vastly different cultures and corral them into some semblance of a cohesive movement. This unification was difficult even before HIV. The gay activist movement of the early 1980s was a stratified melange of diverse individuals who had emerged during three distinct phases of movement development. There were gay liberationists (1969-1975), gay rights advocates (1976-1983), and young gay men who would later claim the rubric "queer" and became a dominant force in the late 1980s. These groups held vastly different analyses of gay oppression and understood political organizing from distinct social contexts.

Gay liberationists, who initiated the grassroots counterculture movement ignited by Stonewall, were not a monolithic group. Dominant cultural forces of the times determined that a newly launched gay movement would carry a banner for radical social change, sexual freedom, and gender-role revolution. Gay liberationists challenged the authority of a wide range of "experts" (doctors, psychiatrists, scientific researchers, and academics) and embraced alternative forms of education that encouraged the empowerment of oppressed peoples. Consciousness-raising groups and protracted collective discourse provided essential forums for coming out and personal reflection as well as an ongoing critique of evolving gay identity.

By 1976, paralleling the mass co-opting of progressive movements by reformist elements, gay liberation was enmeshed in a duel with gay rights advocacy. The ascendancy of gay rights advocates was driven by a desire to integrate gay men and women into the mainstream of American life, while their liberationist colleagues' goal had been the overthrow of the existing order and creation of a new society reflecting antipatriarchal and anticapitalist values. As huge numbers of men began inching out of the closet, encouraged by the movement's highly visible battles against the incipient so-called Moral Majority (Anita Bryant, the Briggs Initiative, the military assault on Perry Watkins and Leonard Matlovich), the precarious balance between radical and reformist elements began to tip, and the world of gay men experienced rapid cultural assimilation. We formed choruses, baseball leagues, and community centers, joined the Democratic Party, and rapidly transformed the counter culture into an upscale, commercialized "lifestyle." By the time the 1980s arrived, bringing with it Reagan-Bush conservatism, the gay population had become entrenched in the identity politics of the period. Modeling itself on the minority status concept popularized by newly empowered ethnic communities, the gay community joined the rainbow quest seeking a piece of the American dream.

The year 1984 serves as a rough dividing line between gay rights advocacy and the rise of what I then termed the "nouveau-homo"— gay men who entered the movement amid the shock and urgency of an epidemic. Neither knowledgable about nor respectful of gay liberation and gay rights before AIDS, these men forged politics rooted in alienated youth culture which, by the late 1980s, would overshadow its counterparts through the coalescing of groups such as ACT-UP and Queer Nation. While utilizing similar in-your-face tactics as gay liberationists, queer activists took uncompromising positions on a wide range of issues. Lacking the Left ideological roots of gay lib and flouting the assimilationist demeanor of gay rights, queer activists introduced a third wildly divergent worldview into the hybrid gay movement.

Hence a canvas illustrating the gay male community that existed in the early 1980s would display a fragile collage centered on the dominant mainstream gay rights advocates attempting to bridge the trenchant radicalism of gay liberation and the nascent disaffection of a new generation of activists. Bitter sex debates did not begin with the epidemic. As the ranks of the movement filled with increasingly diverse men in the decade after Stonewall, tensions erupted focused upon the "excesses" of gay men's sex cultures. Controversies surrounding promiscuity, S/M, intergenerational sex, and public sex riveted community attention and often defined the split perspectives between liberationists, gay rights advocates, and eventually, queer nationalists.[28] At the same time, interactions between gay male activists and lesbian feminist organizers often broke down over vastly different sexual politics.[29]

The rank and file of the gay community before the epidemic displayed a brazen sense of invulnerability to illness that was a reflection of the broader 1960s youth culture. Post-war American life believed that disease had been virtually conquered and that prescription medication held a solution to every malaise. Many young people felt impervious to disease and thought their health could go unaffected by the consumption of vast quantities of drugs and alcohol. While movement leadership had begun to place gay men's health issues as increasingly important priorities for activism, efforts addressing such matters were limited and lacked mass support. Men were encouraged to have regular VD screenings; alcoholism and drug abuse programs targeting gay men were founded; efforts to combat herpes, depression, suicide, and anti-gay violence were just beginning.

Hence the AIDS epidemic was visited upon a politically fractured community that held broadly divergent views on sexuality and an attitude of invulnerability to disease and illness. How did we develop systems of AIDS education and prevention amid such challenges? When the limited data available to us about a new, life-threatening terror was filtered through systems already identified as enemies of gay men (the medical establishment, scientific researchers, and powerful media conglomerates), how did gay men relate to the information product delivered to our doorstep? With many strings manipulating the limbs of marionette community leadership, whom was one to trust? The gay doctor whose livelihood and status was entangled with the success of AZT? The gay public health bureaucrat who must serve dual masters of medical science and city politics? The gay organizational director who tried to bridge the conservatism of his Board with the radical demands of his clients? These were the serious challenges that confronted AIDS prevention efforts even before they got out of the starting gate.

THE FIRST GENERATION OF SAFE SEX EFFORTS

Before assessing the safe sex efforts of the 1980s, it's important to recall the historical context because most assessments are ignorant of the everyday life of the organized gay community of the period and apply inappropriate criteria to a community in its infancy. Early prevention work was initiated by people who didn't think of themselves as educators. Education was just one small item on the job description these men and women held as volunteer activists in the gay community. Most had neither degrees in public health nor book-knowledge of educational theory; they often didn't consider themselves "experts" or "leaders" or seek such status from their efforts.

Their prevention work consisted mostly of utilizing preexisting grassroots venues (community-based media, organizations, and commercial establishments) to disperse information and promote discussion among gay men about an issue with tremendous relevance to their lives. The first generation of HIV prevention targeting gay men was comprised of informal, grassroots efforts championed by individual gay men, lesbians, and bisexuals. They were conceptually rooted in two community-based systems which were well established by 1981: the gay male sexually transmitted disease (STD) clinic movement and the women's self-help movement. Both were grounded in theories of nonhierarchical education and based on the empowerment of oppressed people. Tactics of revelation, truth telling, and personal disclosure of matters previously considered private, were transferred directly from these two movements to AIDS prevention.

Whether using speculums to peer into vaginas, attending workshops on breast self-examination, or participating in mass rituals utilizing menstrual bloods, women in the 1970s refused to accept the "experts'" vision of their lives. The feminist chant of these years, "Our bodies, our lives, our right to decide" extended well beyond reproductive rights and struck at a core tenet of modern inquiry: women demanded that medical research and health science be placed in the service of feminist empowerment and no longer function as agents of sexist repression. Required reading of the period, including the Boston Women's Health Collective's *Our Bodies, Ourselves,* Betty Dodson's *Liberating Masturbation,* and the Santa Cruz Women's Health Collective's *Lesbian Health Matters,* utilized basic self-help models.[30] Medical and physiological information, when serving to increase knowledge and expand the individual's locus of authority, could be part of a journey toward communal liberation.

Gay men's clinics that sprung up in the decade before AIDS likewise were focused on self-examination, demystification of body parts, and community self-care. Simply walking into Boston's Fenway Community Health Center, Chicago's Howard Brown Memorial Clinic, or Los Angeles' Gay Community Services Center during a "gay men's VD clinic" represented a major step toward self-identity and personal power. I recall looking around the waiting room at the Fenway at several dozen men of different ages, classes, and ethnicities and feeling solidarity and pride. Despite the risks of those years, each of us had seized the moment and claimed status as sexually active gay men. The culture of gay male STD clinics emerged from conscientious grappling with issues of community ethics, individual morality, and a long-held mistrust for established health care systems. Debates during these times centered upon methods and ethics of informing sex partners of a positive VD test, the discovery of vast, uncharted erotic zones (e.g., the nipple as sex organ), and the medical establishment's questionable potential for providing competent and non-judgmental services to homosexual men.[31]

The majority of gay men during this period of time lacked access to quality, gay-sensitive health care. The huge legacy of distrust of professional providers ensured that most gay men were not open about their sexual orientation or sexual activities with their physicians.[32] Even in cities that were quickly becoming known as gay population centers, gay physicians were at the early stages of organizing to improve health care access and quality of care for gay men. Most homosexual physicians remained closeted within the medical establishment; most providers were uncomfortable when confronted with openly gay patients. Openly gay physicians who worked within non-gay practices or mainstream health centers faced daunting uphill battles against institutionalized homophobia. Some left the mainstream and opened gay-specific urban practices. Doctors who attempted to improve services for gay men during this period experienced enormous frustration. One emergency room physician working at a medical center adjacent to San Francisco's Castro District recalled documenting nearly two dozen specific sexually transmitted diseases among his gay male patients and attempting without success to draw the attention of the medical establishment to health concerns within the population.[33] Conferences on issues ranging from mental health, suicide, and addiction to sexually transmitted diseases and domestic violence routinely ignored gay concerns. Homosexuals simply did not exist for mainstream systems and institutions.[34]

The earliest AIDS prevention efforts targeting gay men grew out of this soil. They were unfunded, community-based, grassroots efforts determined to alert a population which was alienated from the medical profession and unaccustomed to responding to health warnings. Few cared what was going on in the gay population. Before public officials initiated governmental funding, or Hollywood celebrities donned red ribbons, or an entire system of AIDS-focused agencies was founded, preexisting structures in the gay community responded in a haphazard, erratic, yet statistically significant manner.[35] From 1981-1985, a fractured network of local gay organizers performed heroic early efforts to get the word out about a frightening new disease. The Sisters of Perpetual Indulgence, San Francisco's drag sorority, produced and distributed early brochures on sexual safety with funding from a gay Democratic club. Dignity/Boston, a gay Catholic group, initiated early public forums to broadly communicate the limited available information. The undercapitalized gay press served as the primary mass conduit for information about gay cancer, GRID, and eventually AIDS during 1981-1985.[36]

These early documents–brochures, conference agendas, articles, and advertisements–reveal tensions between liberationist and assimilationist viewpoints existing within the community even before the key players in contemporary prevention policy (politicians, public health officials, academic researchers) came onto the scene. Because sex was the primary suspect for transmission from the beginning, it is not surprising that the brackish pool of internalized homophobia and shame about sex immediately spewed forth from segments of the community. Do we discourage promiscuity and trumpet the benefits of monogamous coupling? Should we attempt to get information to men who have sex in public parks and truck stops or should we shut down these venues? Is it time to put a lid on the talk about sexual liberation? Should we sanitize gay sexuality if it is going to be within eyesight of the general public?

These tensions were not resolved in the early years of the epidemic and remain with us today. Yet because the early efforts to communicate information were under the aegis of individuals and groups rooted in the local gay community, the new disease was conceptualized within specific cultural contexts unfamiliar to mainstream observers. Some have faulted these initial efforts as contradictory and lacking a single cohesive message. Yet in the early 1980s, much of the information about the disease was ambiguous. Information vehicles rooted in gay liberation tried to present the new health threat in a "sex-positive" context, suggesting ways to modify sexual activity while continuing to support erotic freedom. Sources based in gay rights advocacy were likely to choose more conservative approaches and discourage men from having multiple partners or engaging in kinkier sex acts. These early efforts ensured that men who participated in burgeoning gay-identified cultures could receive information from sources aligned with differing values and beliefs; this benefit accrued to the community because of the lack of operative centralized authority. These were also years when activists wrestled individually and collectively with the question of whether "gay cancer" was going to be a temporary, limited phenomenon, or whether Larry Kramer's dire predictions would come true.[37]

PROFESSIONALS TO THE RESCUE

In a very short period of time, history has forgotten the early efforts. By 1985 responsibility and authority had shifted from the anarchic grassroots to the increasingly centralized gay and AIDS health care systems. The money that accompanied this centralization precipitated a philosophical and financial turf war. Its two primary components—gay men's VD clinics established in the early 1970s and their upstart infant sibling AIDS organizations—hashed out bizarre divisions of duties. Some gay clinics gave birth to AIDS organizations that eventually became autonomous (Boston's Fenway Community Health Center spawned Massachusetts' AIDS Action Committee, for example). Other gay clinics were themselves transformed into powerful AIDS groups (Washington, DC's Whitman-Walker Clinic or Chicago's Harold Brown Memorial Clinic). In some cities, independent efforts founded new organizations (New York's Gay Men's Health Crisis and San Francisco's Kaposi's Sarcoma Foundation, now the San Francisco AIDS Foundation), which then attempted to forge relationships with preexisting gay health services. Who was best qualified to lead prevention efforts targeting gay men, we asked ourselves: gay clinics with a relatively long-term knowledge of the community or AIDS organizations that rapidly were becoming seen as the experts on AIDS?

As the community became overwhelmed by the cyclone of madness increasingly referred to in polite society as the "health crisis," formal organizations seized the reins of prevention efforts from the grassroots. Mixing private financing from the community (altruistic donors, raffles in the bars, splashy events, and donation booths in gay neighborhoods) with trickles of funding available from government sources, well-intentioned community organizers naively assumed the mantle of "health educators." These men and women were often community-based activists who understood prevention work from the perspective of advocacy and organizing, yet they answered to an increasing number of masters whose views were not those of gay liberationists. It was precisely at this juncture that competing interests effectively began to create tremendous dissidence with gay male prevention efforts.

There is a tendency to blame one faction or other for what occurred during the early years of the epidemic: the rapid spread of a virus through the community, the closing of bathhouses and sex clubs, the "degaying of AIDS." Some claim that the gay community did nothing during these years and that gluttonous erotic appetites of men confounded judgment. Commercial interests held hostage the gay community because they saw the disease as a primary threat to the burgeoning lifestyle industry of sex venues and products. Others insist that rigid anti-sex and homophobic tendencies focused the community agenda on flashpoint issues such as bathhouse closures rather than on well-considered, culturally appropriate campaigns. Everyone is blamed by someone: people who did nothing, people who did something, and people who tried to do everything. Rarely do we consider these early years for what they were: a time of profound crisis for an unsuspecting and newly defined community which, due to its very brief and localized history of haphazard, grassroots organizing, defiantly resisted centralization, "management," and traditional models of authority.

One of the first casualties of the professionalization of gay male prevention efforts was candid discussion about men's sex lives. In the face of a mounting epidemic and a burgeoning brochure industry cranking out lists of do's and don'ts, men began lying, dissembling, and telling half-truths. It became clear very rapidly which subjects were appropriate to discuss and which ones, under the constraints of safe sex guidelines, had become heretical. The probing discourse concerning gay male sexuality initiated in the 1970s was relegated to increasingly small and isolated pockets. A decade of gay liberation and communal erotic exploration was convicted of the crime of contagion. We had come out of the closets, seized control of our bodies, and it had brought on us decimation. After years of throwing off the shackles of gay doom, they were snapped again onto our wrists, tighter than ever.

Once the plague was raging and shock took hold of the steering wheel, it became difficult to recall or refer to the lessons of gay liberation. Under mounting conditions of terror, divisions within individual psyches and within the community grew wider rather than narrower. The gay movement could only pretend to be of one mind or a single worldview. Stratifications of race and class were deepening. The masses of men who had streamed into the community during the Anita Bryant years struggled for control of AIDS organizing efforts with gay liberation pioneers. Men coming out in the 1980s in the wake of the epidemic held entirely different priorities and visions.

Grassroots efforts dwindled and were replaced by professionally coordinated safe sex campaigns that soon became the recipients of significant funds. This second generation of education strategies (frequently discussed in the literature as the first generation, ignoring the earlier informal, community-based efforts) ironically was conceived amid an orgy of multiple partners and a spiral of conflicting loyalties. Gay liberationists wrestled with gay health advocates; government funders grappled with rising gay politicos; closeted gay people in the public health system argued with the clones of the gay ghetto. Debates over philosophies of education, the relationship between sexual behavior and knowledge, and the transgressive nature of homosexual desire were shunted aside. Questions concerning who maintains sovereignty and authority over individual sexual conduct became moot points. Health educators, physicians, and community activists jumped into the void and took up the reins.

Wracked by shock, fear and internecine warfare, is it any wonder that the concept, design, and messages of gay men's HIV-prevention efforts seem like a hybrid of questionable origin? With such formidable barriers, skills of compromise, manipulation, and political power-brokering became paramount qualifications for prevention leaders. As grassroots efforts erratically eked forward, the inflow of funding into gay health clinics and AIDS organizations ensured that they were rapidly eclipsed, and such efforts became a relic of the past.

The compromises forged by the newly installed prevention leadership represented a distinct change in direction for the gay community. Cindy Patton succinctly summarized this shift:

> Professionalized health education displaced authority for understanding and enforcing safe sex standards from the people who engage in sex, and placed that authority instead in the hands of medical experts.[38]

This shift effectively decentered long-held gay liberation values. Individual gay men weren't positioned as active agents promoting their individual sexual empowerment and assuming responsibility for their choices. Instead they were considered transgressive bad boys who needed to be manipulated, cajoled, and sometimes coerced into proper conduct. Promiscuity became a dirty word. Posters, leaflets, and billboards appeared urging men to "wear your rubbers every time." Communal sex spaces were closed or patrolled by "safe sex monitors."

Two distinct kinds of prevention efforts emerged during this time period. They were exemplified by Gay Men's Health Crisis' *800 Men* campaign which provided information and exercises to assist men in "eroticizing safer sex," and San Francisco's *Stop AIDS* which focused on motivating gay men to engage in safer sex through "altering community norms."[39] Work which facilitates open, unpoliced dialogue among gay men is uncommon. The Stop AIDS model during various periods in different cities has provided spaces for empowering discussion among men uninterrupted by subtle, directive-based manipulations by facilitators; at other times it has been reworked (and sometimes renamed) to be little more than a classroom session dictating "proper" sex conduct. The vast majority of education work with gay men has not even attempted to encourage authentic dialogue and has focused on leader-directed delivery of information and manipulation of gay men through "exercises." Models developed in this arena skillfully have displaced gay men from subject to object in sexual discourse and have viewed gay bodies and erotic life as at-risk territory to be colonized by health educators. Research literature of critical importance to uninfected gay men was delivered directly to health educators (often themselves gay and bisexual men) who filtered it through public health paradigms, synthesized it into terse messages, and then allowed it to reach the eyes of the gay citizenry. It was as if the gay rank-and-file could not be trusted to make informed decisions. Enormous funding was pumped into public relations and marketing–billboards, pamphlets, advertising, t-shirts–leaving more participatory forms of education, which might encourage self-determination and empowerment, as the unwanted stepsisters of prevention.

Over the past decade, prevention advocates have experimented with innumerable strategies to encourage "safety" while maintaining what they believe to be the integrity of gay male erotic diversity. They have worked tirelessly to distribute brochures, pass out condoms, and create new, attractive posters. They have created endless campaigns: Safety Net, Lifeguard, 800 Men, Hot, Horny & Healthy, Safe Company, Hot and Sexy, Mother CARES, L.A. CARES, West Hollywood CARES. . . . They have tried to teach us to "eroticize safe sex," "grieve our sexual losses," and "accept a condom as a friend." Yet the methods they have used left many gay men's sexuality devalued and their intelligence insulted. This has created the community we inhabit today: cities populated by vast numbers of gay men who distrust, disbelieve, and do not follow guidelines set forth by our own community organizations.

NOTES

1. For discussion of the opening of a bathhouse in New York City see Amy Pagnozzi, "Gay Group Measures Prevention in Lives," *Daily News,* February 15, 1995; "City Hall Targets Sex Clubs," *Daily News,* editorial, February 13, 1995; Jonathan Capehart, "Getting Undressed, Going Undercover," *Daily News* February 13, 1995; "GMHC Statement on Safe Sex and HIV Prevention in Commercial Sex Establishments," Gay Men's Health Crisis, media release, February 17, 1995; Mark Schoofs, "Beds, Baths, and Beyond," *Village Voice,* March 28, 1995, 13.

For debate on the opening of bathhouses in San Francisco see Keith Griffith, "Who Sets Your Rules for Safer Sex," *Bay Area Reporter,* March 24, 1994, 6; Coalition for Healthy Sex, "Sex in Tight Places," *Bay Area Reporter,* May 5, 1994, 6; Michael C. Botkin, "Some Modest Proposals," *Bay Area Reporter,* April 21, 1994, 22; Allen White, "Irresponsible Claims of Irresponsible Behavior," *San Francisco Sentinel,* March 23, 1994, 10; Phillip Matier and Andrew Ross, "Jordan Vows to Slam Door on Gay Bathhouse Plan," *San Francisco Chronicle,* March 21, 1994, A15-A16; "A Killer Proposal," *San Francisco Examiner,* March 22, 1994, A16; Tim Kingston, "Tempest in a Tub," *San Francisco Bay Times,* April 7, 1994, cover story; Sidney Brinkley, "Bathhouse Battle Steams Up," *Washington Blade,* April 1, 1994, 16; Thomas M. Edwards and Thomas F. Lundquist, Letter to the Editor, *San Francisco Independent,* April 12, 1994, 11; Michael Colbruno, "Close the Door on the Bathhouse Idea," *San Francisco Sentinel,* March 16, 1994, 4; Jim Provenzano, "Steam-y Town Meeting on Sex Clubs," *Bay Area Reporter,* March 3, 1994, 21.

2. Kathy J. Harowski, "The Worried Well: Coping in the Face of AIDS," *Journal of Homosexuality* 14(1,2): 299-306; Walt Odets, "The Secret Epidemic," *Out/look* 14:45-49 (Fall, 1991); H. Gochros, "The Sexuality of Gay Men with HIV Infection," *Social Work* 37(2): 1051-1059 (1992). B. R. Simon Rosser, PhD, "Facing Our Challenges, Celebrating Our Lives: Lesbian and Gay Health in the '90s," paper presented at the 1995 National Lesbian and Gay Health Conference in Minneapolis. Included study results indicating that the majority of men studied suffered at least one type of sexual dysfunction.

3. See Dee Livingston, "Group Counseling for Gay Couples Coping with HIV/AIDS," in *The Second Decade of AIDS,* eds. Walt Odets and Michael Shernoff (New York: Hatherleigh Press, 1995), 69-84. See also Mark Schoofs, "Can You Trust Your Lover: Gay Couples Weigh the Risk of Unprotected Sex," *Village Voice,* January 31, 1995, 37-39.

4. John L. Martin, Laura Dean, Marc Garcia, and William Hall, "The Impact of AIDS on a Gay Community: Changes in Sexual Behavior, Substance Use, and Mental Health," *American Journal of Community Psychology* 17(3): 269-293 (1989).

5. Jim [pseud.], "An HIV-Positive Man Reclaims Sex," *Bay Area Reporter,* February 10, 1994, 14.

6. Mireya Navarro, "Healthy, Gay, Guilt-Stricken: AIDS' Toll on the Virus-Free," *The New York Times,* January 11, 1993, B6.

7. John Gagnon, "Losing Ground Against AIDS," *The New York Times,* January 6, 1994.

8. "HIV Prevention Efforts Fall Short," *San Francisco Sentinel,* March 29, 1995, 18.

9. Paul Robinson, "The Way We Do the Things We Do," *The New York Times* Book Review, October 30, 1994, 3.

10. Walt Odets, *In the Shadow of the Epidemic: Being HIV Negative in the Age of AIDS.* Durham, NC: Duke University Press, 1995, 39.

11. Jonathan G. Silin, "Dangerous Knowledge," *Christopher Street* 10(5):36 (1987). Used with permission of the author.

12. See my analysis on page 277.

13. Albert Memmi, *The Colonizer and the Colonized* (New York: Orion Press, 1965), ix.

14. These remarks were made at the National Gay and Lesbian Task Force's Creating Change Conference, November 1992, in Los Angeles.

15. Silin, "Dangerous Knowledge," 36.

16. Cindy Patton, *Inventing AIDS* (New York and London: Routledge, 1989), 44.

17. Jay P. Paul, Robert B. Hays, Thomas J. Coates, "The Impact of the HIV Epidemic on U.S. Gay Male Communities," in eds. Anthony R. D'Augelli and Charlotte J. Patterson, *Lesbian, Gay, and Bisexual Identities Over the Lifespan: Psychological Perspectives on Personal, Relational, and Community Processes* (London: Oxford University Press, 1994), 3.

18. Robert De Andreis, "Restoring a Subculture Named Desire," *San Francisco Sentinel,* February 16, 1994, 18.

19. Michael Colbruno, "Close the Door on the Bathhouse Idea," *San Francisco Sentinel,* March 16, 1994, 13.

20. John Rechy, "The Outlaw Sensibility in the Arts: From Drag and Leather to Prose; the Mythology of Stonewall; and a Defense of Stereotypes," (keynote address presented at Queer Frontiers Conference, University of Southern California, March 26, 1995).

21. Audre Lorde, "Uses of the Erotic: The Erotic as Power," in *Sister Outsider* (Freedom, CA: Crossing Press, 1984), 54-55.

22. *Ibid.,* 56.

23. Muriel Dimen, "Politically Correct? Politically Incorrect," in ed. Carole S. Vance, *Pleasure and Danger: Exploring Female Sexuality* (Boston: Routledge and Kegan Paul, 1984), 142.

24. Amber Hollibaugh, "Desire for the Future: Radical Hope in Passion and Pleasure," in ed. Carole S. Vance, *Pleasure and Danger: Exploring Female Sexuality* (Boston: Rutledge and Kegan Paul, 1984), 406.

25. Dimen, "Politically Correct? Politically Incorrect," 147.

26. Lorde, "Uses of the Erotic," 57.

27. John D'Emilio, *Making Trouble: Essays on Gay History, Politics and the University* (New York and London: Routledge, 1992), 262-263.

28. These controversies and debates were documented in the pre-AIDS era most thoroughly in the pages of *Gay Community News* (Boston) and *The Body Politic* (Toronto).

29. Attempts to form a national gay and lesbian grassroots organization after the 1979 National March on Washington for Lesbian and Gay Rights broke down over these issues with most (though not all) women and men dividing along gender lines. For one classic lesbian-feminist viewpoint of gay male culture of this era, see Adrienne Rich, "The Meaning of Our Love for Women is What We Have Constantly to Expand," in *On Lies, Secrets, and Silence: Selected Prose, 1966-1978* (New York: Norton, 1979), 223-230.

30. Boston Women's Health Book Collective, *Our Bodies, Ourselves* (New York: Simon and Schuster, 1976); Betty Dodson, *Liberating Masturbation* (Body Sex Designs, 1975); Mary O'Donnell, Val Leoffler, Kater Pollock, and Ziesel Saunders, *Lesbian Health Matters!* (Santa Cruz: Santa Cruz Women's Health Center, 1979).

31. See Steven Epstein, "Democratic Science? AIDS Activism and the Contested Construction of Knowledge," in *Socialist Review* 21(2):39 (April-June 1991).

32. R.D. Fenwick, *The Advocate Guide to Gay Health* (Boston: Alyson, 1982), 59; discusses the problem of diagnosing sexually transmitted diseases because of "the gay patient's lack of candor about his sexual proclivities."

33. Stuart Fleming. Conversation with author, Pacific Grove, CA, February 12, 1994.

34. I am grateful to Dr. Stuart Fleming for providing me with an original copy of "A Report to the Executive Committee of the Medical Staff to Ralph K. Davies Medical Center Concerning a Comprehensive Gay Health Service," (January 8, 1979). This report documents the limited pre-AIDS understanding of lesbian and gay health issues among health providers at a medical facility in San Francisco's Castro District and some of the political machinations of advocates attempting to improve health care for this population. It includes as Appendix C, a study by Bay Area Physicians for Human Rights entitled "Perception of Health Issues by Sexual Minority Consumers" which presents survey results from 1978 gay street fairs in San Francisco. Among the findings of interest to this book are "Approximately half of the sexual minorities currently had no established basic care physician," (p. 2) "almost half . . . believed they were not currently receiving adequate medical care for their needs," (p. 2) and "One-third of those sexual minorities who had never disclosed their sexual orientation to a doctor had not done so because they feared disapproval" (p. 3). Finally, while 92 percent of the sexual minority men answered that they "know about" gonorrhea, and 83 percent were informed about syphilis, the awareness of amoebiasis and giardiasis were much smaller (22 percent and 10 percent respectively) (p. 11).

35. Patton, *Inventing AIDS,* 28.

36. For more detailed discussion on early brochures and gay press coverage, see Edward King, *Safety in Numbers: Safer Sex and Gay Men* (New York: Routledge, 1993), 47,57-59.

37. Larry Kramer, "1,112 and Counting" and "2,339 and Counting," in *Reports from the Holocaust: The Making of an AIDS Activist* (New York: St. Martin's Press, 1989), 33-51, 68-74.

38. Patton, *Inventing AIDS,* 42.

39. Silin, "Dangerous Knowledge," 37-39; provides an analysis of these two programs.

Chapter 5

Lies, Secrets, and Sex Lives

Please don't talk about being true,
And all the trouble we've been through.

—Alicia Bridges, "I Love the Nightlife"

Didn't you notice a powerful and obnoxious odor of mendacity in this room? There ain't nothin' more powerful than the odor of mendacity.

— Big Daddy in the MGM film
Cat on a Hot Tin Roof

Gay men know a lot about lying. We have been lied to and lied about. We have been subtly encouraged to lie, asked outright to lie, and forced to lie against our will. We have been told that we were lying when we were telling the truth. We have been told that we were telling the truth when we were lying.

The history of gay liberation could be written as a history of resisting mendacity. The wall that came tumbling down at Stonewall had been built with bricks of falsehood and mortar of denial. Coming out of the closet represented a refusal to continue deceiving ourselves about primary aspects of life and identity. The "SILENCE = DEATH" mantra of AIDS activism is rooted in core queer awareness that by not speaking we are complicit with our genocide: we allow the fallacies of the heterosexual hegemony to stand as facts. Our rage at a "Don't Ask, Don't Tell" solution to the military ban has its genesis in visceral knowledge that silence, used to protect the status quo, directly leads to our suffocation.

Gay men recognize the powerful and obnoxious odor of mendacity as if we have a sixth sense. We are able to intuit deception before it is identified by our conscious minds. We don't always confront it or name it, but when we smell it, we immediately look for the nearest door.

In a landmark essay, "Women and Honor: Some Notes on Lying," (1975), Adrienne Rich asks a question of lesbians which might be asked of gay men twenty years later:

> Does a life "in the closet"–lying, perhaps of necessity, about ourselves to bosses, landlords, clients, colleagues, family, because the law and public opinion are founded on a lie– does this, can it, spread into private life, so that lying (described as *discretion*) becomes an easy way to avoid conflict or complication? Can it become a strategy so ingrained that it is used even with close friends and lovers?[1]

Can lying become a strategy so ingrained that it is used with an entire community searching for information and instruction? This is the question we must ask after a dozen years of epidemic politics. Has mass response to the collective nightmare been to tell our individual truths, no matter how conflicted or complicated? Or have tactics of "lies, secrets, and silence" been marshaled to address one of the most critical aspects of contemporary gay men's lives?

EDUCATION OR SOCIAL MARKETING?

Safe sex education is not a simple matter of grappling with lists and microbes and specific erotic acts. In an analysis of school-based sex education programs, Jonathan Silin writes:

> Effective sexuality education itself, education that empowers students by building their sense of entitlement and decreasing their vulnerability, must be based on our willingness to listen to and work with the experiences students bring with them. This requires giving up presuppositions about the nature of sexuality and the outcomes of our efforts in favor of a sociohistorical appreciation of the ways in which sexual meanings are constructed and changed. . . .[2]

HIV-prevention efforts at their best would be like effective sex education, like effective education: modeled on acknowledging both the autonomy and interrelationship of individuals and respecting people's ability to weigh meaning and consequence with internal impulse and use the best judgment possible to make decisions. Far-ranging information that enumerates social context is provided which places trust in the empowerment of the individual who has the authority and responsibility to transform education into action. Since Foucault we may have insisted that knowledge is power but, since the emergence of epidemic conditions, certain kinds of queer knowledge have been shifted slowly and quietly into the province of the elite.

Bright ideas follow a long, circuitous route before becoming locked in as established tenets of safe sex education. There are periods of discovery, debate, and analysis, followed by trial, retrial, and then refinement. Input may be received from various targeted populations, social marketing executives, medical researchers, political activists, and public health officials. Occasionally mental health professionals, community organizers, and sex educators vie for influence. Creating safe sex campaigns amid such hubbub, along with the ever-shifting sands of a perplexing and expanding epidemic, seems like an impossible task. That the results of such efforts have had flaws does not diminish the considerable achievement of churning out coherent programs under hostile conditions.

The past decade has produced a body of seasoned workers who have participated in several generations of prevention efforts targeting gay men. This prevention leadership, comprised primarily of gay and bisexual men working as community organizers, health educators, and public health researchers, has struggled in earnest to bridge competing analyses of gay male sexuality and sex cultures amidst intense media scrutiny and the erratic whirlwind of politics. Educators have faced an obstacle course of restrictions every step of the way. Working in the field of gay male prevention has involved overcoming specific community taboos, anti-sex funding restrictions, and homophobic local and national statutes. This has been no small task.

Almost universally, prevention workers have refused to pretend that specific taboo sex acts do not take place between gay men, even though mainstream America might consider such activities bizarre or offensive. Few health education programs targeting gay men explicitly condemn promiscuity. Ironically, it has been individual gay men who have occasionally expressed outrage at the inclusion of watersports, fistfucking, or S/M in brochures that target homosexual men. Educators have recognized correctly that credibility with crucial power bases in the organized gay community would be undermined if gay sex were "de-kinked" to win mainstream acceptance.

Prevention leaders' overt support for the diversity of sexual activity pursued by gay men has overshadowed a more subtle and perilous shift: the covert usurping of authority for sexual conduct from the individual gay man. This has been most pronounced when prevention efforts have been conceptualized and developed using a framework of public relations rather than education. Why does a community which draws consistent parallels between itself and social change movements to liberate racial minorities choose corporate public relations strategies rather than educational theories developed to empower oppressed groups as models for HIV-prevention efforts? The language that has been developed for safe sex education now speaks of "campaigns," "audiences," "focus groups," and "messages." Gay men appear as consumers to be pitched specific messages, as if their erotic desires have much in common with consumer urges for Pepsi Cola, a Big Mac, or Jeep Cherokees. Dialogue and reflection are superseded by seven-second sound bites and four-word slogans on the sides of buses.

Gay everyman has been displaced from being the subject at the center of a process of engaged participation, to an object passively awaiting enlightenment. The installation of gay man as units to be manipulated, molded, or motivated that has occurred in HIV-prevention work, contradicts gay and AIDS activists' critique of science as hoarding knowledge to maintain established power relations:

> Rather than conceiving of scientific knowledge simply as a resource that can be monopolized or shared, radical AIDS activism seems implicitly to point toward an awareness that different ways of generating knowledge can establish different sorts of force fields of power relations. . . . From the Foucaultian standpoint, the political strategy of simply disseminating scientific

knowledge in a "downward" direction–creating a community-based expertise–seems potentially naive, or at a minimum, insufficient. In the worst-case scenario, such a strategy transforms the recipient of knowledge into an object of power.[3]

What does this mean in practical terms? After a dozen years of AIDS-prevention efforts in epicenter cities, gay men regardless of race, class, and age, may be more familiar with catchy marketing lines which bombard us on billboards, t-shirts, and bus shelters, than the physiology of our penises. Men identified with the gay community are able to parrot a simple list of safe sex do's and don'ts, but may not be capable of answering simple questions about the ways in which infection might occur through a specific sex act. Marketing strategies often encourage men to consider sex acts as narrowly defined and circumscribed, requiring only a simple, discrete adjustment to be made safe, like an automobile with bad brakes. Yet erotic activity is complex and variegated, difficult to categorize and control, and filled with competing meanings. Gay men may understand that anal sex without a condom is not safe, but may be unable to answer specific questions pertinent to managing their own risk (Is there HIV in precum? How much risk if he pulls out? How likely is it for an HIV-negative top to get infected through anal sex with his HIV-positive lover?).

Men who have embraced gay identity and desire are commonly independent thinkers who question authority. Without these qualities, we would not have been able to inch out of the closet. Many of those who have lived quietly and appear to conform to mainstream cultural expectations maintain private erotic lives of persistent self-discovery and self-definition. Gay men are not lambs. Our iconoclastic nature makes it difficult for us to be duped and we sense when we are being treated without respect. When the complexity of human sexual response is simplistically reduced, our trust may be rapidly eroded.

When meaningful, defining activities such as oral sex or anal intercourse are reduced to terse slogans and marketing messages that become primary tactics in gay male prevention efforts, it may feel patronizing and insulting to some gay men. Many campaigns have stripped significance and value from sexual activity and reduced complex acts to a few key messages: (1) never swallow semen; (2) men should pull out before ejaculating; (3) a latex condom and water-based lubricants should always be utilized with anal sex. We have heard these suggestions repeated over and over in many different mediums. Urban gay men may have received these messages thousands of times. Advertising droning on and on with the same five-word slogan is not the same as the pedagogical process called education. The creation of a foundation of information, skills, motivation, and empowerment is a thing very different from marketing.

We are bombarded with messages telling us to always wear a condom when having anal sex. How much risk is involved in anal sex if I am uninfected and am getting fucked by a lover who is also uninfected? How does my risk change if he hasn't been tested for a year and has been fucked without condoms by several tricks? If he tells me he's monogamous but isn't, am I likely to become infected? What if he was afraid I'd leave him if he told me he's positive, so he lied and told me he's negative?

If an HIV-positive man wants to fuck me, how do I evaluate the comparative risk of his wearing no condom and pulling out before orgasm with the risk of his wearing a condom and ejaculating inside me? What is the actual level of my risk of infection, if I penetrate a friend whom I know to be infected? The prevention leadership's assumption that any level of infection risk provides enough rationale and motivation to stop the activity altogether might be motivated by sincere desire to protect us and keep us alive, but may reveal false assumptions about the easy expendability of anal sex. Surveys which show that over one-third of the uninfected urban gay men are occasionally engaging in unprotected anal intercourse, while being fully aware of the risk involved, provide evidence that knowledge of infection risk is inadequate motivation.[4]

If anal sex has been swiftly and sternly dealt with in prevention as an easily expendable or exchangeable activity, intense ambivalence has circulated around oral sex. While clinical and anecdotal evidence appeared in the early and mid-1990s which argued (successfully to my mind) that HIV was transmittable through cocksucking, such infections seemed to occur in men who had particularly susceptible oral cavities due to specific medical conditions or men who had fellated and ingested the semen of large numbers of men in short periods of time (often accompanied by popper usage). Yet the queer man-on-the-street easily gained the impression from terse safe sex slogans that unprotected oral and anal sex held comparable levels of risk. Perhaps no aspect of gay male sexuality in the 1990s is as conflicted and as journalistically muddled as oral sex.[5]

In attempting to streamline, simplify, and mass-market safe sex messages, prevention leaders are motivated by their schooling, training, and experience in various fields. They believe that the most effective way to reach masses of gay men with crucial information is through social marketing. This may be correct, but it may not be the most effective way to change sexual behavior. Men who find great value, pleasure, or meaning in the act of getting fucked and receiving semen need extensive information concerning the details of sexual transmission, as well as well-developed skills at erotic negotiation. Slogans and simple marketing lines are no substitute for dialogic education with active participation. The manipulation of transmission information and educational methods ultimately may be considered exploitative:

> To act paternalistically is to guide and even coerce people in order to protect them and serve their best interests, as a father might his children. . . . The intention of guarding from harm has led, both through mistake and through abuse, to great suffering. The "protection" can suffocate; it can also exploit. Throughout history, men, women and children have been compelled to accept degrading work, alien religious practices, institutionalization, and even wars alleged to "free" them, all in the name of what someone has declared to be their own best interest. And deception may well have outranked force as a means of subjection: duping people to conform, to embrace ideologies and cults–never more zealously perpetrated than by those who believe that the welfare of those deceived is at issue.[6]

Gay men may have been inculcated in safe sex behavior but inculcation has fallen short of ensuring protected sexual activity. The reduction of acts coded with meaning and historical context into consumer goods, underlies the gradual erosion of gay men's trust in community prevention efforts over the past decade.

MAKING LOVE OR MAKING MADNESS?

My lover and I went to bed last night with the shared expectation that we would be having sex. We had kept this Friday evening free of social obligations, lit Sabbath candles, and enjoyed a leisurely dinner of salmon and rice. Half an hour after tidying the kitchen, we found ourselves lying on twin sofas, reading contentedly, until bedtime arrived, and we headed into the bathroom one at a time for evening ministrations.

Safe sex campaigns tiptoed after me into the bathroom, quietly whispering into my ear. I washed my hands and scrubbed my face, but did not brush or floss my teeth. Such dental care activities within four hours of deep kissing with an HIV-positive lover could be hazardous. Where did I read this? How did the four-hour limit become lodged in my brain? If I anticipate that sex may occur on a certain day at a certain time, I count backwards four hours and mentally schedule my brushing and flossing. Am I putting safe sex guidelines to good use with my dental care? When organizations produce brochures, do they intend to infiltrate my bathroom privacy? Did they base this specific recommendation on research and scientific data or simply the authors' best guess? If research was used which purports to show that HIV may be transmitted through abrasions in the mouth, how sound were the researchers' methodology, analyses, and conclusions?

After finishing at the sink, I undress in the bedroom, pull back the sheets, and fold myself into bed. It's my lover's time in the bathroom now. I can hear the water running and the sounds of him washing up. Is he brushing his teeth? Will he be flossing before coming to bed? We once talked about hazards of transmission through deep kissing (Are they real or imagined? I still don't know) but we've never formally agreed to avoid flossing before having sex. Is he being as circumspect as I? Why haven't we developed an agreement about pre-sex dental care? Do we have the information we need to do so? Do we believe the information or does something get in the way?

I hear my partner turning out lights, stripping off his clothes, and tossing them helter-skelter on the floor. In this couple, I am orderly and he is messy; he would say that he is laid-back and I am anal. Does the care we put into sexual safety follow similar roles? He crawls into bed, shimmying up like a frisky seal. As he cranes his neck over to kiss me, our arms wrap around each other. We snuggle and embrace.

My favorite erotic activity is kissing. I have always loved making out with a guy. Something about the subtle interchange of power, the wet pressure of mouths meeting, the angles we twist into to avoid a direct hit of the noses, has charged kissing with tremendous erotic significance for me. I like to keep my eyes wide open and I have often asked my partners to do likewise. Face to face, eye to eye, and mouth to mouth, I find tremendous delight in kissing.

We begin with light pecks on the lips, and I move my mouth over, kissing the side of his cheek, his temple, his eyes. Soft busses all over his face, as I feel passion mounting within. My mouth swoops down to his neck, shoulder, and ear, the smooches becoming more intense and wet. My teeth chew at his neck, as I feel his body relax into me, turn one way and another, and give himself over to sensation. Then my mouth is back again on his own, lips opening, tongue slowly stealing into his mouth.

Kissing is a zone of contention between us. After we had been together about a year, emerging signs indicated that my lover had barriers to deep kissing. He'd offer me his neck instead of his mouth, or he'd cut short the smooching and pull quickly toward the genitals. So much came into play here: Who had power in the relationship? Did I deserve to have the kinds of sex I wanted? What happens when one partner's favorite activity is disliked by the other partner? After various nonverbal communications which revealed an incompatibility in this area, I voiced concern and we shifted from nuzzling negotiations to verbal deliberations.

At first, my partner insisted he had never really liked kissing with the passion and the perseverance I seemed eager to maintain. How had I missed this during our initial year together? Had I gotten so caught up in my own head and my own fantasies that I simply hadn't noticed? Was my lover so immersed in the romance of it all that he simply didn't assert his own preferences? As we delved deeper, I came to understand that as issues of commitment and power shifted and he felt increasingly secure in the relationship, my lover was more able to assert and negotiate the kind of sex with which he felt comfortable.

Still, something nagged at me, something undefined but definitely stuck in my brain. As my partner continued talking, voicing his own needs and defending his desires, he also began speaking of his concerns about HIV transmission between us. While our relationship had deepened and grown more committed, the difference in antibody status between us seemed to assert itself in new ways. He told me that, while he always had feelings about potentially infecting a sex partner and had harbored these concerns for me since we'd met, over the past few months as our relationship solidified, he'd felt an increasing sense of protection toward me. If I became infected through our sex together, he could not live with himself. And somehow, deep kissing between us prominently raised his red flag.

What do I really know about deep kissing and HIV transmission? If kissing is such an important activity for me, why haven't I used my library card and sought out the latest research information? I remember the early years of the epidemic, when we suspected that this new disease could be transmitted easily through kissing. I had vowed that—if this were the case—I would be willing to acquire the disease rather than eliminate deep kissing from my life. Ten years later, I find myself in love with a man whose prediliction against wet kissing finds justification in a few lists of safe sex guidelines.

What meaning is lost to me by my lover's reluctance to engage in deep kissing? Does eliminating this act have no effect on our erotic life together, or does it transform our sexual relationship and alter its meaning for me? How is he affected by the knowledge that I want to kiss him in ways he doesn't want to kiss me? Who gets to decide whether or not HIV-transmission concerns are allowed to dictate our activity in this area—the partner with HIV, the uninfected partner, both, or neither?

As we continue gentle, sensuous kissing, safe sex warnings dart into my head: Be careful about deep kissing. Sores in the mouth or tears in the gums can be points of entry for HIV. Is French kissing on the "safe" or "potentially risky" column on safe sex menus? The awareness that I am an uninfected man, having sex with an infected man, comes over me. Visions of contagion, infection, and infirmity dance before my eyes. I fight back thoughts which taint my lover as dangerous. All I'm trying to do is make love with my lover—can't I do it in peace?

I feel his hands moving over me–arm, side, chest, belly. Fingers rake through the hair on my stomach, gently but firmly pressing into my body. As he reaches for my cock, I realize it has hardened; it springs forth as I feel the touch of his fingertips surrounding the shaft. I move my hand between his legs and grasp his balls, firmly tugging at them, twisting them to the side, tightening my fist and squeezing them.

We are two men–one HIV positive and one HIV negative–holding each other's genitals. We are doing something which we know from four years' experience gives both of us pleasure. This simple act is on no one's list as hazardous. Does the manipulation of our cocks and balls offer a harbor sheltered from fear and thoughts of illness? Can we find, in this erotic exchange, a moment free from the tensions that arise from kissing? If I simply stroke my lover's crotch, and nuzzle my face in his armpit, am I able to eke out some peace?

He knows how much I like my body touched. As I roll over on top of him, he brings both his hands to my chest and rubs me firmly. My hands move up to his stomach, then to his sides, then over to his chest. We grab at each other, energy sparking between us. I lower my mouth to his and kiss again. Do danger signals flash quickly someplace in the back of my brain? As I begin to rub up against him, my lover reaches down and adjusts our cocks so that the friction is pleasurable for each of us. He knows that I can easily climax in this way–cock against cock, chest to chest, eye to eye. It is among my preferred positions for orgasm–I feel close to him, in control and out of control simultaneously, and I can watch this handsome man's eyes reflect into mine. But tonight he's going for something else and he moves me off him before climax approaches.

My lover has an enthusiasm for dicks that I have never developed. Watching me rub myself is an intensely erotic experience for him, to my mind, charged with years of Catholic schooling in the sin of masturbation. He positions me so that I am kneeling between his legs, masturbating my cock up against his balls. At the same time, he is grabbing his own dick, moving his fingers swiftly up the shaft and down over the head. I press into his balls more insistently, thrusting a bit, then pulling back, then thrusting again.

As his excitement mounts, I focus my attention on my partner's pleasure. I know that the sound of my voice, the speaking of specific words, will heighten his arousal. I bring my fingers back to his testicles and grab them firmly, while the other hand plays up and down his thighs, flirting past his anus and over his cheeks. Should I put a condom on my finger if I intend to go any closer? What risk is involved if the tip of my finger probes an inch up his ass? Is it laziness which keeps me from reaching next to the bed and grabbing a condom, or the hassle of ripping open the wrapper and applying the rubber over my finger? Perhaps it is certain ideas that would be introduced explicitly into our erotic encounter by the appearance of the condom–a warning signal which flashes "DANGER!" or a floodlight shining on us, like construction work crews opening a manhole after midnight. Do I imagine that the television talk show on which this sex act is occurring, would suddenly put the words "AIDS-carrying homosexual" under my lover's head, and "As-yet-uninfected homosexual" under mine?

My partner's orgasm is approaching and I swiftly insert my finger in his ass. He pushes it away, bringing it back to his balls. I grab them roughly, bend my head over, and kiss him on the neck. I nibble down to his shoulder, then to his chest, and my teeth surround his nipple and lightly chew. As my tongue flicks against it, his body suddenly begins to spasm. My teeth clamp him harder, and I hear the moans erupt out of his chest, escalating as his orgasm pushes forward. I feel semen splash wet against my arm, my stomach, my cock. I hold him firmly as the quaking continues and his hand jerks up and down on his cock. As his breathing subsides, I loosen my teeth's grip on his chest and my hand's grasp on his balls, and cradle him closely against me.

Do I believe what I've been told about the semen of HIV-infected men? It feels so hot and exciting against me. Do I have breaks in the skin on my arm? Didn't I have some sunburn that was peeling? Can his semen be infecting me with HIV as we hold each other? I thought I felt some of his cum shoot against my dick? Is this hazardous to my health? Should I get a towel and clean it off, before continuing? Would a towel really help, or do I actually need a shower to effectively remove the microscopic HIV? What is my lover thinking? Does he share these concerns? Or is he ready to drift off to never-never land before I get to orgasm?

My cock is still erect. I push other thoughts out of my mind, and focus on my lover. I breathe deeply and smell him. I press against his thigh, and our mouths meet. His arm comes around my body and strokes the back of my head. This excites me. I pull back from him and look into his face, our eyes meeting, smiles playing off each other. My breathing becomes rapid. I am excited by our bodies up against each other and I feel my climax approaching. I bear into his body, thrusting myself hard against his stomach, as I feel myself letting go. My orgasm explodes between my thighs, and I feel semen erupt out of me, our bodies trapping the fluid between his leg and my stomach, as if we were a sandwich–my lover, me, the semen.

How has AIDS prevention informed this sexual encounter? Has it caused thoughts of danger and illness to intrude into a previously pure connection, or have these thoughts been visited on me by the simple arrival of a sexually transmitted epidemic? Have prevention campaigns helped me reduce the risk in making love with this HIV-positive man? Most people would view this encounter as relatively high on the safety list of sex between HIV-positive and HIV-negative men: we had no oral sex and the anal involvement was swift and superficial. Do I know enough about how HIV is transmitted to navigate through an encounter like this without the frequent intrusion of AIDS into my mind? Would some people claim our lovemaking isn't really sex at all? Am I too caught up in my head during sex to enjoy it fully?

When I lie back in bed afterwards, goodnight kisses given and lights out, am I kidding myself when I tell myself I've been safe? Do I deliberately minimize the risk of getting my partner's semen on me because I like how it feels? Am I in denial about the potential hazards of the deep kissing I so desire? Or am I mad–after engaging in what seems to be close to fully safe sex–to be thinking about this stuff at all?

THE LIES WE TELL OURSELVES

Ethicist Sissela Bok, in a study of lying, writes:

> I shall define as a lie any intentionally deceptive message which is *stated*. . . . Deception, then, is the larger category, and lying forms part of it. . . .

> I propose . . . to look primarily at clear-cut lies—lies where the intention to mislead is obvious, where the liar knows that what he is communicating is not what he believes, and where he has not deluded himself into believing his own deceits.[7]

When prevention workers speak about how to have safer sex, where do they get their information and how accurate is it? Do the gay men who serve as health educators believe the advice and instruction they offer is true? Are those who write the text of educational brochures aware that they may be manipulating or deceiving other gay men? Do they follow their own advice 100 percent of the time?

Whether directly stated, implied, or merely tossed into the marketplace of ideas, a series of half-truths, blatant distortions, and outright lies have been simmering in the stew of safe sex discourse for a dozen years. Gay men have been expected to believe that:

- Sucking dick and getting fucked present equivalent risk for HIV infection when performed without condoms.

- Rimming is an easy way to catch HIV.

- Good gay men practice safe sex 100 percent of the time.

- Condoms are fun!

- Swallowing semen is dangerous. Spit it out!

- The top is as likely to become infected through anal sex as the bottom.

- Anal intercourse without protection is never acceptable.

- A latex condom is the only way to make fucking safer.

- HIV-positive men shouldn't have unprotected anal sex together because they can catch new strains of the AIDS virus.

- Massage, foot rubs, and hugging are forms of sex.

Kernels of truth are embedded in many of these statements, along with certain questionable assumptions about gay sex, the process of education, and the ability of gay men to responsibly assume authority for sexual conduct. A subtle but pronounced message has been foisted on gay men suggesting that all intimate sexual activity between men is unsafe and should be modified or avoided. It sometimes appears some health educators are reluctant to consider *any* gay erotic activity acceptable. Rimming might transmit certain parasites or hepatitis, but is not likely to cause HIV infection. Condoms are just one way to reduce transmission risk from anal sex. Footrubs may be great, but they do not in themselves constitute sex.

Beyond total abstinence from specific practices, quick, in surface answers to questions about sexual transmission don't provide men with the knowledge necessary to manage risk.

The message "Always wear a condom" is frequently flouted by HIV-positive men who have been told repeatedly that protection is necessary to prevent exposure to "additional strains" of HIV. What research data suggests gay men risk exposure to diverse strains of HIV? Dr. Jay Levy, a prominent AIDS researcher has written recently,

> Thus far, there is no evidence that repeated exposure to HIV through multiple HIV-positive partners, intravenous drug use, contaminated blood, or blood products affects the progression of disease or causes infection by more than one HIV strain.[8]

There may be existing information regarding anal exposure to specific non-HIV pathogens which would compel some HIV-infected men to use condoms, but it has yet to be widely promoted among gay men. Is a person more likely to alter behavior by directly reviewing research or by hearing simplified conclusions of "experts?"

The ordinary gay citizen is not assisted with gaining access to scientific data or sociological surveys about HIV prevention; this is not considered his purview. Rarely are uninfected men encouraged to read or provided with access to original research findings. Three assumptions ensure that the common man remains at a distance from original research: (a) the prevention leadership is able to interpret scientific reports and draw conclusions better than laypeople; (b) gay men will not commit the time and attention needed to review, analyze, and integrate research findings; (c) gay men do not have the intelligence, judgment, and maturity to interpret scientific data and put it to use.

This failure to distribute available information about life and death matters may be experienced by some gay men as disempowering and undermining. The resulting vacuum limits men's options and keeps them locked in a tight space of confusion, ambivalence, and helplessness:

> A lie, first, may misinform, so as to obscure some *objective,* something the deceived person wanted to do or obtain. It may make the objective seem unattainable or no longer desirable. . . . Lies may also eliminate or obscure relevant *alternatives,* as when a traveler is falsely told a bridge has collapsed. At times, lies foster the belief that there are more alternatives than is really the case; at other times, a lie may lead to the unnecessary loss of confidence in the best alternative.[9]

The gay community has prioritized the provision of substantial, cutting-edge research information on infections and treatments (medical, holistic, and experimental) to HIV-positive people. The work of groups such as Project Inform and *AIDS Treatment News* illustrates that complex scientific and community-based research can be communicated quickly and effectively to laypeople, and that a mass market exists which hungers for that information. Uninfected gay men have parallel needs that are equally pressing for research findings concerning sexual transmission of HIV, yet the relationship between prevention groups and scientific research has evolved quite differently. One group of researchers has identified this problem:

> The traditional "trickle down" model of disseminating research findings–which presumes that findings published in scientific journals will eventually be discovered and used by applied or community entities–is inefficient for transferring promising prevention technologies from research settings to field applications in the midst of an epidemic.[10]

Some men might experience condoms as "fun," but the vast majority of men of every sexual orientation experience them as pleasure reducing, cumbersome, and haphazard.[11] One gay man summarized the feelings of many when he said:

I would like to say . . . "I'm Mr. Righteous here, and yes safe sex has been incorporated in my life and it's not a problem." Bullshit! It's a problem. I don't like having to think about condoms. I don't like having to think about it in the middle of passion, when he's rubbing my asshole with his cock, and I've got to say, "Stop! Oh no! It's time to go get the condom now!" I mean, I don't want to deal with that. I do. But I don't want to.[12]

For most gay men, condoms alter the experience and meaning of anal sex. Marketing claims to the contrary do not change the authentic experience of individual men.[13] Instead, it may create dissonance between what is known to be true and what is claimed by educators, what men say and what men actually experience. Cheerleading fools few people and, in the process, may undermine confidence in education. How have gay men's relationships to prevention efforts been transformed by the manipulation of known experience? When social-marketing campaigns minimize problems associated with condoms do they result in more men using them or fewer?

Prevention workers often maintain that their chief aim is to find simple, appealing ways to capture a specific educational concept and mass market it to specific communities. This is only one of the available public health models of community education.[14] For example, programs modeled on group discussion offer a different methodology but have the additional challenge of attracting active participation. If a significant commitment of time is required in order to allow for protracted dialogue on complex sexual matters, even fewer men may participate. Do gay men willfully avoid placing themselves in situations where they will be active subjects in an educational process? Structured inquiry and formalized discourse with gay men are relegated to physicians, test-site counselors, and therapists. Reflection, consideration, and dialogue more commonly take place informally between gay men in social settings. In a sense, the bulk of the safe sex education of gay men occurs the way learning about sex has always occurred for American males: on the street, behind the bushes, through the media.

At the most basic level, a reexamination of the theoretical foundation of AIDS educational work is in order. Is it more effective to simplify information and reduce complexity rather than present detailed theories and data in all their ambiguity? Are gay men able to take in significant information, sort through intricacies and conflicts, and implement new patterns of behavior, or are they simply too fried at this stage of the epidemic? Do prevention workers believe that educated, middle-class gay men might be able to handle complicated information, but that uneducated, working-class, and poor men need things simplified? Have prevention efforts considered marketing as a critical adjunct to education, or have they followed contemporary America's penchant for replacing education with marketing?

These days, nothing causes greater outrage in the gay community than deception in the sexual arena. One-on-one erotic couplings are crucial encounters with negotiation, veracity, and trust. Men who deliberately deceive sex partners about their antibody status have been vilified. Those who promise to withdraw before ejaculation and then don't are branded unethical. Friends who tell us they're 100 percent safe and subsequently seroconvert are angrily accused of everything from being mentally insane to being a traitor to the cause. Yet community-wide safe sex education efforts often offer platitudes and half-truths as substitutes for complex factual information.

Gay men have been pulled into a spiral of confusion and doubt. One man's expression of frustration captures this sentiment:

> I'm still not sure exactly how it's transmitted. I'm not sure who's lying to me and who's not lying to me and it seems like every month or every two months they come up with something new, there's a different type of AIDS. It keeps on changing, the virus changes. If the virus changes, I'm sure that the way it is transmitted can also change, so it's like being in constant limbo.[15]

It is this specific juncture–the nexus of expecting full personal disclosure and honesty in our private encounters while promoting gross simplification and prevarication in our public efforts–that increasing numbers of gay men are judging as hypocritical.

WHAT HAPPENED IN 1985?

The misrepresentations introduced to gay men through safe sex education, however well-intentioned and motivated by desire to contain the spread of AIDS, are dangerous precisely because of the role they play in undermining confidence in community education efforts and continuing the transmission of HIV. A key myth about gay men and safe sex which developed in the late 1980s illustrates the long-range perils of tampering with statistics and manipulating sexual conduct. This myth, succinctly stated, claims that safe sex education almost completely halted gay male transmission of HIV in the mid-1980s.

In 1985, AIDS educators in the gay community began to declare victory over the transmission of HIV and touted a dramatic decline in new infections as a sign of successful education efforts taken up by a "responsible" gay community. Sweeping statements such as, "AIDS education and prevention campaigns have resulted in the most profound modifications of personal health-related behaviors ever recorded,"[16] were issued by AIDS researchers, educators, and community advocates (including me) attempting to milk this achievement for all it was worth: justifying expanded federal funding, rallying heterosexual participation at donor events, and presenting a "good boy" image of the gay community in the mainstream media. Gay men's supposedly successful efforts to reduce new seroconversions in the mid-1980s in epicenter cities rapidly were melded into a sacred cow, which neither permitted thoughtful analysis nor encouraged independent evaluation of relevant data.

The documented statistical decline in seroconversions between 1985-1988 is commonly attributed to gay men's belief that the epidemic was going to be "solved" quickly and that the cessation of anal sex or the use of condoms were temporary measures. If men could simply spend a few years "playing safely," a cure would be found and utopia could reconvene. This analysis maintains that most gay men rose to the occasion presented by the epidemic and exhibited heroic restraint by ceasing unprotected intercourse.[17]

Yet as the 1980s rolled on and a cure wasn't discovered, seroconversions again began to occur. By 1990, anecdotal reports and initial statistical information were forcing prevention workers to come up with an explanation for the apparent backsliding from heroism. Thus the earlier analysis was extended to incorporate a portrait of long-restrained gay men who, due to governmental failure to produce a cure or a vaccine, became "pent up" to the point where they could hold back no longer. In a mad orgy of abandon, these men unleashed their carnal cravings, leaving behind reason and tossing care to the wind. Once frustrated desires had been "gotten out of the system," men supposedly again calmed down and behaved themselves. After another period of time, however, backlogged erotic desires would emerge again and demand fulfillment.

What does this popularized understanding of communal erotic life say about gay men's sexuality? Is desire a *need,* like a starving man's appetite for food? Is sexuality something to be alternately restrained or unleashed? The words and images that have been used to explain gay men's sexuality reveal a conceptualization of sex as a demonic, threatening force, like a tiger waiting to lunge. It is common for individual gay men to describe their attempts to modify erotic behavior using similar concepts and words:

> I think part of it is just fatigue. [HIV's] been around for ten years, and people are tired of restraining themselves. And a sex club is very, very decadent, very much a way to let it all hang out. And people are taking advantage of it.[18]

Any discussion of the *meaning* that specific sexual acts bring to one's life is absent from our understanding of desire. If the act of being fucked, and having a man climax inside, provides some men with a visceral sense of intimacy, trust, or being possessed, how does the introduction of a latex barrier transform the significance and symbolism of the activity? What new meanings and values arise from reconstructed anal sex?

Most campaigns to encourage gay men to use condoms skirt the issue of signification altogether, or imply that a change from unprotected to protected is insignificant and meaningless. Yet swallowing semen or being fucked have tremendous meaning and provide significant pleasure for individual gay man. A forty-year-old gay man in Boston who is HIV negative said:

One part of my love of sex is swallowing cum. I feel as though the person–their seed–is inside of me, even though I'm not going to have a baby. It's valuable. I don't know if it's tribal, ancient, or what, but I think it's important to be able to drink another man and have him drink you. My very first lover fucked me, and as he was coming, he said, "My seed is in you for eternity." I felt a warmth of love when he said that, and when I fucked him, I said the same thing.[19]

A San Francisco gay man spoke about a parallel meaning he derives from anal intercourse:

It is sort of a complete giving of yourself to that person, where you're totally exposed. I think that's one issue that's never been really addressed by the gay community. And it's like a spiritual dimension, like Catholicism, if you don't have, like, risky sex. If you don't have that semen get in there, it's not even considered genuine. It's not considered integrated. And I think that we take it so lightly–"Oh, well, just use a condom. No big deal." But I think maybe it is a big deal in terms of that total giving of oneself to another person. That you're totally giving yourself to them. Exposed to them.[20]

Many gay men hear a subtle but familiar message from safe sex campaigns: the meanings gay men find in their sexual congresses are spurious, trivial, or expendable. Homosexual desires are not worthy expressions of affirmation for life and connection–they are perverse, corrupt, and decadent, like homosexuals themselves. The integrity of esteemed erotic acts is devalued and men are ordered simply to find other methods of fulfillment. Does the value of health and longevity of life inherently override long-treasured erotic expressions? Are men able to put aside desires which seem primal because an epidemic is raging? Does something about the epidemic ironically *increase* some men's needs for whatever it is that unprotected anal sex means to them?

Far-reaching efforts to expand the use of birth control or discourage youth drug abuse have shown that the deconstruction and reconstruction of behavior patterns and identities are complex, long-term tasks.[21] Changing the sexual behavior of a vast and diverse population may not be the easy and quick task educators imagined it to be in the 1980s—we may find that it takes many years and several gay generations to occur. The common explanation of the declining seroconversion rate among gay men in the mid-1980s may reveal subtle, unconscious beliefs that sex between men—and particularly anal sex—is unnatural, offensive, and illness-linked. Hence men are expected to sacrifice or exchange it for some other act quickly and easily. While some gay men may have been able to modify their sexual activity quickly and completely, other factors may offer at least a partial explanation for the statistical decline during the mid and late 1980s.

If safe sex education about unprotected anal sex deserves primary credit for declining seroconversions during these years, one would expect men to maintain a relatively stable level of sexual activity and simply avoid or modify specific acts. Yet behavioral risk reduction studies of this time reveal otherwise. Research in several cities shows a significant decline in overall sexual activity for gay men, not simply acts considered to be unsafe.[22] A San Francisco study concluded that "Men in non-monogamous relationships and men not in relationships reported substantial reductions in high-risk sexual activity, but not a corresponding increase in low-risk sexual behavior."[23] In New York City, one study showed gay men's number of different sexual partners declined by 78 percent, and sexual activity "involving the exchange of body fluids and mucus membrane contact" fell by 70 percent.[24] One summary of the findings of AIDS prevention studies appearing before 1988 concluded: "there is little actual evidence that an individual's knowledge and attitudes toward AIDS significantly shape his or her behavior."[25]

As the number of deaths mounted and spectral visages haunted gay ghettos, the entrenched denial of the early years slowly withered and the full horror of the epidemic slowly came into focus. I believe the dawning realization of mass, cataclysmic impact caused many urban gay men to freeze and shut down on many levels. At the same time, as sex between men was held responsible for mass death, conflicted feelings about sex came to the surface, brought on paralysis, and played a role in reducing sexual activity. Not only did specific venues close their doors, but men brought great ambiva-

lence about gay sex into the waning sexual marketplace. I believe
that a fall-off in the level of sexual activity which occurred during
these years is attributable in large part to systemic, collective shock
and shut down and the accompanying rise of mass ambivalence
toward gay sexuality among urban gay men. In short, we were
scared sexless.[26]

It is difficult for many gay men to remember their lives and
sexualities during the early years of the epidemic. We forget the
overwhelming confusion and powerful fears of this time period. A
classic example of early grassroots safe sex organizing provides a
glimpse into this particular window in time. The late author John
Preston challenged gay male writers to create "erotic stories about
safer sex." With the assistance of Alyson Publications, then a newly
established publisher of gay and lesbian titles, Preston edited the
Hot Living anthology in mid-1985. Reading the book's introduction
is like time-traveling back to the madness that encircled gay men at
that particular time:

> There are a number of questions about how AIDS is trans-
> mitted. Can it be carried in saliva? If so, kissing is out. Is any
> cock sucking at all a major risk or is it really a question of
> swallowing semen? Is any fucking bad; is there such trauma to
> the walls of the rectum that it is automatically going to pro-
> duce a state where AIDS will be more likely?[27]

The uncertainty about the risks of kissing exemplifies the incredible conundrums of gay erotic lives: Do we give up the act which
often holds meaning of affection, passion, and love? How is the
meaning of erotic life transformed when kissing is proscribed?
What impact does this have on our relationships and our feelings
about gay men? What message do we take away from sexual encounters where we avoid kissing another man?

At the time Preston's book was published, the HIV antibody test
was not widely available. Many gay men were living with uncon-
firmed fears that they already "had it." No accurate sense of the
incubation period for AIDS was available. Preston writes, "The
time span between exposure to the disease and its manifestation can
be as long as five years."[28] Extraordinarily complex psychic elements were introduced into gay men's efforts to "play safely."

Preston addressed gay men's confusion and fears during these years and offered hope and encouragement:

> In this volume are contributions by some of the best known gay writers today. . . . They've come together here to give you one very essential message: Sex is not over with. There are ways to have sex that are enjoyable, and that are desirable. . . . We were in a psychic winter. Our mourning, residues of our socially enforced guilt, and our fear, all produced a sense of despair when the AIDS crisis began. The crisis is far from over. But we can be better prepared to answer the crisis if we can regain some of the sense of empowerment and validation that sex gives us.[29]

Key commercial gay sex venues closed or were forcibly shutdown around 1984-1985 including, amid national debate, all of San Francisco's bathhouses.[30] In addition to providing opportunities for gay men to realize desires, these establishments held tremendous symbolic value for gay men's sexuality.[31] As individual men experienced the death of peers, and as the community as an entity faced the enormity of annihilation, shock drained erotic energy. Men had less sex of any kind with fewer partners.

To take away credit for the drop-off of new seroconversions from education efforts of the time may seem heretical and mean-spirited. This is not my intent; certainly education played a role. Yet despite the development of an entire industry under the rubric of safe sex education, can we really claim that extensive educational efforts have occurred? Education requires systemic instruction and behavior-change education demands that this occur over time. Limited funding, political repression, and homophobic approbations against gay male sexuality have ensured that the prevention system targeting gay men is focused on marketing, public relations, and distribution of second-hand information rather than instruction, dialogue, and reflection. After a decade of prevention efforts, the most committed gay man might have experienced fifteen hours of dedicated HIV education.

It is difficult to locate established educational programs that offer gay men substantial hours of participatory education. Much-touted local programs such as "Hot, Horny, and Healthy," "Stop AIDS," or "Lifeguard" may require a total of ten or fifteen hours of education, and, at that level of commitment, often have difficulty attracting men. When one considers the total behavior change expected of gay men, fifteen hours of education seems like a fraction of the requisite time. Instead of blaming education and insisting it has failed, it would be more apt to acknowledge that appropriate education has not been permitted to occur.

In the mid-1990s, gay men are beginning to pay the price for the myth we naively created a decade ago. Did the community-wide belief that HIV transmission had ceased encourage some men to feel invulnerabile to the hazards of infection? Did a failure to understand fully the seronconversion fall-off in the mid-1980s allow gay men to deprioritize prevention and encourage limited governmental funding of gay male education efforts?[32] Having proclaimed to the world-at-large that we had halted unsafe sex acts, how do we now explain escalating conversion rates among urban gay men? If we were "virtuous" and "responsible" in 1985, are we evil and irresponsible in 1995?

NOTES

1. Adrienne Rich, "Women and Honor–Some Notes on Lying," in *On Lies, Secrets, and Silence: Selected Prose 1966-1978* (New York: Norton, 1979), 190.

2. Jonathan G. Silin, *Sex, Death, and the Education of Children: Our Passion for Ignorance in the Age of AIDS* (New York: Teachers College Press, 1995), 79. Used with permission of the author.

3. Steve Epstein, "Democratic Science? AIDS Activism and the Contested Construction of Knowledge," *Socialist Review* 21(2):55 (April-June 1991).

4. Jeffrey A. Kelly, et al., "AIDS Risk Behavior Patterns Among Gay Men in Small Southern Cities," *American Journal of Public Health* 80(4):416-418 (April 1990) surveyed men entering gay bars in three small Southern cities and found "condoms were used by the insertive partner in only 51 percent of all anal intercourse occasions." Walt Odets, "AIDS Education and Harm Reduction for Gay Men: Psychological Approaches for the 21st Century," *AIDS and Public Policy Journal* 9(1) (Spring 1994) indicates that one-third of men surveyed in San Francisco self-report unprotected anal sex. Odets acknowledges the historical under-reporting of "severely stigmatized behaviors" through surveying and estimates that 45-53 percent of the men in San Francisco are engaging in unprotected anal sex. Michael Warner, "Why Gay Men Are Having Risky Sex," *Village Voice,* January 31, 1995 reports on a study by Project ACHIEVE at the New York Blood Center which indicated that, of the gay men surveyed, 30 percent self-disclosed getting fucked without a condom in the previous three months and 38 percent fucked without a condom.

5. Among the key scholarly and journalistic writings on oral sex between men are Alan R. Lifson, Paul M. O'Malley, Nancy A. Hessol, Susan P. Buchbinder, Lyn Cannon, and George W. Rutherford, "HIV Seroconversion in Two Homosexual Men After Receptive Oral Intercourse With Ejaculations: Implications for Counseling Concerning Safe Sexual Practices," *American Journal of Public Health*, 80(12) (December 1990), 1509-1511; Jeffrey Pudney, Monica Oneta, Kenneth Mayer, George Seage, III, Deborah Anderson, "Pre-ejaculatory Fluid as Potential Vector for Sexual Transmission of HIV-1," *The Lancet*, 340 (December 12, 1992), 1470; Kenneth Mayer and Victor DeGruttola, "Human Immunodeficiency Virus and Oral Intercourse," *Annals of Internal Medicine*, 103(3), September 1993, 428-429; Gabriel Rotello, "Watch Your Mouth," *Out*, (June 1994), 148-168; Aras van Hertum, "Oral Sex Riskier for Those with Dental Problems, Study Reports," *Washington Blade*, November 27, 1992, 8. Cindy Filipenko, "Oral Sex Risk Debate Continues to Rage," *Bay Area Reporter*, September 22, 1994, 25; Wendell Ricketts, "Safe Sex Sucks," *S.F. Frontiers*, April 13, 1995, 12-15.

6. Sisella Bok, *Lying: Moral Choice in Public and Private Life* (New York: Vintage Books, 1978), 215-216.

7. *Ibid.*, 14, 16-17.

8. Jay A. Levy, "The Transmission of HIV and Factors Influencing Progression to AIDS," *American Journal of Medicine* 95:97 (July 1993).

9. Bok, *Lying*, 29.

10. Jeffrey A. Kelly, Debra A. Murphy, Kathleen J. Sikkema, and Seth C. Kalichman, "Psychological Interventions to Prevent HIV Infection Are Urgently Needed: New Priorities for Behavioral Research in the Second Decade of AIDS," *American Psychologist* 48(10):1029 (October 1993).

11. Walt Odets, "Psychological and Educational Challenges for the Gay and Bisexual Male Communities," (paper presented at the American Association of Physicians for Human Rights' AIDS Prevention Summit, Dallas, TX, July 1994), 5.

12. Communication Technologies, "Assessing the Attitudes and Opinions of San Francisco Gay/Queer/Bisexual Men: Results from Twelve Focus Groups," (A report to the San Francisco AIDS Foundation), unedited draft, February 26, 1993, 59-60.

13. For a comprehensive and original discussion of the "origins and moral content of the code of behavior among gay men that has developed around the condom," see David L. Chambers, "Gay Men, AIDS, and the Code of the Condom," *Harvard Civil Rights/Civil Liberties Law Review*, 29(2):353-385 (Summer 1994).

14. Rafael M. Diaz, Associate Professor of Psychological Studies in Education at Stanford University, developed a course titled "Theories of Self-Regulation and Behavior Change" which cites three distinct modalities: "developmental approaches," "social-cognitive approaches," and "empowerment pedagogy."

15. Communication Technologies, "Assessing the Attitudes and Opinions of San Francisco Gay/Queer/Bisexual Men," 54.

16. Ron D. Stall, Thomas J. Coates, and Colleen Hoff, "Behavioral Risk Reduction for HIV Infection Among Gay and Bisexual Men–A Review of Results from the United States," *American Psychologist* 43(11):878 (November 1988).

17. For an early article which considers the formidable challenge of transforming sexual behavior and begins to interrogate the construct of sexual restraint see Michael C. Qudland and William D. Shattls, "AIDS, Sexuality, and Sexual Control," *Journal of Homosexuality* 14(1/2) 1987.

18. Communication Technologies, "Assessing the Attitudes and Opinions of San Francisco Gay/Queer/Bisexual Men," 59.

19. "Frank Ruggero" quoted in William I. Johnston, *HIV-Negative: How the Uninfected Are Affected by AIDS* (New York: Insight Books-Plenum Press, 1995), 211-212.

20. Communication Technologies, "Assessing the Attitudes and Opinions of San Francisco Gay/Queer/Bisexual Men," 61-62.

21. For a discussion of birth control, see Linda Gordon, *Woman's Body, Woman's Right: Birth Control in America* (New York: Penguin, 1990). For a discussion of attempts to discourage youth drug abuse, see Eli Ginzberg, Howard S. Berliner, and Miriam Ostrow, *Young People at Risk: Is Prevention Possible?* (Boulder: Westview Press, 1988), 3-15.

22. Stall, Coates, and Hoff, "Behavioral Risk Reduction for HIV Infection Among Gay and Bisexual Men," 878-879.

23. Leon McKusick, William Horstman, and Thomas J. Coates, "AIDS and Sexual Behavior Reported by Gay Men in San Francisco," *American Journal of Public Health* 75(5):493 (May 1985).

24. John L. Martin, "The Impact of AIDS on Gay Male Sexual Behavior Patterns in New York City," *American Journal of Public Health* 77(5):578 (May 1987).

25. Marshall H. Becker and Jill G. Joseph, "AIDS and Behavioral Change to Reduce Risk: A Review," *American Journal of Public Health* 78(4):408 (April 1988).

26. I am grateful to William I. Johnston for this succinct term summarizing our collective feelings during that period of time.

27. John Preston, ed., *Hot Living: Erotic Stories About Safer Sex* (Boston: Alyson, 1985), 10. Used by permission of Alyson Publications.

28. *Ibid.*, 12.

29. *Op. cit.*, 13.

30. Stephen Cook, "Baths Ended Era of Sex on the Sly, Court Told," *San Francisco Examiner,* November 15, 1994, B1.

31. Historian Allan Bérubé has brilliantly documented both the symbolic and functional role of bathhouses in gay male cultures. See Allan Bérubé, "The History of Gay Bathhouses," *Coming Up!,* December 1984; also Allan Bérubé, "Don't Save Us From Our Sexuality," *Coming Up!,* April 1984.

32. In 1988, San Francisco's Stop AIDS program declared their work essentially completed and went into a three-year hiatus before being resurrected due to rising seroconversion among local gay men.

Chapter 6

Sodomy Emerges Victorious

Human sexuality is a complicated phenomenon. A cursory examination will not yield the entire significance of a sexual act.

—Pat Califia
"Feminisim and Sadomasochism"

When I'm bad, I'm so, so bad.

—Donna Summer, "Last Dance"

We may be witnessing the creation of a new urban gay male life cycle.

Hank Homo (primarily white, but not always; primarily middle class, though not always) spends his childhood in the Midwest (or the South, or New England, or Colorado) with a dawning sense of being "different" which blooms in adolescence into full-blown alienation. He fools around with guys in high school, sneaks out of his college dorm on Saturday night to visit the nearest gay bar, and shortly after graduation, comes out of the closet at age twenty-one.

Hank spends the next few years exorcising demons of self-hatred and addiction, immersing himself in queer culture of the nearest small city, and trying on different kinds of gay identities. At twenty-five, seeking to fulfill a seemingly unquenchable thirst for gay life and a heightened queer identity, he packs his bags and gets on a Trailways bus (or a plane, or in his used '78 Chevy Nova) and heads for San Francisco (or New York, or Los Angeles, or Chicago . . .). He finds a roommate situation in the Castro (or the East Village or West Hollywood or New Town . . .), a gig as a barback at a neighborhood bar, and a gym filled with hundreds of other mid-twenties homo-migrants.

He knows what's safe and what's not safe and wears a red ribbon on his leather jacket lapel. Hank throws himself into "the life" with gusto, good humor, and the best intentions. He discovers the dance clubs and the sex clubs, is jerked off in the showers at his gym (or the park at night, or the tea-room in the department store), and picks up men on subways, streetcorners, and at the corner market. He's feeling good, he's feeling hot–finally attractive and at home in his body. At twenty-eight years old, he's living the kind of life he's always dreamed of: out and proud as a gay man, immersed in a gay-positive environment, sharing in a communal culture of plea-sure and freedom and affirmation.

One night (or day, or afternoon) he goes home with a man he's dated a few times (or a man he met on the street, or his ex-lover, or his ex-lover's new lover), and gets caught up in a moment of pas-sion (or too much to drink, or wanting it so bad . . .) and he engages in sex he knows he's not supposed to engage in and never has before (or only has had a few times, or has had quite a bit lately). He frets about it for days (or weeks, or years) and before he knows it, he's at the HIV test site, scared shitless, waiting to get the results.

At thirty he hears the news he's feared for years (or expected to hear for years): he finds out he's infected with HIV. From age thirty to thirty-three, he's in denial and tells himself HIV is "chronic and manageable" (or the test was wrong, or that there'll be a cure soon). From thirty-three to thirty-six, he's mildly symptomatic, and learns to meditate and eat right (or begins taking AZT, or becomes religious, or joins ACT-UP). At thirty-seven he's diagnosed with KS (must have been those poppers, or the speed, or all the semen swallowed, or bad genes) and gets on several experimental treat-ments (or withdraws into severe depression, or writes a column for the local gay paper, or moves back to the Midwest, the South, or New England). He recovers his health for a while, joins a healing circle (or a twelve-step program, or a phone sex line, or a new compact disc club) and tells the world he's "gonna beat it!" His energy begins slipping away, he loses weight (or eyesight, or bowel control, or mental functioning), becomes increasingly debilitated and homebound.

Two months before his fortieth birthday, Hank Homo succumbs to HIV disease, another soul caught up in a truncated life cycle increasingly prevalent in gay male worlds.

SEX STAGES A COMEBACK

During the 1980s, a generational divide emerged within urban gay male communities, distinguished not only by age but by relationship to the onset of the AIDS epidemic. Younger men who had come out after the epidemic began, by 1985 had embarked on the early stages of community development. This movement of queer men could be found between 1985-1990 making connections, redefining identities, and inventing new social venues and cultural semiotics. During these same years, the men who had constituted gay male cultures of the 1970s were watching the social and sexual worlds they had constructed fall to pieces; many were sick, dying, or experiencing deep emotional and psychological reactions to the epidemic. As the decade came to a close and the epidemic showed no signs of ending, both populations experienced internal shifts in the ways they framed identity, constituted desire, and occupied the queer public sphere. A resurgence of sexual activity slowly became evident among both of these gay male populations nationwide.[1]

By 1985, many gay men over the age of thirty were facing decimation beyond their wildest imagination. Over 10,000 had been diagnosed with this frightening new syndrome and tens of thousands more were infected with HIV and feared for their lives.[2] Even more men had lost lovers, best friends, neighbors, coworkers, and entire social networks. The expectations they had held for themselves and for the gay community in the 1970s at best had been interrupted; more likely dreams were being dashed to pieces. Profound changes in sexuality appeared including dysfunction, sexual anorexia, or sex addiction.[3] As the extremity of life in the epidemic twisted gay male psyches–and as these men approached middle age–many entered a sexual winter and found diminished interest in erotic desire, commercial sex cultures, and life in the gay community.[4]

This same period (the mid-1980s) was undoubtedly troubling for young gay men attempting to emerge from the closet and enter community life amid the reappearance of linkages between gay identity and lethality. The experiences of teenagers and men in their early twenties coming out amid this twisted connection between illness and sexual identity has yet to be fully documented. As the late 1980s arrived, an assortment of new publications, organizations, and cultures emerged out of the networks of young self-defined queers. Adopting distinctive styles, music, activism, and icons, queer men created venues and identities which found new ways to grapple with core issues: gender, power, social organization, sexuality, and AIDS.

By 1990, men of these two distinct generations were feeling a shared resurgence of libido. In urban centers, younger men had successfully made inroads and established their own commercial venues: dance clubs, sex clubs, gyms, coffee shops, backroom bars. With the beachheads secured, a few years of experience in the rough and tumble of the epidemic behind them, and the increasing mainstream visibility of gay and lesbian issues, queer men surged into communal life with gusto. For all their attempts to separate themselves politically and culturally from the preexisting gay community, queer men placed sex at the center of their communal culture, as urban gay men had done a generation earlier.

Jay Paul and colleagues describe a "generation gap" between these two populations of gay men:

> Historical changes in the gay community as a consequence of the AIDS epidemic have contributed to a "generation gap" between older and younger gay men. Every generation feels the need to assert its independence from previous generations, yet the highly threatening nature of AIDS may have intensified the younger generation's motivation to separate themselves from their gay elders. In some communities, this was exemplified by the emergence of age-segregated social groups (e.g., San Francisco's "Boy Clubs"). This has also been evident in the development of a new aesthetic among younger gay men, who created both a new look and a new club scene

that may feel quite alien to those who came out in the seventies period of gay male "clone."[5]

As the younger generation's new cultural venues became institutionalized, signs that the previous gay generation was entering a period of sexual revival became visible. Men who had stayed away from commercial sex venues for years found themselves revisiting old haunts. Some men began participating in parties, dance clubs, and other social venues dominated by the younger generation of queers. By 1995, New York magazine could report on the revived sex culture of Manhattan:

> The change in attitude is clearly visible around the city. The return of vintage seventies promiscuity has sparked a small boom in theaters, dance clubs, bars, and a variety of other venues that have back rooms and private cubicles for sex. Places like Club 82, the Crow Bar, and L.U.R.E. (Leather, Uniforms, Rubber, Etc.) are flourishing. So are private clubs, which meet at secret locations that change from week to week and have names like Excalibur and Carter's Prime. There are also weekly theme evenings, like Muscle Knights, where you check your clothes at the door. . . . A Chelsea club called Zone DK has been checked more than nineteen times over the past year and a half and during virtually every visit, inspectors saw customers having unprotected oral sex. . . . At a joint called Jay's Hangout in the West Village, inspectors reported both oral and anal sex. . . .[6]

Social discourse about sex issues, which had seemed frozen in a state of moral conservatism in the mid-1980s, began to thaw. Studies of gay men's sexual activity began to show a steady upswing at the close of the 1980s; more men had started to have more sex with more partners. At the same time, these surveys revealed that more men appeared to be engaging in what had become known as "high-risk" activity.[7]

RELAPSE AND RECIDIVISM:
THE RE-PATHOLOGIZING OF ANAL SEX

Caught in the crisis of the week of the late 1980s, AIDS researchers and educators hardly had time to plan for or notice the dramatic shifts in the communal sex lives of gay men. It was only after 1990 that epidemiologists began to confront data documenting a serious increase of new infections among gay men in epicenter cities.[8] Once the alarm was sounded, health educators and community leaders initiated efforts seeking new directions and creative methods of what was rapidly termed "preventing relapse."

The choice of terms such as "relapse" and "recidivism" by public health researchers and community health educators exposes biases about gay male sexuality common to dominant prevention paradigms. One therapist revealingly told *Time* magazine:

> There is an awful lot of safe-sex recidivism. People who know what they are supposed to do and have been doing it for a while are finding it irresistible to return to their dangerous old ways.[9]

While the denotation of "relapse" is simply "to revert back to a former state," the term's popular usage with cancer patients and alcoholics brings with it connotations of "regressing after partial recovery from illness" and "backsliding into bad habits." Relapse implies disappointment, error, and failure.[10] "Recidivism" refers to a tendency to return to previous patterns of criminal behavior. Value-laden constructs such as "relapse," "recidivism," and "high-risk," became essential building blocks of gay male HIV education, and subtley undermined gay men's trust in prevention professionals: these are the identical constructs that historically have been used to pathologize gay men's sexual orientation.[11]

Pre-epidemic societal fear of and disdain for male homosexual acts were amplified by HIV and served to distort prevention efforts. Punitive and judgmental responses to the epidemic emerged out of the mix of fascination and revulsion which mainstream American culture harbors toward anal sex. A decade before the epidemic, French theorist Guy Hocquenghem explored the paradoxical linkage between homosexuality and anal eroticism:

The desiring use of the anus made by homosexuals is the chief, if not the exclusive one. Only homosexuals make such constant libidinal use of this zone. . . . Homosexual desire challenges anality-sublimation because it restores the desiring use of the anus. . . . Homosexuality primarily means anal homosexuality, sodomy.[12]

Many believe that visceral ambivalence toward anal intercourse is triggered by "contradictory" functions of the anus. One gay psychologist has written:

It is understandably confusing that the part of the body which is supposed to be so unsavory is also extremely sensitive and potentially among the most enjoyable. Especially for a child, the discovery that the anus is considered bad and repulsive must be confusing, since the idea is in direct contradiction to his or her pleasurable experience.[13]

If anal intercourse and the depositing or receiving of semen were bad habits, illnesses, or sins, the use of the term "relapse" might be appropriate. If such activities were to be considered legitimate sources of pleasure and expressions of desire between two men (or, for that manner, between two individuals of any gender), "relapse" may be considered a phobic term likely to spur the transmission of guilt through the discourse of safe sex.[14]

By accepting sexphobic and homophobic attitudes toward anal sex without challenges, prevention efforts in the 1990s reinforce judgments of gay men and devalue acts considered by many to be sacred. As Susan Sontag explained:

An infectious disease whose principal means of transmission is sexual necessarily puts at greater risk those who are sexually more active—and is easy to view as a punishment for that activity. True of syphilis, this is even truer of AIDS, since not just promiscuity but a specific sexual "practice" regarded as unnatural is named as more endangering. Getting the disease through a sexual practice is thought to be more willful, therefore deserves more blame.[15]

Because anal intercourse and oral sex are potential transmission routes (although under differing circumstances and with vastly differing levels of risk), gay men have been encouraged to consider them expendable activities. A supposedly lethal epidemic is expected to provide the requisite motivation for sweeping behavior changes. It is assumed that the contemporary gay male sexual consumer will order from an erotic menu which doesn't include activities that have historically and transculturally held tremendous meaning. Most safe sex campaigns insist on condom usage with oral sex. The acceptance of semen into any orifice seems out of the question.[16]

Few "experts" are telling white, middle-class, married heterosexuals to stop vaginal intercourse. It took the New York State Public Health Council until 1994–almost fifteen years into the epidemic–to acknowledge that activity's role in HIV transmission and add it to the list of sex acts banned in that state's sex clubs.[17] Because vaginal intercourse is a core-defining act of heterosexual identity, an identity privileged in American culture, it is seen as natural and valuable. Vaginal intercourse is considered symbolically and literally life-giving and life-affirming–qualities few would attribute to anal intercourse. Telling heterosexual men and women to cease vaginal sex entirely would be mocked. At most, educators tepidly suggest the use of condoms during vaginal intercourse. And when heterosexual couples don't use them, it is attributed to faith in monogamy, the imbalance of power between men and women, and women's fears of provoking a man by the mere mention of condoms.[18] The defining role vaginal intercourse plays in the creation of heterosexuality and the reinforcement of bifurcated gender roles may be a large factor in failure to use condoms. Receiving semen provides many women with identity as a heterosexual woman; ejaculating semen into a woman provides many men with identity as a heterosexual man.[19]

During the International AIDS Conference in Amsterdam in 1992, I attended a presentation on condom use by heterosexual hemophiliac couples where the man was infected and the woman was not. In one study, most couples never used condoms during vaginal intercourse. The audience of doctors, researchers, and health providers nodded sympathetically with understanding. A later presentation that discussed unprotected anal intercourse between men brought on expressions of shock, disgust, and outrage. Heterosexuals infected through sexual activity are seen as sympathetic unknowing victims, a stigma quite different than that reserved for homosexual men. Studies which reveal that heterosexual couples overwhelmingly fail to use latex barriers during intercourse may be greeted with somber nods of identification and empathy by all except feminist health advocates.

The inability to fathom the complex cultural ways in which specific erotic acts between men are constituted lies at the root of societal incredulity that gay men are becoming infected at this stage of the epidemic. Why does it seem staggering and unbelievable that a man would allow himself to get fucked without protection? What makes people believe that swallowing semen is something that men will be able to give up for the rest of their lives? How do we feel when we realize that men we know, love, and respect, have unprotected anal sex? What is it like to realize that we desire these same acts?

Walt Odets, in an essay on unsafe sex between men, insists:

> We have to acknowledge that there *are* positive reasons that people have unsafe sex, that there are emotional reasons, that aspects of a relationship and intimacy are expressed in unsafe sex. For some people, the "exchange of bodily fluids" is what sex is all about.[20]

Why are sexual acts that may cause illness judged more harshly than non-erotic activities which lead to infirmity and death? Sontag identified the way Americans judge AIDS-related behavior:

> The unsafe habits associated with cancer, among other illnesses—even heart disease, hitherto little culpabilized, is now largely viewed as the price one pays for excesses of diet and "life-style"—are the result of a weakness of the will or a lack of prudence, or of addiction to legal (albeit very dangerous) chemicals. The unsafe behavior that produces AIDS is judged to be more than just weakness. It is indulgence, delinquency—addictions to chemicals that are illegal and to sex regarded as deviant.[21]

Gay men who never enjoyed anal sex and those who have been fully able to alter their sexual activities to ensure safety are often among those dumbstruck when they hear about the surge in new infections. When one's long-prized erotic repertoire holds little risk of infection, condemnation of others may come quickly. If one's sexual behavior has proven malleable, it may be easy to expect others to do likewise. Gay men who cannot intellectually grasp the complex factors which motivate men to have unprotected sex can be firm and furious in their indictments. The level of outrage and self-righteousness may suggest an intense identification with the men they purport to judge.

Is it possible for men to make anything resembling an authentic choice to be anally penetrated without a condom in the middle of this epidemic? For those who value life above all else, it may be impossible to resist pathologizing men who maintain different priorities in the middle of an epidemic: a value system which privileges pleasure, unfettered abandon, or specific modes of semen transfer over longevity of life seems unimaginable. Hence many "make sense" of the newly infected by insisting they are driven by low self-esteem, a death wish, or some kind of addiction (alcohol, drugs, sex . . .). While I suspect many men who seroconvert do not do so out of reasoned choice or an intellectually rooted desire to actualize personal values, I do not believe that all newly HIV-positive gay men are victims of poor mental health. Fundamental distinctions in the ways gay men conceptualize life in the epidemic are rarely acknowledged or discussed, yet may be a primary source of the varied responses to risk and safety.

Because prevention strategy has emerged from public health behaviorist approaches to education, the current attempts to explain unprotected sex occur within limited frameworks of understanding the ways desires are constituted. Some look for environmental factors which cause a man to take risk and blame bathhouses, sex clubs, drug and alcohol use, prostitution, and the gay ghetto. Most explanations ignore the existence of the vast unconscious mind which may contribute to human action. Many insist that if individuals are reasonably "intelligent," informed about safe sex, and provided with condoms, they will use them 100 percent of the time. When men violate these expectations, AIDS educators insist they "haven't gotten the message," or "lack common sense." Perhaps something else is going on.

Author Richard Rodriguez has written, "To grow up homosexual is to live with secrets and within secrets."[22] These days many gay men may live within a very specific secret: sexual desires and activities are sources of great comfort and pleasure which may be needed now more than before the epidemic. While treated as exchangeable and expendable by many prevention campaigns, specific acts in fact provide considerable meaning and value to gay men's lives and identities.

At least one group of researchers, in attempting to understand why educated gay men continue to engage in unprotected anal sex, grasped the complex ways sexual desires are constituted:

> Important differences in beliefs about the value and relative importance of particular sexual behaviors may exist between those men who comply with safe sex recommendations and those who do not. . . . Some health belief items hint at interesting attitudinal factors in those men engaging in high-risk sex. That is, there is no compelling reason why placing a high value on sexual expression should be associated with participation in high-risk sex. . . . Do these measures hint at some as yet unidentified processes important to participation in high-risk sex?[23]

Most explanations of unprotected sex ignore the rich web of social and cultural relations out of which emerge human activity. R. W. Connell and colleagues offer innovative and pragmatic approaches to understanding these matters in a series of articles linking postmodern theory about sex and desire with HIV prevention for gay men. Decrying medical and public health's stranglehold on HIV education, they write:

> Sexuality must be understood as inherently social, not merely as a biological-phenomenon-with-a-social-context. Many social relationships are in considerable part *constituted* by sexuality, forming networks and institutions which, like all other forms of social structuring, are dynamic in historical

time. Such evolving patterns of social relationship form the crucially important contexts of particular sexual practices.[24]

Connell and colleagues, in a study of homosexual desire and sexual activity among working-class men, further articulate the socially-constituted meanings of specific sex practices:

> The HIV epidemic did not arrive from outer space to disrupt a settled, static community. It arrived through sexual practices already being reworked into a set of social relations already in motion, indeed substantially reshaped in very recent history. The response to HIV/AIDS was therefore likely to be diverse, reflecting the unevenness of the changes and the variety of life situations homosexual men found themselves in.[25]

Recent work on urban gay male social history illustrates the imbrication of social relations with sexuality. Before the advent of AIDS, men undertook enormous risks to have anal sex.[26] Men have been willing to face the scorn of families, the loss of employment opportunities, and the threat of street violence for sex with other men. Penetration and the receiving of semen hold vastly different meanings in diverse cultures.[27] Why would the risk of HIV infection be motivation enough for men to exchange one sex act for another, as if simply replacing chocolate with vanilla ice cream?

It has become common to claim that gay liberation is about gay men's right to love other men. The right to love has historically posed less of a threat to Western societies than the right to fuck. Particular expressions of male love in America have been highly esteemed for a long time: entire institutions such as the church, military, Congress, and competitive sports are constructed around the elevation of manly love. Gay liberation was ignited by a drive to free the *erotic* power between men. Activist pioneers were advocating not solely affection and "domestic partnership," but the right to be fucked.[28] Masses of men emerging from the closet over the past twenty-five years have clamored for sexual freedom and the urban cultures they created elevated the value of communal sexual options. AIDS educators who have underestimated the powerful meanings of anal sex, oral sex, and semen exchange to significant numbers of gay men may have imperiled the effectiveness of their efforts.

UNSAFE SEX AND ME:
EROTICIZING THE FORBIDDEN

Except for brief periods in my life, I have never been monogamous. The men with whom I have lived and loved have shared my interest in continuing to have sex with other men. While my lover and I went through a period of time during the early stage of our relationship when our strong passions for one another naturally narrowed our focus, for most of our time together, we have enjoyed "extramarital relations."

I have never used a condom. Because I have not engaged in anal sex since 1983, I have not felt the need. Attending countless workshops has instructed me in their use, explained the differences between varying brands, and forced me into relay-race games which required me to put condoms quickly and efficiently onto bananas, dildos, and my fingers. Despite this training, I can't pretend to be an expert in condoms or anal sex.

Yet I have occasionally found myself in situations where men expect me to fuck them. This has created occasional awkward and disappointing encounters, and I now am sure to make it clear before going home with someone that anal sex is not going to occur. Still, I find myself with men who hope I will penetrate them.

While on a recent trip to Houston, I met a handsome man in a bar and struck up a conversation. After an hour of informal chit-chat and flirtation, he invited me back to his apartment. As I've learned to do in this situation, I agreed but asked him for a few minutes of conversation about our erotic preferences for the evening. I am acutely aware that such discussions can squelch desire before even getting to the bedroom, but experience has taught me they're worth the risk.

In this case, it was a very good idea. After I asked the gentleman what kinds of sex he was partial toward, it became clear that he had one thing in mind. "I really need to get fucked tonight," he told me in a slow, sexy, Southern drawl. "I want you to fuck me long and hard. . . . "

My heart sank when I heard these words. I knew I had to fess up. But I didn't want to risk alienating him and losing the chance to get him in the sack.

"Well, pal, I don't really have anal sex anymore," I said softly. "It's never been a favorite activity of mine and, with current concerns about safety, I've cut it out of my sexual repertoire. Are there other activities that we may be able to enjoy together?"

The man's expression changed dramatically. His face turned disappointed, even angry. "I'd use a condom with you," he offered. "It's fine for me if you want to be safe. I just need your dick deep in me tonight."

I considered his proposal only for a split second. "No way," I replied firmly. "I haven't fucked or been fucked in a long time and I'm not looking to start again now. Do you have any interest in cocksucking?" I asked, hoping an alternate interest could be agreed upon.

He turned and looked away from me and took a swallow of his beer. "I was really hoping you'd fuck me," he admitted. "I'm really good at it," he promised, looking back at me and grinning. His hand reached out and began rubbing my crotch through my jeans. "I would really show you a good time," he continued, "and I know you can show me a really good time. What do you say?"

It was clear that he thought I was simply teasing. I had to chuckle to myself at the dilemma I found myself in. Here was the man that I found most attractive in the bar and he was very interested in me. The sparks between us were evident. Yet our sexual desires were clearly not compatible. I was not willing to give him what he wanted, and he was very much focused that evening on a single, specific act.

I took his hand off me and turned to face him. "I'm really sorry, pal, but I am not kidding you," I insisted. "This is not something that I'm open to being talked into. I'm really good at certain other sexual activities," I bragged, laughing inside at my own overblown self-promotion, "but it's clear that tonight we are looking for two different things."

With that statement, I shook his hand, and walked into the crowd to cruise for a more compatible partner. Yet for the remainder of the evening, this gentleman kept giving me the eye, dropping by to flirt, and making his offer once again. It was clear that we both recognized our dilemma, though we also hoped the other would be swayed as the hours passed by.

I have great respect for men who enjoy getting fucked. At different times in my life, I have envied them and wished I could share their interest. There is something about the transgressiveness of receiving anal sex which has fascinated me, even as I keep the activity at a distance. As I've listened to men speak about the transformative powers of getting fucked, I often find myself relating to feelings and thoughts which seem to fall out from the act. The relationship between receptive anal intercourse and alternative visions of masculinity and male identity has struck me as particularly appealing. A penetrated man remains a man, but he may be different from men who don't get fucked. As a man in the latter category, I feel that difference acutely.

I occasionally have phone sex with a man who shares my interest in talking about unsafe anal intercourse. While he occasionally "tops" me during these telephone fantasy sessions and ejaculates up my butt, more often I am the one doing the fucking. This man enjoys setting the scene together and is especially excited when he is put in the position of telling me that he doesn't want me to use a condom.

Because I am familiar with his desires, I always am sure to say something like, "I didn't bring any rubbers with me, pal. Do you have any handy?" or "Before we go any farther, I've got to get a condom from my wallet and put it on. . . . ."

This is usually followed by him saying, "No. No condoms today. I need to feel your dick in me, without a condom. I need to feel you shoot cum up my butt. I need it inside me. I need to feel your sperm in me."

He enjoys repeating this statement in a variety of ways. In fact, I believe that the most exciting parts of our phone sex conversations are those where he is urging me to fuck him without protection. Something in the words, in his description of "needing sperm" and "needing to know you're in me without anything between us," is highly charged for both of us. We've had great phone sex for over a year and essentially have performed the same act in our fantasies, dozens of times.

I have talked to other men through phone sex lines who have also eroticized unprotected anal sex. By this I do not mean that they simply like to talk about having anal sex and don't include the ritualistic putting on of the condom as a part of the fantasy. I am speaking about men who find it exciting to consciously not use protection, and to articulate, often repeatedly, that condoms are not going to be used and that sperm is going to enter the anal tract. One man shared his fantasies, which focus on forcing me to have unprotected intercourse: he likes me to beg him to use a condom and then he refuses. Sometimes he enjoys telling me that he will use one and then not following through on his promise. I find this exciting as well.

Over the past few years, I have noticed an increasing prevalence of this kind of fantasy on phone sex lines. It has caused me to wonder about some things. If men who never meet one another in the flesh get off on buttfucking without condoms, do men who do meet also eroticize unprotected anal sex? I am again not referring to men who enjoy anal sex and prefer simply not to introduce a condom into the scenerio. The focus of my interest is on men who may be fucking and getting fucked and their erotic experience is heightened by a conscious and articulated refusal to use condoms.

I have spoken to one friend who is turned on by such activity and despite living in a major city heavily impacted by HIV since the start of the epidemic and being primarily a sexual "bottom," he still tests HIV negative. He attributes this feat to his commitment to surviving the epidemic and his ability to construct a satisfying erotic life through his powerful imagination and good judgment. He maintains that he is careful to select uninfected men he trusts as his sex partners for these fantasies.

I wonder whether labeling a specific sexual act "forbidden" heightens men's erotic interest in the act. As a man who has never enjoyed getting fucked and who has experienced varying levels of discomfort and pain during my few ventures in this area, I have noticed an escalating interest in getting fucked appearing in my masturbatory fantasies since the early years of the epidemic. How common is it for humans to eroticize the exact activities which they are told not to actualize? Is something about a gay culture filled with explicit warnings about anal sex hazards, channeling young gay men's erotic desires more strongly toward anal intercourse? In a world where many gay men have staked out terrain as "sexual outlaws," has unprotected anal sex become the defining act of renegade status?

Culture and Sexual Meanings

Penetration and the receiving of semen hold vastly different meanings in diverse cultures. By examining these practices across cultures through the lens of varied disciplines, anthropologists, folklorists, sociologists, and other researchers provide a sense of the ways in which sexual meanings emerge out of specific historical contexts and are socially and culturally constructed. What they haven't seemed able to do is show how sexual meanings are able to shift or be transformed over time.

Alan Dundes examines the relationship between German national character and shit, toilet training, and anal eroticism in *Life Is Like a Chicken Coop Ladder: A Portrait of German Culture Through Folklore*.[29] Using a wide variety of sources–folktales, children's rhymes, historical accounts, jokes and riddles, poetry, art, letters–Dundes makes a compelling case for linking German character with issues of control, and rooting this connection in childhood practices of toilet training and swaddling. Dundes asserts that "genital matters are commonly expressed in terms of anal equivalents" in German folklore (p. 52), and his book offers a rich collection of examples of the diverse meanings which surround anality and grow out of a wide range of cultural factors.

Yet Dundes doesn't limit his explorations of anality to Germany. A recent essay explores connections between anal penetration and sports, war, and games in cultures such as Argentina, Spain, Iceland, and the United States.[30] In another piece examining folklore surrounding the Gulf War, Dundes and Carl Pagter illustrate popular conceptions linking receptive anal intercourse with degradation:

> In terms of the psychology of warfare, it is not enough to deprive one's opponent of his masculinity. Rather the opponent must be totally humiliated by being feminized as well. This is why, we would argue, several of the items portray the Iraqi soldier or Hussein himself as the victim of anal penetration. The play on "Saddam elected to receive" is a clear sign

of his prospective loss of masculinity–in football parlance, he is about to take it in his "endzone."[31]

Dundes continues his examination of these themes in an essay which compiles and analyzes jokes surrounding the O. J. Simpson murder trial. He again illustrates the linkage of anal intercourse with feminization and racism:

> What is O. J.'s new name going to be?
> Orangina.

> O. J. is introduced to his new cellmate, a huge, nasty-look-ing guy doing five consecutive life sentences. He says to O. J., "Look here, we gonna get something straight right off da bat. Are you gonna be da husband or da wife?" O. J. thinks fast. If he says "wife," he reasons, he'll get it up the wazoo in a matter of nanoseconds, so he says, "I'll be the husband." The guy then says, "OK. then. Now get down on yo knees and suck yo wife's dick."[32]

Dundes folklore research on anal intercourse provides evidence of the vast and complex ways in which specific erotic activity–which contemporary HIV educators often view as an isolated, "free-floating" practice lacking rooting in specific cultures–is bound up in a range of social practices. The message his body of work delivers to contemporary HIV prevention efforts is that sex acts are not discrete entities separated from the web of culture and should not be expected to disappear or be radically transformed easily and quickly.

In a similar manner, Gilbert Herdt's book *Guardians of the Flutes* presents a portrait on the Sambia of New Guinea which focuses upon mass ritualistic oral insemination of boys and uncovers Sambian cultural belief that, by receiving semen, the boys will grow "big and strong."[33] Parallel acts performed between males of similar ages in most North American cultures would be policed as acts of violation, abuse, and perversion. One could argue that the central ideals Herdt illuminates through Sambian boy-insemination–"how culture struc-tures sexuality, how individuals' desires also harness culture, and how the rituals of boy-inseminating might form the crucible" of specific gay male identities, communities, and ways of life?

The literature on "Dhat Syndrome" in South Asia provides another example of ways in which distinct cultures confer specific meanings upon similar sexual activities. Dhat syndrome has been defined differently by different researchers in different locations. One medical team described Indian Dhat syndrome in this way:

> The Indian Dhat syndrome is a culture-bound symptom complex. The clinical picture includes severe anxiety and hypochondriasis. The patient is preoccupied with the excessive loss of semen by noctoral emissions. There is a fear that semen is being lost, and mixed in urine.[34]

Another researcher insisted on renaming the syndrome as "semen anxiety" and discusses similarities and differences in the ways in which "semen anxiety" is manifested and takes on varied meanings in varied cultures (Chinese, Sri Lankan, Pakistani, distinct Indian cultures).[35] One study which compared "semen-loss syndrome" in Sri Lanka and Japan found that in the former nation, people "consider semen loss to be detrimental to mental and physical health," while in the latter, complaints about "lost semen" and a belief system surrounding the experience hardly existed.[36]

Within a specific theoretically "unified" area (South Asia or the United States, for example), sexual practices may take on different meanings and be embedded in strikingly different cultures. United States HIV-prevention efforts using public health paradigms, commonly have ignored or simplified sexual meanings, discounted the deep significance of culture, and privileged rational forms of decision making over the role of either the unconscious or a matrix of social and cultural relations as key to behavior change.

THE MYTH OF AN EPIDEMIC ON THE WANE

By 1991, people responsible for HIV-prevention activities targeting gay men in epicenter cities began to panic. After several years of conceptualizing unprotected anal sex as "relapse," and attempting to develop "solutions" to the "problem," the information that new seroconversions were mounting again among gay men began to circulate beyond the privatized spaces of AIDS educators (conferences, academic journals, professional networks) and enter the public sphere through the mainstream media.

Many educators had first learned about new infections among previously HIV-negative gay men informally, as they heard of friends and colleagues who had recently tested HIV positive. Few addressed the matter directly because it challenged the entrenched mindset of the gay community: the spread of HIV had been virtually halted among gay men in the mid-1980s. Organizations provided no targeted services for newly infected gay men, placing men who seroconverted in 1991 in general support groups for HIV-positive men.[37] These individuals found themselves in the awkward position of either adhering to the group norm by pretending they seroconverted in the early 1980s, or being honest and raising the ire of the group members who had become infected "before they knew better." The community at the time simply couldn't cope with the idea that this epidemic had instituted a "rolling admissions" policy, and that an end was not in sight.

When individual gay men became ready to investigate the matter more closely, their efforts were initially conducted quietly, away from public scrutiny. Many community advocates felt that, if word leaked out that gay men were engaging in unprotected anal sex, governmental funding for AIDS efforts would be undermined significantly. Between 1991-1993, a small but steady stream of research studies and focus groups were initiated in San Francisco to probe sexual behavior and psychological motivation among gay and bisexual men of all ages.

In November 1992, San Francisco's AIDS prevention leadership quietly met "to identify the causes for continuing high rates of HIV infection among self-identified gay and bisexual men in San Francisco, and to decide how AIDS prevention efforts can be strengthened to deal with this emergency."[38] They convened a dozen focus groups comprising 119 gay and bisexual men; reports from these groups were analyzed by local AIDS prevention workers. A series of fourteen recommendations emerged, including "the need for evolving AIDS prevention efforts," "addressing emotional and psychological issues interfering with safe sex," and "providing greater care and support for gay and bisexual men."[39] In the tight circle of San Francisco's AIDS prevention workers, the awareness that education efforts needed to be reconceptualized was dawning.

A front-page story in *The New York Times* in 1993 titled "Second Wave of AIDS Feared by Officials in San Francisco" was responsible for bringing the new infections to the public's attention. Reporter Jane Gross, having reviewed public health reports, transcripts of focus group sessions, and epidemiological data, wrote:

> Among every 100 uninfected gay men here, there were 18 new infections in 1982, a rate that dropped to less than 1 in 1985. That has nudged back up to 2 out of 100 now, and is twice that high among men younger than 25. That increase, is viewed as alarming by health officials and is the clearest sign of a corresponding increase in unsafe behavior.[40]

Gross cited surveys which "indicate that one of every three gay men in San Francisco is engaging in unsafe sex, primarily anal intercourse without condoms," and explored the possible causes of what she dubbed a "second wave of AIDS infection."

The New York Times piece rocked San Francisco's AIDS system like another earthquake, precisely because it pierced the heavy public relations armor which the system had been amassing for years. A city that prided itself on getting down to business and halting new infections a decade ago, now found the myths it created visibly exposed on the front page of the nation's newspaper of record. Over the next few months, the news of a possible new wave of infection seemed to deepen the level of depression and despair among the city's gay men, while sending local prevention leaders into increasingly frequent postures of defense. As one leading AIDS advocate privately told me, "Everyone knows that the City's AIDS organizations don't have a clue about what to do about new infections, but they'll keep getting funded because they're the only game in town. Even the health department knows that it's flushing its prevention dollars down the toilet."[41]

Three months after *The New York Times* piece appeared, the City's AIDS prevention leadership struck back. In an act with boundless repercussions, the Department of Public Health's AIDS Office convened a press conference and declared that the AIDS epidemic in San Francisco had peaked and was now on the wane.

Hailing "dramatic reductions in new HIV infections which occurred a decade ago and which were achieved as a result of successful prevention campaigns waged in San Francisco during the past 10 years," the City's chief epidemiologist presented information showing that the number of annual AIDS diagnoses had dropped 50 percent in 1993, and would continue to decline over the following five years.[42]

Local newspapers hailed the news with lead stories and front-page headlines, one declaring in bold letters, "S.F. AIDS Epidemic Waning." In almost celebratory tone, the paper's AIDS-beat reporter wrote:

> The AIDS epidemic that has ravaged San Francisco for the past decade has begun to recede, surrendering to aggressive efforts of disease education and prevention, a new study shows. . . . Ten years ago, The City's tightknit and well-educated gay community launched a "safe sex" AIDS prevention campaign that dramatically changed behavior and sharply curtailed new HIV infection rates.[43]

The *Examiner* article seemed like a pep rally for the City's AIDS prevention efforts which had been so painfully undercut just three months earlier in *The New York Times* cover story. "These figures show that prevention works," the chief epidemiologist stated, in the *Examiner.* "Our prevention efforts—targeted at specific populations—have altered the course of the epidemic in The City." A gay journalist was quoted as saying proudly that the fall-off of new AIDS cases was "very much an accomplishment of my community. We did a remarkable job of stopping a very sharp and high degree of transmission." Another community advocate hailed the announcement, stating, "It's good news, but we can't take a break."[44] To top it all off, the following day's *Examiner* included a laudatory editorial, championing local prevention efforts and proclaiming "Education Cuts AIDS Spread."[45] It seemed almost as if the press conference were timed to show to legislators in Washington, DC, who were debating the federal AIDS prevention budget, that education programs had been effective and that funding increases were merited.

What seems cynical about this particular press conference is that it was used successfully to buttress the sagging reputations of local

AIDS prevention efforts without promising substantive new directions. A despairing community was fed fabricated pap to lift its spirits and rekindle a sense of pride. Evidence was never presented which empirically linked the fall-off in new cases to education efforts and a close scrutiny of the reported data suggests different conclusions. While letters to the editor appeared to challenge the headline's assertion,[46] and a special hearing of the city's Board of Supervisors Health and Budget Committees was held to discuss the report—mainly to chide AIDS office staffers for releasing the projections and unintentionally justifying a decrease in federal and state prevention dollars[47]—it was impossible to erase the headline from the minds of the masses. True or not, AIDS was now on the wane in San Francisco.[48]

The report shows that by 1997, more than 26,700 AIDS cases will have been diagnosed in San Francisco, nearly all among gay and bisexual men. An additional 18,000 gay men will have been infected but not diagnosed. Hence the study shows that in the first sixteen years of the epidemic, 45,000 residents will have been infected with HIV, diagnosed with AIDS, or killed by HIV disease.[49] This figure represents an astounding 60 percent of the estimated 75,000 gay men in San Francisco at the start of the epidemic.[50] With no further analysis, one might conclude that AIDS prevention efforts saved 40 percent of the gay men in San Francisco from becoming infected—a sizeable portion yet still significantly less than a majority of the gay population.

However, the assumption that all gay men are at significant risk for HIV infection—a belief seemingly held by the entire mainstream media and frequently exploited by gay male prevention leaders who know otherwise—is not borne out by studies of gay men's sexual behavior. Only a handful of cases of HIV transmission have been documented through oral sex.[51] The vast majority of gay men who have become infected with HIV are generally believed to have contracted it through anal sex. Yet studies have consistently shown that between 10 percent and 50 percent of gay men never engage in anal sex.[52]

During the decade before the epidemic was identified, Guy Hocquenghem wrote:

Homosexuality is always connected with the anus, even though—as Kinsey's precious statistics demonstrate—anal intercourse is still the exception even among homosexuals.[53]

If one assumes 20 percent of the gay men in San Francisco do not engage in either receptive or insertive anal sex (a conservative estimate, I believe), the remaining 80 percent of gay men become the "at-risk" population for HIV transmission. If 80 percent of the city's gay men are at risk and 60 percent of the city's gay men will have been infected by 1997, "successful prevention campaigns" can be credited with "saving" only 20 percent of the gay and bisexual men's population—the other 20 percent of this population were never seriously at risk. Put another way, of the 60,000 gay men in San Francisco at the start of the epidemic who were at risk because they engage in anal sex, 45,000—or 75 percent—have been infected and 15,000—or 25 percent— remain uninfected.

This is a significant number of at-risk gay men remaining uninfected. However, plaudits given to AIDS prevention efforts, the repeated use of adjectives such as "successful," and "historic," and phrases such as "the most profound modifications of personal health-related behaviors ever recorded," seem disrespectful to the 45,000 lives whom such efforts apparently failed to save.

The recent decline in new infections to under 1,000 a year is also being attributed to prevention efforts, but additional factors may be just as important. This "small" amount of seroconversion may simply indicate that the population of gay men in San Francisco who engage in anal sex has been saturated with HIV. Those men who don't desire to engage in anal sex—either due to dislike, aversion, or simple lack of experience—are not at significant risk for HIV infection, yet repeatedly are statistically appropriated by prevention leaders to buttress their claims of protecting large numbers of gay men from infection.

In his powerful and insightful book *Safety in Numbers: Safer Sex and Gay Men,* Edward King lists the concept "saturation" as one of the "myths about behavior change."[54] While King states that "this theory cannot be conclusively ruled out in large American studies . . . due to the extremely high prevalence of HIV in such cohorts," he argues that "the levelling off in infection rates among gay men which is consistently seen in studies around the world occurred at different levels of seroprevalence in different countries." King also cites the saturation theory's failure "to take account of the shifting nature of the population of gay men at risk."

I respectfully disagree with King here, but we don't have the research we need to argue. I believe that levelling off at different levels of seroprevalence could be expected to occur because different percentages of men engage in anal sex in different locations. I suspect that gay men in cities well-known as gay centers might get fucked more than gay men in smaller cities and towns. This is suggested in a multicity study of pre-AIDS gay male sexual behavior at VD clinics which indicated that while 82.1 percent of the study's San Francisco participants engaged in receptive anal intercourse with ejaculation during a four-month period in 1978, and 77.8 percent of the Los Angeles men did likewise, the percentage fell to 68.3 among the St. Louis participants and 66.6 in the Chicago group. I do not believe that specific sex practices are participated in by men across geographic areas and across cultures, and initial data comparing black gay men and white gay men bear this out.[55]

Rather than being an example of a city which has initiated successful, targeted prevention campaigns, San Francisco may be a city which shows the profound draw of anal sex and semen exchange for gay men, despite mass attempts to discourage the activity. This is particularly evident when one reviews projections of HIV prevalence among young gay men which indicates one-third will be HIV positive before they are thirty.[56]

SHAME STAGES A COMEBACK

In a climate where public attention has begun to focus on escalating seroconversions among both young gay men and older men who had remained uninfected for a decade and a half, AIDS educators are feeling a great deal of pressure. Although many leaders of gay men's prevention programs are knowledgeable about HIV, gay culture, and social marketing, most seem to have a limited understanding of the serious challenges which have historically stymied educators attempting to influence human sexuality. Unsure of how to respond to seroconversion increases, and targets of escalating criticism from certain sectors of the gay community, some AIDS educators are defaulting to tactics of fear-mongering and shaming to stem the tide of new infections.

An essay widely discussed in San Francisco exemplifies panic as a tactic to use to marshall community support. Two local HIV prevention leaders published a piece in the community forum section of a local gay newspaper. Titled "It's Not Acceptable, in 1993 . . . " the article initially acknowledges the importance of anal sex to many gay men:

> As humans, we communicate deeply through sex. And in a world where it sometimes feels like we lost everything else–civil rights, friends, lovers, basic dignity–it's easy to feel we're being asked to relinquish our most primal means of communication and pleasure.
>
> We're afraid, in fact, that we'll lose the profundity of fusion. Coming in a guy's butt is the closest we'll ever get to that guy; similarly, having someone come inside us triggers a primal sense of oneness. The wholly natural human drive for completion through sex is, for some of us, deeply buried in our unconscious. So the call to safe fucking, while intellectually palatable, seems unconsciously unbearable. Who wants a barrier–even a latex one–to come between us?[57]

After such affirmation, the authors' tone and message shifts, launching into a polemic laden with assumptions and judgments which increasing numbers of gay men do not appear to share:

> But we're living with an epidemic. In an epidemic, "normal" human behavior gets suspended in deference to staying alive. And it's easy to forget there's power in life-affirming protected sex, and there's power in taking care of each other.
>
> So we need to revisit our public/private norms. Two guys fucking unsafely are, in a way, fucking all of us; if we watch, we're joining in. The questions then arise: what do we do? Tap the two on the shoulder and ask them to stop? Report them to the club owners? Report the club to the city? Join in? Or do nothing? What's clear is that our silence is our death. It's time

to show care and take responsibility for each other by intervening.

Is it true that under epidemic conditions "normal" human behavior gets suspended in deference to staying alive? In other contexts, Sissela Bok has analyzed the impact of prolonged threats to survival on individual choice. She initially seems to reach a similar conclusion:

> In extreme and prolonged threats to survival, as in plagues, invasions, and religious or political persecutions, human choice is intolerably restricted. Survival alone counts; moral considerations are nearly obliterated . . . the luxury of alternatives is out of the question. The overwhelming justification is, once again, survival. It appeals to the most powerful aspects of the principle of avoiding harm—the battle against personal extinction. At such times, the spread of deceptive practices cannot be a consideration insofar as it has already taken place.[58]

Yet Bok probes deeper and raises important considerations surrounding the use of deception and manipulation with a population undergoing extreme threats to survival:

> But to say that the long-term threats to survival strain morality is not to say that hindsight cannot make out differences in adherence to principles of justice or veracity at such times. Nor, obviously, is it to say that those who *impose* or tolerate such burdens for their fellow human beings must not be judged. It is merely to say that there comes a point of human endurance and of long-term threat beyond which justice is inoperative for sufferers, and where their adherence to moral principles cannot be evaluated by outsiders.[59]

Gay men may be at one of these points. While some men protect themselves amid the deepening catastrophe of AIDS, more men than usually acknowledged do otherwise. Defining the men who opt for safe sex as healthy, moral citizens with significant self-esteem and those who don't as self-destructive, drug-addicted, bad people is facile. While not simplifying the complexity of factors that may motivate an individual to participate in activities which threaten health or shorten lifespan (smoking, excessive drinking, eating fried foods, refusing to exercise), is it possible to value the meanings of an activity and the pleasure and satisfaction it affords over safety and longevity of life?

Gay men who seroconvert display a broad range of feelings about their new status. A forty-year-old gay man in San Francisco, who had recently tested HIV positive, said:

> There are some times when AIDS seems like an incredible relief. I feel that I'm saved. I never have to worry about what I'm going to be when I grow up. I no longer have to deal with really frightening issues like, how graciously will I grow old? Sometimes I think, well, this solves a lot of things for me, doesn't it?[60]

Another San Franciscan, a thirty-two-year-old airline mechanic who recently seroconverted, told *The New York Times*:

> "I thought if I was HIV-positive I'd be so much gayer. . . . People are looking for the red badge of courage, and you get that when you convert."[61]

I was initially caught off guard by the calmness and clarity of friends who had tested positive after years of testing negative. My own judgments led me to explain their composure as rooted in the seroconversions' confirmation of long-standing, internal sense of doom or deeply entrenched feelings of worthlessness. I tried to see how these men were different from me and how my psychology may have protected me from infection. When men explained what they claimed to be their reason for having unprotected sex, my ears shut off and I discounted their analyses as rationalizations. Only when one man challenged my arrogance did I begin to hear these men's heartfelt formulations and I was startled. Some of these men claim to have made reasoned, defensible decisions regarding sexual conduct and found peace with themselves in the face of seroconverting. I was left raging inside and confused.

By stating "It's easy to forget there's power in life-affirming protected sex," the authors of "It's Not Acceptable" seem to suggest that the erotic is a source of power which serves as a prime motivator of our sexual congresses.[62] Are they speaking of the energy and fulfillment which may be generated by desire, or the social and political strength which may accrue to the gay community by showing the public-at-large that we comply with safe sex guidelines? For those of us who have remained uninfected, what kind of power do we garner from protected sex? While I suspect that men gain both personal and communal power through the fulfillment of specific erotic desires, I am dubious that the marketing of power in this manner can be used effectively to regulate gay men's sexuality.

Specific sexual acts have vastly different meaning for different individuals. This is true cross-culturally and true within specific cultures. All men who enjoy fucking another man do not experience a sense of power from the act, and those who do might have differing experiences and values of power. The many permutations of meaning from specific acts are affected by a wide range of factors. It has become common to simplify the meaning of anal sex (the top seeks power and/or control, the bottom seeks surrender, both seek fusion) or semen exchange (intimacy, closeness, merging), although conversations with gay men reveal an incredible multiplicity of meaning from the same specific act.[63] Anal intercourse with a latex barrier may provide some men with feelings of power and safety, while other men may experience the identical activity as conveying danger, contagion, or disempowerment.

The authors' argument veers across a decisive line when they insist, "Two guys fucking unsafely are, in a way, fucking all of us; if we watch, we're joining in." The use of "fucking" for both anal sex and as a colloquial term for "injure" or "wound" may belie superficial sex-positive posturing. In what ways is the greater gay community undermined when two men engage in unprotected anal sex? Perhaps the authors believe that the gay community as an entity is harmed by "allowing" unprotected anal sex to occur in public venues because the heterosexual public may judge us as irresponsible. How should community conduct be influenced by an imagined sense of the values of other populations? The moral issues here are complex and difficult to sort through, but the authors seem to divide morality into stark black and white.

Scapegoating is a dangerous tactic to employ in the midst of a sexually transmitted epidemic. Psychologists believe that scapegoating occurs when groups or individuals psychologically split off a piece of themselves and charge it with conflicted significance.[64] Do we envy the men who are having unprotected sex? Are we angry because they have left us out? Do we blame them for our own infection or that of our friends?

Over the past ten years, a prevention strategy has been institutionalized which attempts to regulate desire and sexual activity largely through moralizing, peer pressure, and public relations. Under the guise of encouragement and social marketing, this approach employs outside forces of guilt and shame to influence individual conduct. It encourages the manipulation and simplifying of information and it glosses over ambiguity. Historic precedents have shown that human sexuality is difficult to control and resistant to such regulation. At this point, many gay men apparently are rebelling:

> I think what is going on in the heads of some men I talk to is internalized homophobia. I have it too. How could I not? I was raised being made to feel afraid, ashamed, embarrassed, and guilty about the feelings I had for other men. AIDS education for gay men often makes us feel afraid, ashamed, embarrassed, and guilty if we have unsafe sex. It's reinforcing something that does not need reinforcement.[65]

An uninfected gay man who oversees HIV testing and counseling for a metropolitan health department voiced concern about the manipulation of gay men under the guise of shifting community norms:

> The lie is that everybody is practicing safer sex. That's the lie we have lived with in the gay community. It's simply not true, and the thing that worries me is that people don't know where to go to get help. I don't like community norms that feed into people feeling bad about themselves, not being able to talk about what is really bothering them.[66]

Writing about his adolescent homosexual explorations in the 1950s, Jonathan Silin links the way information about sexuality has been kept hidden from teenagers with the manner in which HIV prevention information is used to control sexuality:

> Memory is personal and painful. It reminds me that the knowledge I was acquiring of my body and its desires was dangerous knowledge—dangerous for what it said to me about myself and my future and dangerous to others for what it said to them about the nature of sexual possibilities. But memory is also political and powerful. It tells me that throughout history dangerous knowledge, knowledge that challenges accepted behavioral norms and values, has always been controlled and managed by those in positions to do so. . . .
>
> I have become increasingly concerned about a subtle but perhaps more disturbing kind of violence—a type of violence that occurs when governmental and social agencies try to control sexuality through informational and educational campaigns.[67]

It is time to challenge this kind of symbolic violence against gay male sexuality. New prevention methods utilizing viable alternative strategies merit consideration. Is it possible to develop tactics which fully affirm the right and responsibility of gay men to serve as agents assessing and managing their own sexual risk? Can we provide men with anything that approximates effective education and then trust them to reconstruct their erotic lives? Is it possible to pursue simultaneously both the external, coercive regulation of sexuality and individualized, reflective decision making and risk management? Or do the two cancel out one another?

NOTES

1. This is best documented in Edward King, *Safety in Numbers: Safer Sex and Gay Men* (New York: Routledge, 1993). See in particular, Chapter 4, "Sustaining Safer Sex?," 135-168. King writes, "The data also suggested that the proportion of men engaging in anal sex had increased slightly during the previous year [1988], and this trend was confirmed by follow-up in 1989, 1990 and 1991" (p. 45). One of the first groups to respond to this dawning realization met in November 1992, "to identify the causes for continuing high rates of HIV infection among self-identified gay and bisexual men in San Francisco," and was com-

prised of "a diverse group of AIDS prevention agencies, [San Francisco] Department of Public Health AIDS Office staff, concerned prevention professionals and gay men." See Dana Van Gorder, ed., *A Call for a New Generation of AIDS Prevention for Gay and Bisexual Men in San Francisco* (San Francisco Department of Public Health, August, 1993), 1.

2. Centers for Disease Control, *Morbidity and Mortality Weekly Report: Report on AIDS* (Atlanta: Centers for Disease Control, 1986), 91.

3. Walt Odets, *In the Shadow of the Epidemic: Being HIV-Negative in the Age of AIDS* (Durham NC: Duke University Press, 1995), 23-39.

4. *Ibid.*, 38-39.

5. Jay P. Paul, Robert B. Hays, Thomas J. Coates, "The Impact of the HIV Epidemic on U.S. Gay Male Communities," in *Lesbian, Gay, and Bisexual Identities Over the Lifespan: Psychological Perspectives on Personal, Relational and Community Processes*, eds. Anthony R. D'Augelli and Charlotte J. Patterson (Oxford: Oxford University Press, 1995, 376.

6. Craig Horowitz, "Has AIDS Won?," *New York*, February 20, 1995, 33.

7. A study by Maria Ekstrand of University of California at San Francisco's Center for AIDS Prevention Studies presented at the July 1992 International AIDS Conference in Amsterdam, discussed in Michael Munzell, "Dancing with Death," *San Francisco Sunday Chronicle and Examiner, Image Magazine,* August 23, 1992, 24, reports "37 percent of gay men in San Francisco had unprotected anal sex in one or two years between 1987 and 1990. Another 25 percent had unsafe sex during all three years, making a total of 62 percent that engaged in high-risk behavior." See Maria L. Ekstrand and Tom Coates, "Maintenance of Safer Sex Behaviors and Predictors of Risky Sex: The San Francisco Men's Health Study," *American Journal of Public Health* 80(8):973-977 (1990).

8. Among the earliest articles to shift focus from "gay men have halted (or greatly reduced) HIV transmission" to "we've got an escalating problem on our hands" were Ron Stall, Don Barrett, Larry Bye, Joe Catania, Chuck Frutchey, Jeff Henne, George Lemp, and Jay Paul, "A Comparison of Younger and Older Gay Men's HIV Risk-Taking Behaviors: The Communication Technologies 1989 Cross-Sectional Survey," *Journal of Acquired Immune Deficiency Syndromes* 5:682-687 (1992); Robert B. Hays, Susan M. Keegles, and Thomas J. Coates, "High HIV Risk-Taking Among Young Gay Men," *AIDS,* 4:901-907 (1990); Jeffrey A. Kelly, J. St. Lawrence, T. Brasfield, L. Stevenson, Y. Diaz, and A. Hauth, "AIDS Risk Behavior Patterns Among Gay Men in Small Southern Cities," *American Journal of Public Health* 80(4):410-418 (April 1990).

9. Franklin Abbot, quoted in William A. Henry III, "An Identity Forged in Flames," *Time,* August 3, 1992, 37.

10. Edward King, *Safety in Numbers: Safer Sex and Gay Men* (New York: Routledge, 1993), 142-163, writes extensively about "relapse theory." David Klotz, "Safer Sex Maintenance and Reinforcement in Gay Men," in *The Second Decade of AIDS,* eds. Walt Odets and Michael Shernoff (New York: Hatherleigh Press, 1995), 221, shares a similar concern about the use of this term.

11. George Weinberg, *Society and the Healthy Homosexual* (Garden City, NY: Anchor, 1972) still provides the best analysis of homophboia in the professions of psychology and psychiatry.

12. Guy Hocquenghem, *Homosexual Desire,* trans. Daniella Dangoor (London: Allison & Busby, 1972), 84.

13. Jack Morin, *Anal Pleasure and Health* (Burlingame, CA: Down There Press, 1981), 26.

14. Poet Kenny Fries has eloquently written about the "stigmatization of anal sex" in popular culture. See Kenny Fries, "Pulp Practices," *Metroline,* November 24, 1994, 22.

15. Susan Sontag, *AIDS and Its Metaphors* (New York: Farrar, Straus, and Giroux, 1988), 26.

16. Walt Odets, "AIDS Education and Prevention: Why It Has Gone Almost Completely Wrong and Some Things We Can Do About It" (paper presented at the National Lesbian and Gay Health Conference, Houston, TX, July 23, 1993).

17. Lisa Krieger, "AIDSWEEK," *San Francisco Examiner* February 23, 1994, A2.

18. This is discussed by Anna Quindlen, "Dance of Death," *The New York Times,* February 19, 1994, 13.

19. Andrea Dworkin has written extensively (and problematically) on the sexual politics of intercourse but is at her most succinct in one of her earliest books. See in Andrea Dworkin, *Woman Hating* (New York: Dutton, 1974), the chapter "Androgyny: Androgyny, Fucking and Community," 174-193.

20. Quoted in Michael Munzell, "Dancing with Death," 26. See note 7.

21. Sontag, *AIDS and Its Metaphors,* 25.

22. Richard Rodriguez, *Days of Obligation: An Argument with My Mexican Father* (New York: Viking, 1992), 30.

23. Ron D. Stall, Thomas J. Coates, Colleen Hoff, "Behavioral Risk Reduction for HIV Infection Among Gay and Bisexual Men: A Review of Results from the United States," *American Psychologist* 43(11):882-884 (November 1988).

24. R. W. Connell, J. Crawford, G. W. Dowsett, S. Kippax, V. Sinnott, P. Rodden, R. Berg, D. Baxter, L. Watson, "Danger and Context: Unsafe Anal Sexual Practice Among Homosexual and Bisexual Men in the AIDS Crisis" *Australian and New Zealand Journal of Sociology,* 26(2):189 (August, 1990).

25. R. W. Connell, M. D. Davis, G. W. Dowsett, "A Bastard of a Life: Homosexual Desire and Practice Among Men in Working-Class Milieux," *Australian and New Zealand Journal of Sociology,* 29(1):129 (March, 1993).

26. For an historical account of this dynamic in the early twentieth century, see George Chauncey, *Gay New York: Gender, Urban Culture, and the Making of the Gay Male World, 1890-1940* (New York: Basic Books, 1994).

27. For one anthropological account of semen exchange with different cultural meaning from contemporary North American gay male cultures, see Gilbert Herdt, *Guardians of the Flutes* (Chicago: University of Chicago Press, 1994).

28. For early work documenting gay liberation and sexual liberation see Carl Wittman, "A Gay Manifesto," in *Out of the Closets: Voices of Gay Liberation,*

eds. Karla Jay and Allen Young (New York: Douglas, 1972), and Dennis Altman, *Coming Out in the Seventies* (Boston: Alyson, 1981).

29. Alan Dundes, *Life Is Like a Chicken Coop Ladder* (New York: Columbia University Press, 1984).

30. Alan Dundes, "Traditional Male Combat: From Game to War," in (eds.) Rolf W. Brednich and Walter Hartinger, *Gewalt in Der Kultur* (Passau 1994), 153-177.

31. Alan Dundes and Carl Pagter, "The Mobile SCUD Missile Launcher and Other Persian Gulf Warlore: An American Folk Image of Saddam Hussein's Iraq," *Western Folklore* 50(3):320 (July 1991).

32. Alan Dundes, "From Jock to Joke: The *Sic Transit* of O. J. Simpson," *ZYZZYVA* X.(4): 42-43 (Winter 1994).

33. Gilbert Herdt, *Guardians of the Flutes* (Chicago: University of Chicago Press, 1981).

34. H. K. Malhotra and N. N. Wig, "Dhat Syndrome: A Culture-Bound Sex Meurosis of the Orient," *Archives of Sexual Behavior* 4(5): 519 (1975).

35. James W. Edwards, "Semen Anxiety in South Asian Cultures: Cultural and Transcultural Significance," *Medical Anthropology* 7(3): 51-67 (Summer, 1983).

36. Ratnin Dewaraja and Yuji Sasaki, "Semen-Loss Syndrome: A Comparison Between Sri Lanka and Japan," *American Journal of Psychotherapy* XLV. (1): 14-20 (January 1991).

37. During my tenure as executive director of Shanti Project in San Francisco, I attempted twice unsuccessfully to find a support group for newly infected men among the City's 200 AIDS organizations.

38. *A Call for a New Generation of AIDS Prevention for Gay and Bisexual Men in San Francisco,* ed. Dana Van Gorder, (San Francisco Dept. of Public Health, August 1993), 1.

39. *Ibid.*, table of contents.

40. Jane Gross, "Second Wave of AIDS Feared by Officials in San Francisco," *The New York Times,* December 11, 1993, 1.

41. Anonymous, interview by author, June 21, 1993.

34. *Projections of the AIDS Epidemic in San Francisco: 1994-1997* (San Francisco Department of Public Health, February 15, 1994).

43. Lisa M. Krieger, "S.F. AIDS Epidemic Waning," *San Francisco Examiner,* February 16, 1994, 1.

44. Michael Botkin and Kerrington Osborne, quoted in Lisa M. Krieger, "S.F. AIDS Epidemic Waning," *San Francisco Examiner,* February 16, 1994, A-14.

45. "Education Cuts AIDS Spread," editorial, *San Francisco Examiner,* February 17, 1994, A-20.

46. See Chris Hall, "Despite reports otherwise, HIV is more of a threat than ever," letter to the editor, *San Francisco Examiner,* February 25, 1994, A-20.

47. Michael Colbruno, "Differences Abound Over AIDS Report," *San Francisco Sentinel,* March 30, 1994, 9.

48. This was evident in the coverage given the story by non-local gay media. See Aras van Hertum, "CDC data shows AIDS is slowing among Gay men," *Washington Blade,* March 18, 1994, 27.

49. *Projections of the AIDS Epidemic in San Francisco: 1994-1997* (San Francisco Department of Public Health, February 15, 1994). Edward King, *Safety in Numbers: Safer Sex and Gay Men* (New York: Routledge, 1993), page 11 cites even more extreme infection rates. He provides figures from the San Francisco City Clinic cohort study which indicates that 73.1 percent of the 6,875 gay men in this study were HIV positive by 1985.

50. The number of gay people in any area is difficult to determine. After consultations with San Francisco-based market research professions who have grappled with this question, I settled on a figure of 75,000 gay men in San Francisco by estimating the city's lesbian and gay population at 20 percent of the city's total 1980 population of about 750,000, evenly divided between lesbians and gay men. Recently the San Francisco Department of Public Health has estimated 58,000 gay men in San Francisco. See Sidney Brinkley, "Getting the Message Out," *Washington Blade*, April, 17, 1995, 14.

51. Jay A. Levy, "The Transmission of HIV and Factors Influencing Progression to AIDS," *American Journal of Medicine* 95:91 (July 1993) considers receptive oral intercourse as carrying "a low but still potential risk of HIV transmission." For popular media coverage of the queer debate on oral sex see Cindy Filipenko, "Oral Sex Risk Debate Continues to Rage," *Bay Area Reporter,* September 22, 1994, 25, which cites the Canadian AIDS Society's continued listing of oral sex as a low-risk act in their safe sex guidelines; see also Jeff Epperly, "Still No Easy Answers on Questions About Oral Sex and HIV Transmission," *Bay Windows,* March 3, 1994, 5; Gabriel Rotello, "Watch Your Mouth," *Out* (June 1994), 148-168, presents a case for upgrading oral sex from its current low-risk status to a higher-risk category.

52. Karla Jay and Allen Young, *The Gay Report: Lesbians and Gay Men Speak Out About Sexual Experiences and Lifestyles* (New York: Summit Books, 1977), 464-465, indicates the frequency of gay male participation in the following activities: "fucking your partner:" never (9 percent), once (5 percent), very infrequently (21 percent); "getting fucked:" never (13 percent), once (8 percent), very infrequently (21 percent). James Spada, *The Spada Report: The Newest Survey of Gay Male Sexuality* (New York: Signet, 1979), 328, features the question "Do you enjoy anal intercourse?" and the answers: Yes (76.7 percent), No (12.9 percent), Sometimes (4.4 percent), Depends on partner (1.8 percent), Depends on position (1.6 percent), No answer (3.6 percent); Alan P. Bell and Martin S. Weinberg, *Homosexualites: A Study of Diversity Among Men and Women* (New York: Simon and Schuster, 1978), 328 reports in response to questions about "performing anal intercourse," 78 percent of white homosexual men and 90 percent black homosexual men responded "yes," while 22 percent of the white men and 10 percent of the black men answered "no." The question about "receiving anal intercourse" was answered affirmatively by 67 percent of the white men and 78 percent of the black men and answered negatively by 33 percent of the white men and 22 percent of the black men; Morton Hunt, *Sexual Behavior in the 1970s* (New York: Dell, 1974) includes the figure of 50 percent of gay men reporting participation in anal sex and 50 percent reporting no participation in the act. Edward King,

Safety in Numbers: Safer Sex and Gay Men (New York: Routledge, 1993), 158, cites an Australian survey indicating "for many men, anal sex remains the most pleasurable sexual activity," and a British survey which places anal sex (active and passive) behind masturbation and oral sex in appeal among gay men, and gives figures of 72.5 percent (active) and 61.7 percent (passive) who found anal sex "appealing." For a compelling collection of essays on sodomy from a variety of academic and activist perspectives see Jonathan Goldberg, ed., *Reclaiming Sodom* (New York and London: Routledge, 1994), particularly Leo Bersani's "Is the Rectum a Grave?," 249-264.

53. Hocquenghem, *Homosexual Desire,* 89.

54. Edward King, *Safety in Numbers: Safer Sex and Gay Men* (New York: Routledge, 1993), 63-64.

55. Alan P. Bell and Martin S. Weinberg, *Homosexualities: A Study of Diversity Among Men and Women* (New York: Simon and Schuster, 1978), 108-109. See also Lynda S. Doll, "Sexual Behavior Before AIDS: The Hepatitis B Studies of Homosexual and Bisexual Men," *AIDS* 4:1071 (1990).

56. Donald R. Hoover, Alvaro Muñoz, Vincent Carey, Joan S. Chmeil, Jeremy M. G. Taylor, Joseph B. Margolick, Lawrence Kingsley, and Sten H. Vermund, "Estimating the 1978-1990 and Future Spread of Human Immunodeficiency Virus Type 1 in Subgroups of Homosexual Men," *American Journal of Epidemiology* 134(10): 1190-1205. See also Robert B. Hays, Susan M. Kegeles, and Thomas J. Coates, "High HIV Risk-Taking Among Young Gay Men," *AIDS* 4(9):901-907 (1990); Ron Stall, Don Barrett, Larry Bye, Joe Catania, Chuck Frutchey, Jeff Henne, George Lemp, Jay Paul, "A Comparison of Younger and Older Gay Men's HIV-Risk-Taking Behaviors: The Communications Technologies 1989 Cross-Sectional Survey," *Journal of Acquired Immune Deficiency Syndrome* 5:682-687 (1992).

57. Joe Fera and Wayne Blankenship, "It's Not Acceptable, in 1993 . . . " *Bay Area Reporter,* November 24, 1993.

58. Sissela Bok, *Lying: Moral Choice in Public and Private Life* (New York: Vintage Books, 1978), 117.

59. *Ibid.,* 199.

60. Wayne Blankenship, "Not a Homophobe's Dream—But an Incredible Simulation," *Bay Area Reporter,* January 13, 1994, p. 6.

61. Gross, "Second Wave of AIDS Feared by Officials in San Francisco," 8.

62. For the original landmark essay on this subject, see Audre Lorde, "Uses of the Erotic: The Erotic as Power," in *Sister Outsider* (Freedom, CA: Crossing Press, 1984), 53-59.

63. Young and Jay, *The Gay Report,* 464-480.

64. Sylvia Brinton Perera, *The Scapegoat Complex* (Toronto: Inner City Books, 1986).

65. "Vernon," as quoted in William I. Johnston, *HIV-Negative: How the Uninfected Are Affected By AIDS* (New York and London: Insight, 1995), 225.

66. "James Douglas" quoted in William I. Johnston, *HIV-Negative: How the Uninfected Are Affected By AIDS* (New York and London: Insight, 1994), 266.

67. Jonathan G. Silin, "Dangerous Knowledge," *Christopher Street* 10(5):34.

Chapter 7

Sex Education for the New Millennium

We are at war and yet we are smiling . . . We are at war and we keep performing. . . . My dick is not my enemy.

–Bill T. Jones
AIDS Project: Los Angeles'
"Commitment to Life VII," 1/27/94

Make me feel mighty real.

–Sylvester, "Mighty Real"

I thought that an evening at a San Francisco sex club would give me a feeling for the current "community norms" of a specific gay male population. Blow Buddies, San Francisco's emporium of male oral sex, is well regarded for its work promoting new community norms by both the local health department and the Coalition for Healthy Sex–a local group of gay men who assess local sex clubs' efforts to encourage safe sex. Aware of the limitations of such "participant/observer" research, I decided to investigate nevertheless . . . plus I was looking for a good time. So, on a Saturday night, I took a cab from my home in the Castro to the South of Market district, and arrived at a large, nondescript industrial building without an exterior sign highlighting its function.

I had been to Blow Buddies twice before. Arriving at 11 p.m., I was pleased to find that there wasn't a line of men eagerly awaiting entrance. I was welcomed into the club's foyer, passed the signs saying "No cologne!" and "Safe Sex Only: No Buttfucking, No

Rimming." After purchasing a club membership card (mine had lapsed), and signing the requisite forms, I entered the establishment.

Loud music with a heavy throb was the first thing I noticed. I arrived first at the clothes check booth and relinquished my jacket and t-shirt, to the friendly personnel. This left me wearing only a black leather vest, blue jeans, and workboots. I moved first to a table containing dozens of AIDS prevention materials–brochures from local groups, lists of do's and don'ts, and literature produced specially by Blow Buddies on what they term "safer dicksuckin'."

I assumed this literature contained an articulation of the climate and activities the club was attempting to encourage:

> Condoms are your best bet. Non-lubed rubbers are available free in several locations throughout the club. Blow Buddies and the S.F. Dept. of Public Health recommend you use condoms for dicksuckin'.

> Don't take cum in your mouth. If you choose not to use a rubber when yer fuckin' face, it's better not to cum in your buddy's mouth or take cum (semen) in your mouth. The possibility of HIV infection or re-infection is nil when there is no exchange of body fluids. . . .[1]

I left the literature area and moved past the bathrooms, toward the "play areas." On the way, I passed many safe sex posters, several baskets filled with condoms, and a social area, where gay men sat on couches, relaxing, enjoying refreshments, and watching porn videos. I then entered into a darkened area and my eyes took a moment to adjust. I was in a large space filled with small wooden cubicles, like cupboards, in which men apparently were expected to kneel and give head. Glory holes were drilled into these closets, and other men came by, hoisted out their dicks, and inserted them into the holes in the cubicles. In another part of the room, men stepped up on a raised platform and other men stood below, eager to suck them off in a standing-up position.

While there may have been thirty men in the room, none were talking. The only sounds were the throb of the music and the sounds of cocksucking–slurps, gagging, coughing, moans of relief. Shirtless men of all races and sizes moved in circuits around the room, plugged into an electric energy which seemed focused, determined, almost driven. Eyes darted from face to crotch, and men unabashedly peeked into cupboards, checking out cocksuckers-in-waiting while others were sizing up the meat.

I moved toward the next room and discovered more cupboards, aligned along an elaborate maze filled with several dozen men moving, glancing, stopping, moving, kneeling, sucking, moving, unzipping. Some men were huddled in small groups, while others were in couples. Often unattached men stood by and observed, stroking hardening cocks while others got it on. I recognized a friend whom I'd not seen there on my previous visits. We exchanged nods and kept moving. Occasionally a hand reached out and stroked my chest or grabbed for my dick, but I needed more time to ease into the energy of the club. I saw a sign for the "Whizz Room," a side room reserved for watersports. On entering, I observed two naked men in tubs who were being pissed on by half a dozen guys.

I moved around the club several times as I sought to acclimate myself to the scene. There were several smaller rooms, darkened and lined with leather furnishings. These appeared to be the leather-oriented spaces of the club, designed for men interested in S/M and "power exchange" sex. As my eyes adjusted, I recognized more and more people–colleagues from political work, neighbors from my apartment building, friends from the gym. Everyone seemed plugged into the same intense energy and focused on the same thing–oral sex.

I perched against a wall, situating myself so that I could see and be seen by the masses of men buzzing around. I finally caught the eye of a man who appeared to be in his early thirties–clean cut, trim, and with a very handsome face. I moved out of my position and into one of the cubicles. He followed behind, knelt down, and began to unbutton my jeans and remove my already hardening cock.

I felt his mouth lick the shaft, encompass the balls, and then encircle the head. One of his hands reached up and played with the hairs on my stomach and chest; the other yanked out his own dick and began masturbating. His mouth moved up and down on my cock, sometimes taking the entire length down his throat, at other times simply nibbling the head. I reached my hands down and grabbed at the hair on the front of his forehead, holding his head as

I guided my cock in and out of his mouth. Occasionally I'd hear guttural sounds from his throat and I'd pull out momentarily. Yet he seemed eager to continue cocksucking, and I'd thrust between his lips again and rock rhythmically into his mouth.

While this was going on, several men approached the cubicle and peered in. Some watched for several minutes; others moved on quickly. One man crawled in with us and dropped to his knees, attempting to lick my balls as the original man consumed my cock. This seemed difficult to maneuver, but we each adjusted our postures to accomodate the third party, and I felt my excitement heighten and my orgasm approach.

Because I didn't want to climax during the early hours of the evening, I grabbed at my cock and began to pull it out from the first man's mouth. He resisted, lurching forward to keep the dick in his mouth, sensing my approaching orgasm. I held his head aloof, cradled my cock in my hand, and breathed deeply as the second man continued lavishing attention on my balls. After a minute's rest, I had calmed down somewhat so I inserted my cock into the original man's mouth. This time he took it deep down into his throat and sucked me with a force that caused my excitement to surge. He grabbed at my buttocks and drew me deeply into his mouth. As I felt my breathing heighten, I thrust forward more aggressively; he matched me with his mouth, thrust for thrust.

I knew I was approaching climax, so I yanked the dick suddenly from his mouth and held it quivering in my hand. I looked down at him and whispered, "I'm about to cum. . . . "

He looked at me eagerly. "Give it to me," he insisted and moved his mouth toward my dick.

"Do you want me to cum on your face or in your mouth?" I asked. Meanwhile, the second man was slurping on my balls and bringing me incredibly close to orgasm.

"In my mouth," he demanded, and lunged at my dick. I reached for the back of his head, held it in my hands, and began fucking into his mouth. The waves of excitement rose swiftly in me until I felt myself ejaculate into his mouth. Stream after stream of fluid pumped between his lips and down his throat. Once or twice he gagged a bit, but he caught himself, kept focus, and continued drinking the sperm.

As my hard-on began to subside, I slipped it out of his mouth and held it in my hand.

Both men sat back on their haunches. The ball-eater licked his lips and grinned widely. The cocksucker wiped his forearm over his mouth seeming to savor the sperm. They got to their feet, we hugged as a threesome, then they opened the cubicle door and departed.

I remained at Blow Buddies until three in the morning. During that time, I gave head to three different men. Seven men sucked my dick. I did not witness a single condom in use during oral sex. I did not encounter a single man who refused to participate in unprotected oral sex, and four of the men who sucked me asked me to reach orgasm in their mouths (at most, I can have two orgasms an evening). Of the men I sucked, one came in my mouth.

I left Blow Buddies that evening sexually satisfied, and happy with the ability of gay men to create environments which encourage men to enjoy a lot of sex. But I also left with confusion and questions. Was I foolish to let a single man ejaculate in my mouth? What does it mean that Blow Buddies' literature encourages condom use with oral sex and few men follow suit? What does it mean to claim a norm supporting oral sex without ejaculation in the mouth when the current experience of gay men in public spaces seems to be contrary? What does this say about the relationship between the purveyors of safe sex education and the men they are hoping to reach? And what could this tell us about men's relationship to the norms focused on anal sex, an act not officially permitted in public sex clubs and which occurs apart from witnesses, in privatized spaces?

COMMUNITY RESPONSE TO RENEGADE ACTS

Two men fucking without a condom may have ironically become the newly defined act of the sexual renegade during the safe sex years. Hearing rumors that such activity is increasingly common in private rooms at bathhouses as well as at sex parties and outdoor sex spaces, brings out a range of emotions from gay men: disgust, jealousy, concern, joy, sadness, pity, outrage. How would we react if we came upon two men fucking without a condom? How would our reaction differ if we learned that these men were aware that they were both HIV positive? How would it differ still if both men knew they were HIV negative? If we learned they were both intoxicated? Or if one was forty-five years old and the other twenty-one? What responsibility or right do we have to express these feelings to the men?

The authors of "It's Not Acceptable. . . " believe it is the witness's responsibility to intervene in public sex acts that appear to be unsafe:

> What's clear is that our silence is our death. It's time to show care and take responsibility for each other by intervening. Sex club monitors can't see everything: and who wants to feel "policed" anyway? It's time to take a courageous stand and say "It's not acceptable, in 1993, for us to be fucking unsafely."[2]

The moral issues here are not simple. Complex and competing individual and group interests are involved. A close scrutiny of our individual system of values is essential before branding others' conduct unacceptable. An examination of limits of tolerance for those with different values is also necessary. For those who prize safety, health, and longevity of life above all else, it is easy to assume others share this view. A drive for survival is naturalized and considered shared and instinctual rather than considered socially constructed or individually based. It is difficult for many to imagine a moral system which prioritizes pleasure or whatever meaning one derives from unprotected anal sex over long-term survival. Is there space in this community for such differences, or does the establishment of community norms demand consensus around a value system? If community norms demand consensus, is this possible to achieve within the diverse and fractured gay and bisexual male population?

As public attention becomes riveted on the opening of new bathhouses in cities such as Boston and New York, or new studies of escalating infection rates in Chicago, Denver, and San Francisco, these vexing questions intrude repeatedly into contemporary queer discourse and demand answers.[3] As people stake out positions on the various sides of what is becoming the sex wars of the 1990s, one sobering truth becomes increasingly apparent: there are no easy answers here. As friends continue to die and lovers continue to become infected, psyches spiral through despair, blame, ennui, and fury. Attempts to understand and respond to the situation recycle many of the explanations and arguments of the first decade. To many of us, it feels as if we are sitting through the same bad movie twice.

Amid the increasingly contentious contemporary debates, there are emerging viewpoints and cultural constructs which suggest new possibilites and perhaps new dangers. Several recent journalistic accounts move beyond the "use a condom every time argument" and acknowledge that the expectation of 100 percent compliance won't work with many men. They suggest "negotiated safety," where partners of similar or differing HIV status create agreements on sexual activity boundaries both inside and outside the relationship.[4] Such a community-sanctioned strategy was considered and abandoned earlier in the epidemic and may reflect both an increased understanding of the complexity of sexual meaning and a new openess to considering possibilities of trust and honest communication between gay men.

Men in New York have begun to coalesce around "prevention activism," an idea put forth by Dana Van Gorder, San Francisco's coordinator of lesbian and gay health, at a prevention summit in July 1994.[5] Van Gorder's call-to-arms focused on the creation "of a vast network of ongoing support groups exclusively for HIV-negative men, led in a thorough dialogue not just about safe sex, but about our lives, what it feels like to be HIV negative in our community, what community and personal issues exist in our lives that impact our ability to remain safe, and what things we might add to our lives to make us commit to living longer"; yet, New York's "Gay and Lesbian HIV Prevention Activists" have chosen the more media-hip focus of targeting commercial sex establishments for closure if they fail to comply with the group's eight "guidelines."[6] Hence it is already apparent that the construct of "prevention," when placed alongside "activism," might be expected to provoke a broad range of activities reflecting varying formulations of gay male bodies, desires, and sex acts.

Perhaps the most startling shift in cultural constructs may be seen in an emerging new articulation of the relationship of HIV-positive men to continuing infections. In a controversial essay in *Out* magazine titled "Negative Pride," Michelangelo Signorile describes several HIV-positive men who have "confessed" to him about their feelings of responsibility for infecting others:

> Washington, D.C. queer activist Greg Scott believes that he has infected some of the "many" men with whom he had unprotected oral and anal sex, long after he found out he was HIV positive. Some of these men, he says, have now seroconverted. For several years, during the time that he was at the forefront of AIDS activism as a leader in both ACT-UP and Queer Nation, Scott says he was in denial about his own sexual behavior.[7]

While Scott appears "remorseful" and attributes his conduct to substance use, Signorile's piece is the first mass media account of new seroconversions which begins to confront difficult ethical questions head on and shares responsibility for new infections with both the previously uninfected man as well as the infected man. The danger inherent in this approach is reflected in the headline chosen for the piece when it was excerpted in *The New York Times* on the op-ed page: "HIV-Positive, and Careless."[8]

The terrain is shifting for both HIV-positive and HIV-negative gay men as issues of continuing infection are confronted with few expecting a vaccine or a cure in the next few years. Earlier claims that infected men acquired HIV when no one had heard of AIDS can no longer be made without challenge and place many HIV-positive men in a position of heightened vulnerability. Organizing efforts by HIV-negative men, while offering new possibilities for support, affirmation, and identity, have been quickly interpreted as calls for "viral apartheid," and attacked as draining funds from services for men with AIDS.[9] Serious splits that have been avoided during the first decade and a half of AIDS, again threaten the fragile sense of unity among urban gay men.

What should be done to men who have unprotected anal intercourse? Should they be shamed and stigmatized for "fucking over the community"? Are they to be pitied, or branded as "immoral" and banished from the established gay social order? Do we accept them as they are, without judgment or condemnation? Do they deserve additional education which might assist in making different decisions in the future? These and other vexing questions may lead to very painful answers in the coming years.

Walt Odets frames questions about unprotected anal sex in a different way which may offer an alternative to factionalizing and contentiousness:

> If some feel that the fullest, richest possible life demands behaviors that may also expose them to HIV, who are we, as educators to tell them they are wrong? To attempt to morally shame such individuals who put no others at unwilling risk, to attempt to coerce them into conformity to allay our own anxieties seems to me humanely reprehensible. As educators do we really propose that men live through this tragedy only to be told by us how to feel about it, to have their real feelings denied in public education, and have them described as–or assumed to be–an expression of pathology?[10]

These are no longer theoretical questions. They currently confront the institutions of the gay community nationwide and will serve as increasingly serious challenges to individual moral systems and the collective gay political position in the years ahead. We have become accustomed during the first dozen years of the epidemic to telling the public that all gay men with AIDS were infected before they knew that AIDS even existed. How we raged when the media used the term "innocent victim" to distinguish infected children from gay men! We insisted that infected gay men were also innocent, since they were exposed to HIV before 1981. We vied for inclusion under the category of "innocent" and failed to effectively demolish the construction of a bifurcated scale of innocence and guilt and its application to disease.

In 1994, gay men crossed a line that makes it increasingly difficult to claim unblemished innocence, and increasingly important for us to concentrate on education. Most newly diagnosed gay male AIDS cases are now among those infected after the initial announcements of gay cancer in the early 1980s, since the average time from exposure to diagnosis is roughly ten or eleven years.[11] Try as we might to muster various arguments about sexual transmission initially being unproven, or the lack of early funding for gay male education, we will be confronted more and more by the ramifications of increasing public awareness of post-1981 gay infections. The dynamics of this shift may be profound. Will mainstream America continue to wear red ribbons and attend gala fundraisers when they cannot conceptualize gay men with AIDS as "innocent victims"?

BARRIERS TO ASSESSMENT OF PREVENTION EFFORTS

The first dozen years of formal efforts may not have succeeded at keeping the majority of at-risk men in epicenter cities from HIV infection; this is disheartening, yet should not deter us from developing innovative new programs. Instead this realization might serve as motivation for an ambitious and searching assessment of existing efforts and spur the reconceptualization and redesign of education in the face of continuing epidemic conditions. The mission of education work and its effects on gay men's sexuality must be scrutinized and existing goals, strategies, and methods should be closely interrogated. An evaluation of the achievements and limitations of community efforts offers an opportunity to generate new perspective and original thinking about the relationship of gay men to sexual desire and could be an integral part of the rejuvenation of gay life–including gay erotic life–in America.

How viable have the goals of safe sex education proven to be and how successfully have they been fulfilled? What biases do they contain about responsibility, authority, and power? Do we face the same challenge today as we faced in the early years of the epidemic, or have circumstances changed radically? Are we willing to consider new directions which seem unorthodox and daring? Are we willing to consider anything other than "halting transmission" as the central mission of education?

Evaluating systems of HIV education for gay and bisexual men may prove difficult because individual programs have rarely been scientifically evaluated. In a 1992 comprehensive analysis of interventions targeting gay male sexual transmission of HIV, Jeffrey D. Fisher and William A. Fisher discussed the limits of our current ability to assess program effectiveness:

> Even among the relatively small group of interventions that have been evaluated, there were nearly always serious prob-

lems with experimental design and control groups, reliance on direct, reactive, self-report measures, high subject self-selection and attrition rates, multiply confounded interventions, and failure to assess intervention impact on factors that are presumed to mediate intervention impact. These methodological limitations make the attribution of observed effects to an intervention, or to a specific component of an intervention, virtually impossible in most cases.[12]

The highly politicized nature of HIV education funding and an accompanied daunting process of application and reporting discourage public health systems from setting aside adequate resources and time to engage in the necessary reflective, long-range evaluation and planning. Wars between gay male subcultures (white men vs. men of color, the indigent vs. the middle class, youth vs. middle-aged), an entrenched systemic lethargy, and mindsets drawn repeatedly to crises, present staggering obstacles to big-picture evaluation. Yet this is precisely what must occur if we are going to dramatically shift direction and truly create a new generation of programs with a revised mission.

The backgrounds and biases of those charged with assessing education systems' effectiveness may critically influence evaluation outcomes. It is increasingly common to appoint leaders of existing prevention efforts to committees charged with evaluating current strategies. This may result in a tangled web of turf wars, saving face, and ego massages which distract from balanced assessment. Leaders of AIDS education efforts of the 1980s and early 1990s have accrued significant knowledge and experience, yet these evaluations are studying *their best efforts.* When they are put into the role of evaluator, conflicts of interest inevitably arise. Oversight of educational systems by an entrenched braintrust may restrict the vision of programs to paradigms and systemic models already employed.

Independent evaluators, educators, and social critics from a range of disciplines may offer fresh vision and a different and less uniform collection of biases. The fields of sexology, popular education, and the various branches of psychology have been inadequately mined for insights and models of HIV education. In particular, the fields of developmental, social, and community psychology have been cited as potential sources of assistance in overcoming the barriers currently faced.[13]

The first task for an evaluation team to tackle is to determine the mission and goals of established educational programs. If these are available, some critical questions must be asked. In terms of what we know now about HIV disease, how appropriate is the mission? Has the program been able to meet its goals? If statistical information and scientific data is unavailable, meaningful quantitative evaluation of programs may be impossible. The resources and expertise needed to produce sound epidemiological data must be provided, but evaluators should not fail to consider qualitative methodologies as well.

When information is available, it must be evaluated by individuals with both the expertise and independence to reach conclusions unbiased by the demands and politics of reapplying for funding. Whenever education programs claim a mission of halting or reducing transmission, research methodology must be scrutinized in order to determine the program's ability to measure success. Evaluation is a complex and highly political process where diverse interest groups (public health departments, community-based organizations, elected officials, researchers, educational theorists, marketing professionals, the media) have much at stake. The manipulation of statistics and deliberate misinterpreting of their implications must not continue.

Evaluations might assist us in determining the effectiveness of existing efforts in meeting predetermined goals, but might also allow for consideration of the appropriateness of the goals within an overall vision of prevention. This dual function—assessing individual programs and contextualizing them within a larger vision—is usually absent from prevention work and may result in systemic failure. While the federal government is criticized justifiably for lacking any broad educational or prevention framework for the gay community, the gay community itself has also abrogated responsibility for undertaking such an assessment. Our collective inability to prioritize a community-based vision of HIV prevention and understand its complex linkages to community health, well-being, and sexual functioning leaves such efforts firmly within the authority of governmental entities.

DISTINGUISHING EDUCATION FROM PREVENTION

What should the mission of HIV education be for gay and bisexual men? Is it inevitably linked to preventing HIV transmission? When people use the terms "education" and "prevention" interchangeably, are they conflating two very different (and perhaps inherently oppositional) terms?

It is time to go back to basics in the safe sex education classroom we have constructed over the past decade. An examination of the assumptions and values embedded in our work with men's sexuality is in order. Expectations that the transmission of HIV could be swiftly and dramatically curtailed through the education of gay and bisexual men are challenged by increasing evidence of upswings in seroconversion.[14] Is halting or minimizing transmission an appropriate continuing mission for educational efforts? Do we believe that sexual activity responds to the same public health interventions as smoking, drunk driving, and seat belt compliance? Are there limitations on education's ability to change sexual behavior?

For over a decade, halting HIV transmission has been the primary mission of sex education among gay men. Two distinct disciplines have championed this goal. Public health workers have assumed their traditional American function of disease elimination and become determined to wipe out new infections among gay men. Leaders of the gay community, fulfilling their role of ensuring community survival, have shared this determination. Hence sex education has focused on survival, rather than maximizing men's erotic options, enhancing pleasure, or promoting empowerment. A "methodology of the masses" has reigned, intent on saving the largest number of gay lives. While this methodology has succeeded in blanketing the gay village with condoms and safe sex lists, in cities of greatest impact it has been unable to keep vast numbers of at-risk men from infection. Educational programs aren't meeting their "protection-from-infection" goals and everybody knows it: health educators, gay leaders, public health analysts, even politicians. In the face of such a stunning realization, no one knows exactly what to do.

If transmission of HIV between men has not been reduced to the extent many had expected, it does not necessarily follow that education programs have been ineffective. A review of the distinction between prevention and education may be in order. In an essay examining the ethical dilemmas facing educational efforts, Nora Kizer Bell astutely challenged the criteria used to declare HIV education ineffective:

> The standard is clearly behavior change. Furthermore, it seems equally clear that the bottom line for those in AIDS prevention, the public health goal in AIDS education, is elimination of disease–zero transmission, 100 percent risk reduction. Short of that, public health efforts are said to have failed. This seems an impoverished notion of education. With AIDS/ HIV serious public health and social consequences can flow from a failure to appreciate how likely it is that most educational programs in a democratic society will not bring about complete behavior change–and perhaps equally serious consequences can flow from an expectation that they would.[15]

The goals carved out for safe sex efforts and the timetable assumed for their fulfillment apparently have not been viable. Gay men's general knowledge about how HIV is transmitted has greatly increased and incidents of risk-taking have significantly decreased, yet one single act of unprotected anal intercourse may transmit HIV. A man who never used a condom before 1981 may now insist on condom use 99 percent of the time–an impressive achievement–yet still be unable to keep himself out of the statistics of new seroconversions. One social-marketing professional described the situation this way:

> The overwhelming majority of gay men have made changes in their behavior unparalleled in the history of health promotion. But unfortunately we're dealing with a virus that's so common out there that, well, it's not good enough. Nothing less than 100 percent does it.[16]

As a class, gay men can know the facts about how HIV is transmitted, greatly change behavior patterns greatly, and still become a highly infected population:

> Among population segments with high HIV infection prevalence–including gay men, injection drug users, and sexually ac-

tive heterosexuals with multiple partners (especially in inner cities)–HIV risk is great even with comparatively low rates of risk-taking behavior. Success in HIV prevention often requires helping people make and maintain highly consistent behavior changes, often with very little margin for error or lapses–a challenge virtually unprecedented in the behavioral sciences.[17]

It is facile to claim that AIDS education has failed because of new seroconversions among gay men. There are many possible explanations other than inadequate education for each new infection. A man may have been educated successfully but consciously made a decision to be fucked without a condom. Another might be aware that condoms deter transmission and wants to ask his partner to use one, but lacks assertiveness. These are just two situations which present formidable challenges to our education work when we see it as a panacea.

Equating education with prevention and giving lip-service to individual agency in sexual matters is the core contradiction of safe sex campaigns. It is as if we have been saying, "We support the empowerment of gay men, as long as they make the decisions we want." Empowerment doesn't work this way. Sex education efforts with gay men must be fully committed to the restoration of personal authority in erotic decision making. Activist Mike Isbell succinctly summarized this position to *The New York Times*:

> Once they're educated, consenting adults have the right to engage in whatever sexual activity they choose, even if they harm themselves. It's never been part of the American thinking that we ought to force people to protect themselves.[18]

The purposes of education must be to allow individuals to become knowledgeable about the ways HIV is transmitted and to support gay men's empowerment as they put this knowledge to use in their lives.

THE LIMITS OF DEMOCRATIC EDUCATION

An understanding of the strengths and limitations of democratic education is crucial to understanding the inevitable distinction between education and prevention. Nora Kizer Bell again succinctly captures the complex nature of education work under democracy:

> By its very nature democratic education–that is, education that occurs in the context of a liberal democracy–will eventuate in something less than complete compliance with, or complete assimilation to its instructional mission. . . . A commitment to democratic education means, therefore, accepting compromise in its results. This is especially true in a culture that is pluralistic. . . . Such a conception of education relies heavily on the conviction that not everyone will be attracted to the same options and that, even if they are, they will be able to achieve them to greater or lesser degrees. Furthermore, such a concept of education underscores the value of voluntary choice.[19]

Democratic education provides a framework which helps identify the limitations of equating HIV education with prevention. Men flout a broad and elaborate indoctrination system of "compulsory heterosexuality" in order to self-identify as gay.[20] Is it reasonable to expect these same men to uncritically accept a rigid and defined code of sexual conduct which might significantly restrict their experience of sexuality and the quality of their lives? Men already proven to be transgressive reasonably could be expected to exhibit a broad range of viewpoints, motivation, and ability to actualize defined safe sex practices.

In reconstituting a mission for work with gay men around sexual transmission of HIV, democratic educational theory suggests new ways to define success and failure. Totalitarian states utilize coercive measures to gain behavioral compliance because they are founded upon philosophies of mass social control. In a democracy, education's appropriate aim is to provide individuals and groups with knowledge, skills, and the ability to make choices. The assuming of authority by the individual is particularly important in AIDS prevention because the activities involved in the sexual transmission of AIDS almost without exception involve individual voluntary action and the consequences are focused almost entirely upon the individual participants:

Nearly all transmission involves consensual risk-taking. Nearly every activity that spreads HIV disease is voluntary. Furthermore, most of these activities are inherently private— hence, not easily (or effectively) regulated. While coercive strategies for controlling HIV transmission might have both moral and public health warrant in isolated cases, such as in blood or organ donation, coercion, in general, is not likely to have the desired effect.[21]

Education under democracy aims for people to govern them- selves, invent their own lives, and accept responsibility for their actions. The arrival of an epidemic cannot immediately change long- standing, culturally embedded traditions of individual rights and re- sponsibility rooted in the consciousness of American gay men.

James Baldwin succinctly described how such tensions are en- trenched in the American educational tradition:

The paradox of education is precisely this–that as one begins to become conscious, one begins to examine the society in which one is being educated. The purpose of education, finally, is to create in a person the ability to look at the world for oneself, to make one's own decisions, to say to oneself this is black or is white, to decide for oneself whether there is a God in heaven, or not. To ask questions of the universe, and then to learn to live with those questions, is the way one achieves one's own identity. But no society is really anxious to have that kind of person around. What societies really ideally want is a citi- zenry which will simply obey the rules of society.[22]

Our educational strategy must shift its content and process and become reflective, thoughtful, and dialogic. It must be funded at a level which will allow for long-term, time-intensive work with large numbers of gay and bisexual men and not be contingent upon evidence of rapid mass behavior change. And our strategy must take into account that, in a nation weaving together communities of increasingly divergent values, personal autonomy and individual choice will ensure a broad range of response.

DISPLACING THE UTOPIAN VISION OF PREVENTION

If education is to assume a function of empowerment rather than control, where does this leave prevention?

Prevention becomes a matter distinct from education and those charged with carrying out prevention efforts must see themselves as a distinct, though related, work crew. A mission of empowerment requires educators in some ways to let go of a targeted prevention agenda and trust individual men to forge their own relationship to sex, HIV, and the challenges of contemporary gay life. Risk *management* replaces risk *reduction* as an educational objective.

Once prevention is freed from a narrow focus on education, it may be seen in its full complexity and acknowledged as the daunting challenge it is. To prevent vast numbers of gay and bisexual men from becoming HIV infected requires the acknowledgement of complex motivations and social practices which constitute sexual desire and the multigenerational work likely required to bring about long-term alterations in sexual behavior. While many have cited the development of the birth control pill as swiftly inaugurating an era of sexual liberation, the situation was much more complex.[23] It appears unlikely that a sexually transmitted disease—however lethal—can quell mass erotic activity among gay men in a sustained manner. We neither know about how specific sex acts become charged with meanings nor how sexual meaning changes over time. We pay now for decades of societal failure to research and analyze sexual meaning and erotic activity in America.

Prevention strategies might explore the social context in which sexual meaning is constructed, and focus on methods which afford gay men lives which they feel are worth preserving. The expectation that HIV transmission among gay men will be stopped expeditiously is unreasonable, even utopian, though many of us find ourselves clinging to this expectation frequently. If the infection rate among HIV-negative gay men somehow were to be reduced consistently to 1 percent a year, the population of gay men in American urban centers would continue to be half infected with HIV (the rate was about 2 percent in San Francisco in 1993).[24] This is precisely why efforts to create a vaccine and find a cure must continue with great urgency. It feels heartbreaking to imagine a collective life in the new millennium which includes continuing new seroconversions, yet continuing to expect 100 percent compliance with strict safe sex guidelines is a setup for a continuing spiral of despair.

Nevertheless a broad and insistent chorus of voices—journalists, researchers, health officials, and a substantial segment of gay leadership—publicly promotes this utopian vision of prevention and demands that all gay men practice safe sex all the time. This may reflect long-held (and long-disproven) societal beliefs that knowledge of the causes of disease is all that is required to bring about mass behavior change. Yet sexuality has proven itself to be even more complex than dietary habits, drug use, and other health behavior which historically have been targeted for public health interventions:

> Sexual behavior differs considerably from smoking cigarettes or exercising, and interventions that work well in these areas may not be optimal for promoting sexual behavior change. It seems essential to more closely incorporate models and findings of human sexuality research in AIDS prevention interventions.[25]

A reluctance to grasp complex factors motivating sexual behavior and acknowledge what might be an an essentialist element of primal drive, encourages simplistic approaches and naive optimism about preventing gay male infections, particularly in the political arena. Big city mayors have argued that closing bathhouses and sex clubs earlier would have prevented tens of thousands of gay men from becoming infected. ACT-UP has held Reagan, Bush, and Clinton responsible for not funding prevention efforts at a level which might have saved lives. Randy Shilts faulted gay community leadership for sacrificing masses of gay men by placing public relations before public health and not "sounding the alarm" earlier.[26] Choosing a scapegoat may be an easier task than facing the uncomfortable possibility that, absent coercive measures, unprotected anal intercourse among a significant portion of the gay community cannot be stopped quickly or easily, even when substantial resources are devoted to the effort.

In the boxing ring of AIDS prevention, sodomy has emerged as the victor, vanquishing moralizing, condoms, and public health interventions. At some point, researchers may be forced to acknowledge that sex has more in common with eating, sleeping, and breathing than smoking or drunk driving. If aggressive prevention efforts of the first decade in epicenter cities only resulted in 20 percent of the at-risk gay men remaining uninfected, anal sex and semen exchange must have a powerful draw.[27] If one-third of the young gay men in certain cities who have lived all their sexually active years with the knowledge that unprotected anal sex may transmit a lethal virus are now expected to be infected by the time they reach their thirtieth birthdays, the challenge of prevention work may be more daunting than previously imagined.[28]

A prevention strategy which recognizes many men's powerful desire for penetration and receiving semen might consider a long-range, multigenerational approach to reducing transmission. Such an approach could include a broad two-tiered strategy: the *short-term* objectives will be *educational* and be turned over to the educators who would focus on supporting men in assuming increasing authority and responsibility for their sexual behavior; the *long-term* objectives will be *prevention* and aim to shift sexual meaning over time and assist increasing portions of at-risk men in upcoming gay generations in having lives which are worth living. The short-term work involves sex education focused on working with men on issues of sexuality, desire, identity, power, and their bodies, with no strings attached. The long-term work involves changing the social context in which gay men's lives are situated so that men may construct meaningful lives which are worth preserving and the meanings of specific sex acts may become transformed. The two strategies must be distinct, although prevention depends upon successful education, and both must have realistic goals.

If 80 percent of the at-risk population of epicenter city gay men from the early 1980s have been infected, and one-third of the following generation of at-risk queer men are expected to be infected by the time they are thirty (and many additional men might be expected to be infected before reaching the age of fifty), is it a suitable objective to aim to bring the rate of infection under 30 percent within three gay generations (approximately the year 2030)? While it seems astounding to imagine vast numbers of men continuing to become infected in successive waves and HIV disease becoming integrated as a long-term feature of gay men's life cycles, absent a cure, vaccine, or miracle intervention, this may be the best we can expect.

Gay men have been communicating to prevention leaders for years but no one has been listening. Statistics on gay men's mental health and erotic lives gathered by researchers must be interpreted as a collective statement of encoded demands for new directions for prevention efforts. Existing priorities which place prevention, halting transmission, and survival *by any means necessary,* must be superseded by education, empowerment, and acceptance of the diverse ways men will come to terms with life in the epidemic. Individual agency over sexual behavior–along with the accompanying responsibility–must be supported by freeing men from manipulative and coercive messages hiding behind claims of empowerment. Future efforts might do well to reconnect with the interrupted vision of gay liberation and revive self-determination, personal authority, and individual responsibility as worthwhile objectives. Moralizing must be replaced by reflection; marketing must be secondary to empowerment education; prevention must be superseded by risk management.

STRATEGIES FOR THE COMING YEARS

A new generation of education efforts should be guided by a strategy which aims to support each man in assuming increased authority for his erotic activities and becoming the locus of authority for sexual risk management. The ability of individual men to engage in critical thinking and consolidate thought, emotion, psychology, and interpersonal relations into social and sexual practice must be enhanced through these efforts. At the same time prevention efforts will aim for a long-term improvement in the social context of gay men's lives. A tension might exist between the two, but education and prevention must be allowed to occupy contiguous space on a progressive community agenda.

Social scientists working to refine HIV-prevention models, generally identify three crucial components of prevention:

Information regarding the means of AIDS transmission and information concerning specific methods of preventing infection are necessary prerequisites of risk-reduction behavior. *Motivation* to change AIDS-risk behavior is a second determinant of AIDS prevention and affects whether one acts on one's knowledge regarding AIDS transmission and prevention. *Behavioral skills* for performing specific AIDS-preventive acts are a third critical determinant of prevention and affect whether even a knowledgeable, highly motivated person will be able to change his or her behavior in an AIDS-preventive fashion.[29]

All three areas need to be reconceptualized, broadened, and aligned with new strategy which balances the tensions between individual risk management and the elimination of transmission. Key to this balance may be the development of new ways to think about the ways in which education occurs.

The predominant educational model in America is dualistic: it places the educator as a source of knowledge and the student as a willing receptacle. The instructor imparts wisdom and the student eagerly imbibes. We have emulated this model in much of our safe sex strategies with gay men. Yet a rich body of educational theory has developed over the past twenty-five years which challenges this model's effectiveness with populations that have experienced oppression, colonization, or marginalization. Gay liberation and queer theory have conceptualized gay men as oppressed people whose communal body and sexuality are central sites of colonization. Theories of education which focus on self-determination among oppressed groups provide signposts for future directions of our HIV education work with gay men.

Brazilian theorist and social critic Paulo Freire, in his landmark analysis of literacy education among Third World peasants, *Pedagogy of the Oppressed,* provides an apt critique of the failings of traditional instruction methods to bring about behavior change:

> To substitute monologue, slogans, and communiques for dialogue is to attempt to liberate the oppressed with the instruments of domestication. Attempting to liberate the oppressed without their reflective participation in the act of liberation is to treat them as objects which must be saved from a burning

building; it is to lead them into the populist pitfall and transform them into masses which can be manipulated.[30]

Freire proposes a theory of "liberation education" which emphasizes inquiry, problem solving, and dialogue. Such an educational process would no longer be centered around a teacher or "expert" who has some special access to knowledge; instead, each individual would become the center of a process aimed at achieving *praxis*–the linkage of reflection with action. A partnership is established between teacher and student which aims at collective participation in discovery, problem raising, and critical thinking. This interactive process is rooted in respect for every individual's unique ability to continually make and remake his or her way of life and "emphasizes acts of cognition, not transferrals of information."[31]

As the limitations of established models of AIDS education are recognized, health educators working with populations traditionally considered oppressed are increasingly turning to Freire's theories of pedagogy for inspiration. Kevin Cranston, of the Massachusetts Department of Education, has proposed applying Freireian theories to HIV programs with lesbian, gay, and bisexual youth.[32] Kathy Boudin, an inmate and educator at New York's Bedford Hills Correctional Facility, has utilized Freire's problem-solving methods in literacy work focused on AIDS/HIV as authentic life issues facing the inmate population.[33] Liberation education clearly has much to offer work with these populations, yet provides a compelling theoretical foundation for the much-needed shift in efforts to educate *all* gay men about the sexual transmission of HIV.

Walt Odets has forcefully identified the limitations on the power of educators while powerfully articulating a new mission for our work with gay men:

> For a man living in a lifelong epidemic in which intimacy might become assault and love become death, we have nothing to sell but contemplation itself: the internal space for each man to think and to feel and thus make for himself the best possible decisions that he might. We cannot tell people how to act in the epidemic any more than we can tell them how to feel about it. It has not worked and will not, and if we are concerned with

the quality of gay life in America, rather than just the quantity, that sort of "instruction" is something we should be trying.[34]

Can a new mission which develops the ability of individual men to manage their own risk for HIV infection flow from a model of liberation education? Freireian concepts of "liberation" and "freedom" are not distinct from developing individual authority and responsibility. The aim would be to support gay men's inquiry, reflection, and problem solving around issues of sexuality and health, as was widely discussed during the early gay liberation movement. Tactics of moralizing, shaming, and coercion would be replaced with a process which respects each man's ability to make choices and manage risks. We would be as concerned with the quality of gay men's lives, as the longevity of their lifespans, and we would understand that an interaction exists between the two. We would seek to support the creation of a population of gay men who think and talk about sexual options, acknowledging the complexity of erotic desire, and have the knowledge-base and social support to actualize their own conclusions.

Information

A reconceptualization of the informational needs of gay men might consider three questions: (1) How can research be harnessed to provide the best answers possible to our questions? (2) What can be done expeditiously to maximize access to information? (3) Will gay men devote the time and energy necessary to make the information meaningful to them and integrate it into their consciousnesses?

Many health educators assume urban gay men gained the information needed to protect themselves from infection during the first decade of the epidemic. Whether or not this is accurate, a new mission emphasizing personal responsibility for risk management introduces a wide range of potential gaps in information. Do men understand how their body parts function and how sexual transmission physiologically occurs? Is information available about differential levels of risk which would allow a man to choose between anal sex with a condom and oral sex without? Are gay men knowledgeable about the internal parts of the anus or do they share in the many myths extant in our culture?

The need for additional information is best assessed through protracted conversations with gay men of all classes and ethnicities. It is likely that such interviews will reveal that many gay men understand that condoms should be used with anal sex, mutual masturbation is a safe activity, and that kissing cannot easily transmit HIV. Do these snippets of information represent adequate knowledge which would allow an individual to navigate through sexual encounters? The decisions one makes during a sexual encounter are quite complex and may involve options which require a range of information currently unavailable to gay men. If the choices in all situations were limited to anal sex with a condom or without, the informational needs are simple. When other issues arise–sex between two men who believe they are seronegative and one doesn't want to use a condom, a lover who prefers to withdraw before ejaculation rather than wear protection, an HIV-positive man being fucked by an HIV-negative man–additional information is needed to manage risk.

Once informational gaps have been established, scientific research efforts could be mobilized to provide the best possible answers to the new questions. The methods used to link original research findings and the gay male population cry out for redesign. Instead of individual men raising questions, reviewing findings, and drawing conclusions, "experts" in the prevention system deliver the information and instruct the rest of the population in putting it to use. Rather than serving as the center or the subject in an educational transaction, gay men become passive objects.

Organizations working with gay men might adopt the model of research dissemination developed around HIV treatment issues: newsletters focused on expeditiously presenting cutting-edge research in all its complexity, public forums and time-limited support groups discussing particular sexual transmission issues, informational materials focused on presenting data rather than drawing rigid conclusions about conduct. If snippets of information are going to be produced and widely distributed, it would be best to focus on specific "facts" rather than providing suggestions about behavior:

• What is the seroprevalence rate among gay men in the area in which I live?

- During unprotected anal intercourse, what is the likelihood that an HIV-negative bottom will become infected from an HIV-positive top? What is the likelihood that an HIV-negative top will become infected from an HIV-positive bottom? On what does this depend?

- What is the chance that a trick will be lying about his serostatus?

- If my mouth contains no sores or bleeding, what is the likelihood for infection if I suck off an HIV-positive man?

These questions are some examples of the kind of information many men might find useful in managing their transmission risk. Some might argue that it is difficult to present accurate data on these topics and that if any risk of infection is present, it is the responsibility of the system to discourage men from ever engaging in the act. This is what we have been doing for almost fifteen years—making critical decisions for gay men and discouraging their active participation in the prevention process—and it hasn't worked. We decide that men will make the "wrong" decision if given too much ambiguous or inconclusive data, so information is withheld. It is time to question the ethics of such practices.

One of the major obstacles emerging during the past few years has been the refusal of large numbers of gay men to participate in group processes which encourage peer education and support about HIV issues. While many men in urban centers eagerly filled seats in such discussion groups in the mid-1980s, by the early 1990s, interest was waning. Many educators have concluded that gay men won't give the time needed to educate themselves, and that they prefer to read materials or watch videos, rather than engage in dialogue with other men. At first glance, it is easy to attribute this problem to gay men's burnout around AIDS issues.

An effort must be made to amass community support for a new generation of work on risk management and new methods must be considered to attract the involvement of large numbers of men. Perhaps men don't attend many of the current programs because the content of the programs, the process used, or the outreach methods employed, do not meet contemporary needs. Marshalling community involvement is no simple matter, but there appears to be a huge hunger among gay men for information, affirmation, and community which might be tapped into. There might well be a relationship between the lack of interest gay men show in becoming educated about HIV transmission and the subtle disrespect which has been communicated to the community as they have been positioned as disempowered objects in traditional education paradigms.

Motivation

Sexual behavior emerges from a complicated matrix of social practice and psychological underpinnings which should not be simplistically reduced in attempts to understand what is termed "motivation." Attention riveted on alcohol and drug abuse as contributing factors to new infections among gay men, for example, has often viewed substance use in a simplistic manner. A population of men mired in grief, or traumatized by decimation, or suffering from a range of mild to severe psychological disorders, poses a serious challenge to educators. Long-standing socially constituted conflict around sexual orientation, childhood experiences of abuse, or unresolved existential questions made more pressing by the epidemic, may significantly influence sexual behavior. What impact do escalating anti-gay attacks by the Radical Right have on the erotic lives of gay men? How does the loss of one's entire network of friends affect the will to survive? Do men who maintain multiple identities (black and gay, for example) experience particular barriers of inducements to HIV risk management?

Public health models of HIV prevention have considered "motivation" primarily as driven by "community norms." An emphasis on shifting these norms through marketing and peer pressure has emerged and at times looked like mass queer indoctrination. Gay men are told how we are supposed to feel, what we are supposed to desire, and why we are supposed to enjoy specific acts. Public health leaders may have erred and attempted to manipulate the wrong norm. They have accelerated efforts to imprint moralizing messages on gay men rather than replace external manipulation with empowerment. In the process, extraordinarily complex power dynamics are evoked. Yet discussion of motivation consistently sidesteps significant consideration of sociological and psychological implications.

Reconceptualizing questions of motivation involves starting with the assumption that only individual men can manage their own risk of becoming infected with HIV. Attitudes, social norms, health belief systems all contribute to men's behavior but other powerful determinants of motivation clearly exist:

1. *Mental Health:* Men who are suffering greatly may not be motivated to protect themselves from infection. The unspoken and often denied ramifications of the epidemic on uninfected gay men's psyches must be confronted aggressively. Complex unconscious factors and quality-of-life issues play a major role in undermining many gay men's motivation to stay alive.

2. *Addiction:* Our understanding of the relationship between HIV prevention and alcoholism, drug abuse, and other addictions has come from studies with inadequate methodology and spurious assumptions.[35] The influence of addiction (as distinct from substance use) creates complex challenges. Until we know more about gay men and addiction, and until adequate programs exist to support men in recovery, the ebbs and flows that accompany addiction will maintain a powerful influence over motivation.

3. *Identity Integration:* How do men conceptualize gay identity and how does this interact with other (racial, ethnic, class, religious, sexual, national. . .) identities within the same person? Does being in the closet have an effect on one's motivation to be sexually safe? The diversity of identity-based HIV programs makes it clear that men have differing experiences with multiple identities—how does this influence one's sexual behavior?

4. *Existential Questions:* An epidemic accompanied by huge volumes of death and illness raises profound existential questions among "survivors" which often simmer undetected in the unconscious mind and unaddressed at the community level. Are we able to answer questions about the meaning of life and the existence of order and higher forces? How does rumination on these questions impact motivation?

These are key sites for prevention workers to explore. New work with gay men might include increased emphasis and respect for these factors' influence on motivating risk management. Prevention strategies need to expand opportunities for participation in individual and group psychotherapy, addiction treatment and recovery, peer discussion groups, and self-help organizations. Therapeutic work with gay men will be guided by a commitment to quality of life, trauma recovery, and mental health restoration, rather than a counselor's narrow desire to keep an individual man uninfected with HIV.

Behavioral Skills

Prevention work intended to maximize the behavioral skills of gay men has focused on improving communication during sexual transactions, effective condom use, assertiveness training, and the avoidance of substance use. New areas to consider in the face of a continuing epidemic might include:

- Time-limited, weekly groups that bring together men of similar erotic tastes for facilitated discussion about decision making and risk management in specific situations. Activities could involve reviewing research studies related to gay male sexual practices, role playing negotiation of risk with a new partner, and ongoing peer support among similarly inclined men. The group would aim to provide men with affirmation of sexual desire and meaning, opportunities to rehearse negotiation and assertiveness skills, and up-to-date information on transmission. Every area should offer specific groups for men who like to get fucked.

- Trained sexual surrogates available to work with individuals and gay male couples on sexual decision making and implementation through active participation in erotic exchange. Specific sex therapy approaches have been discounted in current safe sex education work. Surrogates who are knowledgeable about HIV transmission, interpersonal dynamics between gay men, and sexual behavior skills could provide enormous assistance to men who might be knowledgeable and motivated, but lack experience or skills to alter behavior. Surrogates might be particularly helpful with mixed serostatus couples.

- Workshops, parties, and sex venues which support men in the development of skills, experience, and appreciation of specific sexual acts and go one step beyond the current wave of "eroticizing safer sex" seminars. Efforts must be made to include both experience and analysis of specific sexual acts so that meanings may be explored, feelings articulated, and techniques discussed. These events and venues must be carefully designed to ensure that a broad range of gay male sexual experience is discussed and affirmed.

If we believe Freireian theory has much to offer gay men's sexuality, efforts must be made to enhance behavioral skills by keeping the individual at the center of the learning process. Gay men must take the lead in identifying areas needing strengthening and choosing appropriate methods. The power one gains from assuming increased responsibility for one's life and sexual behavior is a critical part of managing risk over the long haul.

LONG-RANGE QUESTIONS

Most major cities and many rural and suburban areas in America have a prevention network targeting gay men. The work before us is to retrain, redirect, or replace many of the personnel, paradigms, and programs of those systems. We need far fewer lists of do's and don'ts and those still needed must target specific undereducated populations (many of which are best involved in emancipatory models of education, rather than brochure-reading). Instead, educators will come to see themselves as *facilitators of learning processes* among diverse gay and bisexual men. No longer claiming to be role models, trendsetters, or sources of wisdom, educators will apply their abundant energies to expanding opportunities, formats, and environments in which men can fully participate in their own education. The sources of nonjudgmental support, which have been the foundation of psychosocial work with people with AIDS since the early days of the epidemic, will be replicated and put to use assisting the uninfected in grappling with the critical questions posed by an ongoing epidemic.

In 1995, education efforts targeting gay men are at a crossroads. We can continue to fine tune traditional models and public health interventions which focus on providing narrowly defined information, motivation, and skills, and pray that existing methods have the desired impact over time. This path may incorporate new safe sex education techniques, inventive social marketing campaigns, and aggressive efforts to manipulate social norms. It may lead to cumulative effects which result in dramatic changes in transmission rates over the next decade. Or it may not.

A different path is open to us—one which provides new strategies and alternative models for working with gay men's sex. Instead of expecting gay men to be "100 percent safe," or to "halt" AIDS transmission, educators can acknowledge the complexity of sexuality and the variegated risks involved in specific sex acts and shift to assist men as they manage their own risk. This route encourages the restoration of authority and responsibility for sexual conduct to individual gay men and provides opportunities for the necessary acquisition of skills, motivation, and personal power.

A change in strategy may lead us to assume a broad mission, focused on assisting a gay population besieged by death and discrimination to create forms of life which are worth living. An emphasis on quality of life, rather than length of life, may offer a modicum of hope and engagement now lacking; simultaneously it also may support a prevention agenda and ultimately lead to reduced HIV transmission.

Reconceptualizing work with gay men's sex opens many new questions. Rather than inquiring, "How can we educate gay men to have only safe sex?" or "Can we shift peer pressure so as to influence private acts as well as public?," we ask "How can gay men create lives worth living?" or "What can community offer to gay men which is engaging, affirming, and life-sustaining?" A rethinking of strategies with gay men may contribute to the regeneration of gay male sexuality as we approach the twenty-first century. It requires the acknowledgment that gay men as a class do not embrace a single answer to the existential questions posed by the catastrophe of AIDS. Some maintain a collective commitment to survival at any cost and some believe there are things more important than longevity. Some men will calmly embrace the role of witness and commit themselves to being around in thirty years to tell the story of how this tragedy was allowed to happen; others will rage at witnessing, and abhor the decades we spend burying our peers.

Men in this epidemic do not share a singular response or a singular fate. Like residents of a mountain village hit suddenly by an avalanche, some will live and some will die and it will not be as predictable as many would like. All we have to offer one another in the wake of disaster is the space for each survivor still standing to tell his true story, and the support all survivors need to forge forward paths of their own determination.

NOTES

1. Blow Buddies Public Service Leaflet, "Safer Dicksuckin'" (San Francisco: BG Productions, 1993), p. 1.

2. Joe Fera and Wayne Blankenship, "It's Not Acceptable, in 1993 . . ., *Bay Area Reporter*, November 24, 1993, 6. "

3. For coverage of a bathhouse opening in New York in 1995, see Jorge Morales, "Curtains for New York Sex Clubs?," *The Advocate*, March 21, 1995, 20. In San Francisco see Tim Kingston, "Tempest in a Tub," *San Francisco Bay Times*, April 7, 1994, cover story. For new infections in Chicago, Denver, and San Francisco see David Olson, "Study: Gay Men Seroconverting at High Rate," *Bay Windows*, January 26, 1995, 3.

4. See Mark Schoofs, "Can You Trust Your Lover?," *Village Voice*, January 31, 1995, 37-39; also Gabriel Rotello, "Beyond Condoms," *The Advocate*, February 21, 1995.

5. Michelangelo Signorile, "Negative Pride," *Out*, March 1995, 106.

6. Gay and Lesbian HIV Prevention Activists, "Goal: To End HIV Transmission in Commercial Sex Establishments" (statement of goals, n.d.); see also Amy Pagnozzi, "Gay Group Measures Prevention in Lives," *Daily News*, February 15, 1995; Gay and Lesbian HIV Prevention Activists, "Gay Group to City Hall: Make Sex Clubs Safe," (media release, March 9, 1995).

7. Michelangelo Signorile, "Negative Pride," *Out*, March 1995, 24.

8. Michelangelo Signorile, "HIV-Positive, and Careless," *The New York Times*, 26 February 1995. Journalists usually have no control over headlines assigned to their stories in daily newspapers.

9. Michael Botkin, "Viral Apartheid," *Bay Area Reporter*, February 23, 1995, 24. See also, Jon D. Barnet, "HIV-Negative Support Group Formed," *St. Louis News-Telegraph*, February 11-24, 1994. Barnet's story discusses an ACT UP/Kansas City's advertisement in a local gay publication which "depicts money

being flushed down a toilet" and has text which reads "GSP [Good Samaritan Project, a local AIDS provider] if you are spending one dime to support this HIV negative group, this is one dime you are taking away from an HIV positive person in need." Also, I am grateful to Will I. Johnston for forwarding to me a letter/leaflet distributed in Boston, dated December 15, 1994 and signed only "an HIV victim" critical of Boston's AIDS Action Committee and Fenway Community Health Center sponsorship of an HIV-negative support group. In part, the letter/leaflet reads, "FCHC's [Fenway Community Health Center's] . . . newsletter of Fall '94 cites that the HIV-negative support and discussion group is co-sponsored by the AAC. In light of limited financial resources of both the AAC and FCHC, recommendation is made for this group to acknowledge priorities and make other private arrangements, if to continue. . . . Kindly cease promoting involving expenditures obviously or otherwise better allocated."

10. Walt Odets, "AIDS Education and Prevention: Why It Has Gone Almost Completely Wrong and Some Things We Can Do About It," (paper presented at the National Gay and Lesbian Health Conference, Houston, TX, July 23, 1993).

11. Jay A. Levy, "The Transmission of HIV and Factors Influencing Progression to AIDS," *American Journal of Medicine* 95:95 (July 1993).

12. Jeffrey D. Fisher and William A. Fisher, "Changing AIDS-Risk Behavior," *Psychological Bulletin* 3 (3): 463 (1992).

13. Jeffrey A. Kelly, Debra A. Murphy, Kathleen J. Sikkema, and Seth C. Kalichman, "Psychological Interventions to Prevent HIV Infection Are Urgently Needed: New Priorities for Behavioral Research in the Second Decade of AIDS," *American Psychologist* 48 (10): 1030 (October 1993).

14. "Summit on HIV Prevention for Gay Men, and Bisexuals and Lesbians at Risk," (San Francisco: American Association of Physicians for Human Rights, 1994).

15. Nora Kizer Bell, "Ethical Issues in AIDS Education," in *AIDS and Ethics,* ed. Frederic G. Reamer (New York: Columbia University Press, 1991), 136.

16. Larry Bye of San Francisco's Communications Technologies, quoted in Michael Munzell, "Dancing with Death," *San Francisco Chronicle and Examiner,* August 23, 1992, *Image Magazine,* 25.

17. Jeffrey A. Kelly, Debra A. Murphy, Kathleen J. Sikkema, and Seth C. Kalichman, "Psychological Interventions to Prevent HIV Infection Are Urgently Needed:" 1024.

18. *The New York Times,* May 16, 1993.

19. Nora Kizer Bell, "Ethical Issues in AIDS Education," in *AIDS and Ethics,* ed. Frederic G. Reamer (New York: Columbia University Press, 1991), 137.

20. An analysis of the systemic indoctrination of women into "compulsive heterosexuality" was initially put forth in Adrienne Rich, "Compulsory Heterosexuality and Lesbian Existance," *Signs: A Journal of Women in Culture and Society* (Summer 1980): 631-657.

21. Bell, 141-142.

22. James Baldwin, "A Talk to Teachers," in *The Graywolf Annual Five: Multicultural Literacy,* eds. Rick Simonson and Scott Walker (St. Paul: Graywolf Press, 1988), 4.

23. Steven Seidman, *Embattled Eros: Sexual Politics and Ethics in Contemporary America* (New York and London: Routledge, 1992), 36-37, 45. See also John D'Emilio and Estelle B. Freedman, *Intimate Matters: A History of Sexuality in America* (New York: Harper and Row, 1988), 338.

24. Donald R. Hoover, Alvaro Muñoz, Vincent Carey, Joan S. Chmiel, Jeremy M. G. Taylor, Joseph B. Margolick, Lawrence Kingsley, and Sten H. Vermund. "Estimating the 1978-1990 and Future Spread of Human Immunodeficiency Virus Type 1 in Subgroups of Homosexual Men," *American Journal of Epidemiology* 134 (10): 1190-1199 (1991). The 2 percent infection rate in San Francisco was reported by Jane Gross, "Second Wave of AIDS Feared by Officials in San Francisco," *The New York Times,* December 11, 1993.

25. Kelly et. al, 1031.

26. Randy Shilts, *And the Band Played On* (New York: St. Martin's Press, 1987).

27. For my analysis which produces this figure, see Chapter 6.

28. Walt Odets, "AIDS Education and Harm Reduction for Gay Men: Psychological Approaches for the 21st Century," *AIDS and Public Policy Journal* 9 (1) (Spring 1994).

29. Fisher and Fisher, 464.

30. Paulo Freire, *Pedagogy of the Oppressed,* trans. Myra Bergman Ramos (New York: Continuum, 1970), 47.

31. *Ibid.,* 60.

32. Kevin Cranston, "HIV Education for Gay, Lesbian and Bisexual Youth: Personal Risk, Personal Power, and the Community of Conscience," in *Coming Out of the Classroom Closet,* ed. Karen Harbeck (New York: The Haworth Press, 1992), 247-259.

33. Kathy Boudin, "Participatory Literacy Education Behind Bars: AIDS Opens the Door," *Harvard Educational Review* 63 (2): 207-232.

34. Walt Odets, "AIDS Education and Prevention: Why It Has Gone Almost Completely Wrong and Some Things We Can Do About It," (paper presented at the National Gay and Lesbian Health Conference, Houston, TX, July 23, 1993).

35. Barbara C. Leigh and Ron Stall, "Substance Use and Risky Sexual Behavior for Exposure to HIV–Issues in Methodology, Interpretation, and Prevention," *American Psychologist* 48 (10): 1035-1045 (October 1993).

SECTION III:
REGENERATING COMMUNITY

Chapter 8

Breeding Lilacs Out of the Dead Land

April is the cruelest month, breeding
Lilacs out of the dead land, mixing
Memory and desire, stirring
Dull roots with spring rain.

–T.S. Eliot, *The Wasteland*

Someone left the cake out in the rain.

–Donna Summer, "MacArthur Park"

In the aftermath of the bombing of Hiroshima, a rumor spread rapidly among survivors suggesting that the powerful poisons released into the atmosphere by the A-bomb's explosion ensured that vegetation never again would grow in the city. Trees and weeds, shrubs and gardens, wildflowers and grasses had been snuffed out along with over a hundred thousand human lives.

Interviews with survivors revealed a powerful connection between the destruction of nature and a profound threat to the human spirit:

> I heard that no trees and flowers would grow. . . . I thought it would be forever. . . . I felt lonely . . . in a way I never had before. . . .

> Without trees and grass you can't live. I was fearful about whether we would die or live. . . .[1]

Yet just seven months after the bombing, as early spring arrived in Hiroshima, the city's cherry blossom trees burst into bloom.

Urban civilization still lay in ruins and inhabitants remained in the throes of sickness and mourning, but trees were flowering, grasses were shooting up through the earth's surface, and nature was being reborn. The impact upon survivors was striking:

> Well, the newspapers and various authorities said there would be no trees or grass in Hiroshima for seven years or so. But when I looked at the rivers and saw how quickly they regained their original beauty, I didn't believe that the city had been reduced to such sterility. . . . I wrote about mud and soil and grass and trees. But I felt the soil of Hiroshima was mixed with the bones of the dead, and the young trees and grass growing out of the ground were–if I can speak metaphorically–the eyes of the dead, looking at the people who had survived . . . When I noticed all of these trees and greens, I began to think more constructively about my present condition and about my future.[2]

After fifteen years of destruction and desolation visited upon the gay urban village by the AIDS epidemic, cherry blossoms are beginning to appear. A renewed sense of order and purpose is creeping back into daily life for many gay men, and a community-wide revitalization is starting to emerge. Unplanned and unexpected–and often with neither recognition nor acknowledgment–a gentle rejuvenation is dawning and bringing with it a new sense of gay community and new relationships between gay identity and sexuality.

At first, signs of regeneration seem odd, out of place, even inappropriate. A friend with AIDS decides to go back to school and earns his college degree. An uninfected gay man who works in the AIDS system teams up with a lesbian couple to parent a child. In the midst of a continuing epidemic, the gay community announces that it is throwing a week of parties and parades to celebrate the 25th anniversary of Stonewall.

Some of us scratch our heads and wonder, how could these things be occurring as a cyclone continuously spins around us? Are these people living in denial? Are they uncaring? How can they flaunt a devil-may-care attitude and go on to other business? What planet have they been living on?

Incidents of individual and communal revival, still subtle and not yet widespread, persistently manifest themselves. A rising tide of evidence of rebirth comes before our eyes daily. A gay man leaves a long career in human services and registers for culinary school, fulfilling a lifelong dream of becoming a chef. Another man rekindles an old interest in gardening, raking through dead weeds and crusted topsoil which had gone neglected for a dozen years. Two middle-aged-men–one HIV positive and one HIV negative–meet, fall in love, and decide to embark on a journey forward together.

Rebirth is occurring in local gay communities throughout the nation, as fragmentary trends coalesce into entrenched cultural phenomena. The reemergence of gay male sex cultures in large, urban centers may be one sign of the community revival. Less-often noted indications of rebirth include the increasing participation by gay men in child rearing and an expanding gay community commitment to programs for gay youth. Rising demands to broaden the movement's political agenda beyond AIDS to include efforts to gain entrance into the military, win the right to marry, and improve media coverage of lesbian and gay issues, reflect an important shift in the way gay men are experiencing their worlds as the epidemic continues.

Many of us expected AIDS to be vanquished by 1990. As initial waves of shock and denial seized control of our psyches in the mid-1980s, we conceptualized AIDS as a short-term obstacle to the gay community's booming process of development. We believed doctors and researchers could expeditiously come up with a cure for any malaise. Our optimistic time frame for containment, vaccination, and cure was abetted by the media, medical researchers, and public health officials. Margaret Heckler, President Reagan's Secretary of Health and Human Services, fueled this optimism-based-on-nothing when she declared victory over AIDS in April 1984, announcing that a vaccine would be available within two years:

Today we add another miracle to the long honor roll of American medicine and science. Today's discovery represents the triumph of science over a dreaded disease. Those who have disparaged this scientific search–those who have said we weren't doing enough–have not understood how sound, solid, significant medical research proceeds.[3]

We knew back in 1984 that we were in for a difficult and painful battle–against disease, mass indifference, and virulent discrimination–but we believed that the alarm clock had been set to go off in about a decade–give or take a few years–and life could return to normal. Our public statements, activist demands, and service system designs, assumed AIDS was a temporal emergency with solutions awaiting discovery.

AIDS is not over. In fact, it is far from over. As researchers, physicians, and community activists attempt to spin the bad news to shield us from despair, gay men have gotten one message loud and clear: the epidemic is likely to be an enduring feature throughout most or all of our lives.[4] HIV disease might become increasingly manageable, but it doesn't appear to be going away. Not only does it seem AIDS will not be vanquished swiftly, but it appears that new infections will continue to occur among gay men. While some of our brains may be able to take in this new reality, our hearts simply cannot. Emotionally, it seems impossible to accept that our lives have become a horror film which appears to be not a one-reel movie, but a never-ending Mobius strip.

THE CIVIL WAR OF THE PSYCHE

Which is it? (choose one):

1. There is no cure. There won't be one. AIDS has become "cancerized." AIDS activists are dead, burnt-out, or bored. Families and friends have convinced themselves of their own helplessness, feeding the hopelessness felt by people with AIDS. AIDS groups are marked by dissent and despair. Too much of the fight against AIDS is driven by greed, ego and power.

2. People with AIDS are living longer and healthier lives. More treatments are available today. A vaccine is around the corner. New treatments are coming on-line soon. AIDS researchers work selflessly for long hours. AIDS activism has

helped drive the campaign for reform of the healthcare system. Astounding individual stories of courage, compassion, and commitment abound.

3. A lot of both.[5]

Thus opened the premiere issue of *POZ*, a publication produced, edited, and aimed at HIV-positive people. In a brief three paragraphs, publisher Sean Strub summarizes the bifurcated war zone currently occupied by people with HIV disease and others affected by the epidemic. The ambivalence and mixed messages which spring out of these conflicting mindsets surround us daily; they can be glimpsed throughout the issue. On one page, a treatment activist gripes:

> Everyone seems bored with activism. The community is getting tired of maintaining a state of emergency on AIDS, and that just won't do. Much like the Los Angeles earthquake, AIDS is a national emergency with a real solution.[6]

Another politico criticizes a mass surrendering to the epidemic:

> Tragically, AIDS has become *cancerized*. People, including many gay men, are concluding that AIDS has become a permanent part of our nation's health landscape. They are giving up on the possibility of a cure. This mindset, if unchecked, will become self-fulfilling.[7]

Advertisers issue contradictory messages on the magazine's pages. A company encourages readers to cash in their life insurance policy, proclaiming, "If You Suffer from a Terminal Illness, Living Well is the Best Revenge." Is AIDS a terminal disease or a manageable illness? A mail-order firm displays t-shirts imprinted with the statement "All I Want Is The Cure and My Friends Back." When a cure is found, will all the friends we thought were dead suddenly be returned to us? This dance between hope and despair, denial and rage, truth and deception is played out every place we look.

Some gay men may continue to occupy this surrealistic world of extremes and contradictions. As the epidemic repeatedly intrudes into their consciousness, offering little relief and no time off, they maintain a powerful and intense political focus on AIDS. Some of these men experience each day as a series of life-or-death episodes, vacillating between terror and rage. Life at ground zero seems like the only option, and they can neither understand nor accept men who create lives which incorporate a different relationship to the epidemic. They may believe a different relationship to the epidemic is neither possible nor morally justifiable. Until the cure is announced and the all-clear signal sounds, they intend to remain alert at their sentry posts and in their bomb shelters, maintaining the single-minded stance of a righteous warrior.

This activist mindset has dominated community discourse for the past decade, insisting repeatedly that a united front demanding an immediate cure and vaccine is necessary to squeeze progress out of the AIDS research bureaucracy, like water from a rock. We have marched in the streets, worn buttons, carried banners, and chided politicians and researchers alike with slogans such as "People Are Dying!," "AIDS is an Emergency," "The AIDS Crisis is Not Over!," and "We Demand a Cure!" We have believed that entrenched scientific, political, and media bureaucracies required compelling public demands to inch forward. We were right. If we had accepted AIDS in 1985 as a permanent part of the landscape of contemporary life, who knows where we'd be today? The continuous pressure asserted by people with AIDS, street activists, lobbyists, and service providers has resulted in more funding, more treatments, more education, and more services.

Framing AIDS as a public health emergency, however, did not emerge out of well-considered, strategic analyses by activists. There was never a meeting held which weighed various formulations of the epidemic and concluded that the emergency model was most appropriate. Instead, the construction of AIDS as a health crisis requiring extreme counter measures and urgent action grew out of a communal psychological reaction to the epidemic during its early years. After the pervasive initial denial was broken through, gay men struggled to accept the overwhelming horrors accumulating all around: contemporaries dying painful deaths, acts of desire becoming acts of contagion, the homophobe's wildest dreams finding fulfillment. It was impossible for most of us to imagine that these bizarre deformations of life could be anything other than temporary features. Our human psyches needed time, information, and historical perspective to fuel through specific psychological stages of coming to terms with the scope of disaster. With rare exception, we have underestimated every aspect of the epidemic since its inception, not because we have been ignorant or uncaring, but because there are limitations on the ability of people to take in and integrate extreme calamity.

The conundrum which makes the psyche ricochet back and forth between states of emergency and acceptance is taking a huge toll on the health and well-being of gay men in America. As long as this schizoid mindset remains dominant, feelings about the epidemic's potential permanence may remain deeply repressed. When gay men maintain a public position that continues to "demand a cure" in the immediate future, do we run the risk of stifling internal voices which cry out otherwise? The psychic hell that dominates gay male lives is defined by two encroaching borders: an escalating emotional and psychological need to adjust to the epidemic's apparent permanence is thwarted constantly by the intellectual and political need to believe that AIDS is temporary. Likewise the AIDS activists' agenda focused on crisis, emergency, and cure is becoming increasingly undermined by internal doubts clandestinely harbored by advocates. Will we awaken soon from this nightmare to find it ended, or will we awaken soon from the nightmare to find that we've accepted it, or will we continue to occupy an ongoing state-of-emergency? Which scenario is more disturbing?

I believe that some kind of psychological adjustment must be encouraged among contemporary urban gay men. While a state-of-emergency mentality appears to offer short-term benefits along with a visible and righteous determination to end suffering, it presents serious risks as well. At this point in our evolving experience of the epidemic, the unceasing, entrenched conception of AIDS as a crisis forces masses of gay men into an untenable state of psychological civil war. The inherent process of emotionally coming to terms with the epidemic is repeatedly short-circuited by an impulse which says, "Resist! Do not accept! AIDS is an emergency! Do not let yourself adjust to its presence or it will be with you forever!"

An editorial in a New England gay newspaper summarizes this impulse. Titled "We Must Never Accept AIDS," editors of Hartford's *Metroline* begin by citing names of colleagues lost to AIDS, and highlighting one particular recent death as an example of the vast human potential stolen by the epidemic.[8] The editorial then captures the paradox of our times:

> It has all become too routine now: the death, the memorials, the obituaries. It is easier not to feel anymore, to accept the fact that death has become an inevitable part of our lives. When Larry Kramer rails that we have all become too complacent in this, the 13th year of the plague, that we no longer think about the end, or how to bring about that end, but rather of merely how to *accept* this horrible reality in our lives, his rage is appropriate. But so many of us, to dull the pain, have shut down, revealing the banality of it all: we have allowed AIDS to become integrated into our lives.[9]

"Acceptance" and "integration" of the epidemic into our lives is equated with complacency and failure to consider ending the epidemic. But is this so? Accepting that AIDS has occurred, gay identity and sexuality have been distorted, community and social order have been transformed, and countless individuals significant to our lives have died would allow gay men to adjust to the new world we inhabit, navigate through its twisted channels, and forge new identities and lives. This kind of acceptance must be distinguished from acquiescence—passive assent without protest or struggle. Yet the editors don't see it this way:

> We must never accept AIDS. While those of us who are living with the virus must, for our own humanity, come to terms with the virus, and accept the inevitability—even the beauty—of death, we as a community must never, ever, come to such an acceptance. For such integration of the plague into our lives only serves to heighten the tragedy, and allows the homophobes and the bigots (and the misguided and the self-oppressed among us) to keep the monolithic, self-perpetuating AIDS industry alive. We must find the strength to find our anger once again, we must be willing to act up, once again, in the streets and in our hearts, and we must not, as a community, permit any more of our best and our brightest to go gently into

that good night. We must, as the poet says, rage, rage against the dying of the light–and against the most frightening outcome of all: the acceptance of AIDS.[10]

While much debate concerns whether death from HIV is inevitable, the "coming to terms" advocated by this editorial may be precisely what is needed at the community level if we intend to regenerate activism and revive determination to find solutions to the challenges of AIDS. This does not necessitate surrendering to AIDS' inevitability and permanence; it *does* mean that community expectations need to be adjusted into the realm of the possible. Playing a trump card of political self-righteousness ("integration of the plague into our lives . . . allows the homophobes and bigots . . . to keep the monolithic, self-perpetuating AIDS industry alive.") doesn't alter gay men's powerful need to emotionally and psychologically adjust to the epidemic. To allow the bigotry of the Radical Right to hold hostage gay men's mental health and quality of life is to exchange psychic health for political expediency. It hasn't worked and it doesn't work.

Psychological adjustment would affirm a series of beliefs which gay men have felt traitorous to even consider:

• Our dead friends are never coming back.

• The epidemic might be a permanent feature of our lives.

• Gay men will continue to be infected with HIV.

• We will experience the deaths of many more friends and lovers.

• Our lives will never return to what they were before the arrival of the epidemic.

• Gay male identity is linked in the public mind with illness and contagion.

• We have been forever changed by this plague.

Admitting such feelings and opinions is frightening, yet most gay men in America are already frequently struggling with these matters in our psyches. We find ourselves saying things like "When the epidemic is over, we are going to . . . " and "As soon as we can return to unfettered abandon, let's go . . . " while inner voices whisper that it's never going to happen. Acknowledging contradictory thoughts feels disloyal, as if we have raised the the white flag of surrender and granted victory to the epidemic. Hence we repress such thoughts and leave ourselves vulnerable to constant retraumatization by the epidemic. Because we have not allowed ourselves to develop new emotional and psychological baselines, each new diagnosis, loss, or death is visited upon a precarious, conflicted psychic foundation.

Remaining in this state of emergency poses tremendous risks for gay men. As the years go by, failure to achieve viable psychological adjustment to the epidemic may result in a deepening psychic state of chronic trauma for many gay men. It is as if we remain in the trenches of war, shell-shocked for fifteen years, or experience repeated aftershocks from the Los Angeles earthquake for an entire decade. Under such sustained pressures, the human psyche is battered beyond recognition and complex mental conditions emerge. Held hostage by a terrorized mindset, human beings make self-defeating and self-destructive gestures. Life in a constant state of crisis, in addition to allowing for little quality of life, leads some gay men into dangerous patterns of addiction, clinical depression, suicidal ideation, and mental illness. Ironically, the continuing conceptualization of AIDS as an emergency with a solution just waiting to be discovered, may be related to unconscious beliefs that becoming infected at this stage is of little lasting consequence because a cure is coming. Increased incidents of unprotected sex and escalating infection rates among gay men may be attributable not to normalizing AIDS but to a failure to come to terms with the ongoing nature of the epidemic.

Is it possible to psychologically adjust to the epidemic as an ongoing feature of life, while continuing to base political demands on the expectation of a magic bullet cure which will vanquish AIDS once and for all? Does the effectiveness and urgency of advocacy diminish if we adapt to the new circumstances of our lives? Will additional treatments, a vaccine, and a cure only come about rapidly if the mindsets of gay men believe they will?

The unresolved question confronted here is about hope. A wrestling match between despair and hope is at the core of this dilemma as it is at the heart of this book. Is it possible simultaneously to maintain sincere hope that the epidemic will come to an end, yet believe that it may last throughout our lifetimes? People infected with HIV face at least one additional question: Is it possible to believe that one can survive HIV disease yet simultaneously adjust to and accept the approach of illness and death?

Gay men today are grappling with these questions, but rarely in a clear-headed manner. No analysis has come forth declaring: "Hey! We thought the epidemic would be over in ten or twelve years and it's not. Sorry. It's become clear to us that we need to switch game plans. While we will continue to press for research and development of treatments, vaccines, and cures, we are also going to encourage gay men as a group to step outside the war zone. Take a breather! You can return in a while, if you like. But you might also consider adjusting your baseline understanding of life to fit the new realities around us. Shit happens. Life is tough. People get sick. People die. Come to terms with it. Face the facts. Some of us will survive. Find a little peace for yourself. You deserve it, after all you've been through."

By the early 1990s, HIV disease had become so widespread, and so difficult to master that many gay men began to shift in their conceptualization of the epidemic. Some treatments for opportunistic infections had proven worthy, but the first dozen years of AIDS research resulted in extending the life of the average person with AIDS only eight months, from twelve to twenty months.[11] We could no longer pretend that AZT was an answer. The illusion that gay men no longer became infected had been dashed. We'd held long-term survivors like Michael Callen close to our hearts as symbols of hope, and then we'd watch them become sick and die. Physicians and scientific researchers began prevaricating in the media, alternately urging us forward to the promised land of a cure, and cautioning us to have realistic expectations and to dig in for the long haul. Is it any wonder our earlier hope began to slip away?

Individual men are discovering that their internal gears have begun to turn and a process of adaptation has been triggered. With little information to understand what is happening, and little public encouragement for the process, many gay men nevertheless are slowly shifting out of a state of emergency and entering a state of psychic regeneration. This kind of psychological shifting can be a period of great turmoil and confusion, uncertainty and doubts, yet it offers new hope and moments of peace, things we've seen little of during the past fifteen years. A new relationship to the epidemic may be emerging for these men, one which falls out of new formulation and understandings of the appearance of the plague in our midst. Where some men's emotional state was once constricted to a narrow band of terror, they now experience a broader range of emotions. Being present in the moment and envisioning a future—tasks which had been impossible while enveloped by chronic trauma—are increasingly common occurrences. The accompanying feelings are exhilarating.

Living in a numbed-out, zombie-like state keeps gay men in a holding-pattern awaiting the time when psyches are ready to begin a process of accepting and integrating the epidemic. Increasing numbers of HIV-positive and HIV-negative gay men have found themselves ready to face the realities of a post-catastrophic world. Our friends have died. We may have gotten infected. The disaster has occurred. The tidal wave hit the shore. The avalanche happened. No amount of denial, optimism, or psychic numbing can reverse its impact. Now the formidable challenge of formulation becomes the task at hand: regenerating one's worldview and psychic functioning on a terrain where the impossible-to-imagine has actually occurred.

THE QUESTION OF FORMULATION

Coming to terms with the meaning of AIDS is challenging on every level—intellectual, social, psychological, spiritual, existential. How could a catastrophe of this magnitude occur? What kind of god or higher power would condemn so many people to suffer so greatly? Why have some of us survived and others perished? How can an act of love and desire become an act of illness and death? It seems almost too much to fathom.

These kinds of profound questions confront every human being still standing in the wake of disaster or atrocity. The complex, multi-level interplay which attempts to put these questions to rest creates a new way for the survivors to see themselves in relationship to the world. Robert J. Lifton described the challenge of formulation faced by hibakusha–the survivors of the destruction of Hiroshima:

> The path beyond anger is formulation. By formulation I do not mean detached theories about the atomic bomb, but rather the process by which the hibakusha recreates himself–establishes those inner forms which can serve as a bridge between self and world.[12]

Lifton highlighted three key aspects of formulation from his study of hibakusha: "the sense of connection," "the sense of symbolic integrity," and "the sense of movement." Gay men who have survived the first fifteen years of the AIDS epidemic are struggling with these same three elements in a parallel process of formulation. How has our relationship to the physical world which surrounds us–people, nature, neighborhoods–been altered, and what does this alteration mean? What significance do our lives have and how has the epidemic transformed their earlier integrity? What do we know now about the role of movement and change in our lives that we did not know before the epidemic and how does this knowledge impact our relationship to ourselves, our community, and the world around us?

A study of the Armenian Genocide explored the ways in which the injustice and tragedy of the event tested the religious faith of survivors:

> On one level, survivors are involved in the task of theological debate and reconciliation, and their innovations in theological discourse should not be ignored. We also believe, however, that the "God issue" represents a deeper attempt to deal with injustice in the world. That is to say, whatever metaphysical status God may have, the debate about God's justice is, for survivors, an internal struggle with the issue of whether the universe is trustworthy.[13]

Working through the difficult questions of formulation requires time, patience, and a great deal of effort. There are also hazards in evaluating, judging, and categorizing formulation after extreme incidents in human history. Why is one person's formulation considered "impaired" and another's "successful"? Formulation is a process, which, once initiated, causes one to interact with the world and experience life in direct relation to one's current stage of "working things through," however incomplete or tumultuous. Gay men's attempt to articulate the meaning of the epidemic often displays the agitation and challenge of formulation:

> AIDS does not exist as a punishment of any group, no matter how self-righteous some of us may feel and no matter how we try to place the blame outside of ourselves. AIDS mirrors to each and every one of us our part in the mass reality we all have had a hand in creating. This experience will not leave us until we all become a part of its solution. This is the gift of AIDS. When this disease has run its course, we will emerge on the other side of this experience as a changed race of people, one that recognizes and practices the loving acceptance of all people.[14]

Men who have emerged from long-entrenched psychic numbing and actively have entered the process of formulation have a great deal to offer the community at this precarious time. If their individual formulation is in process, they may continue to move through routine cycles of guilt, rage, and denial. Those who are able to achieve some kind of mastery over the epidemic may stake out parcels of hope midway between weigh stations of "all-clear" and "crisis time."

Lifton's study of Hiroshima survivors highlights two specific aspects of formulation which merit consideration by gay men.[15] "Psychological non-resistance," involves an active confrontation and acceptance of the catastrophe, along with an acknowledgment that an unexpected and overwhelming force has overtaken one's systems. Through resignation to the devastating reality which one has suffered, continued human existence is affirmed. The second aspect of formulation cited is the "survivor sense of mission," which involves purging survivor guilt through active struggle against the sources of injustice one believes has caused the disaster to occur.

"Psychological non-resistance" and "survivor sense of mission" are active elements of formulation for gay men's regeneration amidst a continuing epidemic. As men face the challenge of integrating extraordinary death and suffering, including, especially for HIV-positive men, issues related to infirmity, psychological non-resistance offers the opportunity to face the recent past head on, without avoidance, romanticization, sentimentality, or drama. Sexual shame, survivor guilt, overarching responsibility, the need to blame, must move toward resolution before acceptance of the epidemic can be achieved. One reaches a psychological and emotional understanding that, while many will be lost to the epidemic, gay life and gay men's culture will continue. The resilience of human life and its ability to transcend overwhelming circumstances ultimately may become affirmed through formulation.

The sense of mission which gay men have found in the epidemic has been extraordinary, but does not in itself reflect effective formulation. Much of what motivates gay men to become involved in activism, fundraising, and caregiving may arise from a powerful need to occupy a constant state of emergency. Comprised of diverse individuals, some likely to be motivated by unconscious and unresolved guilt, the intensity and dysfunction of some AIDS organizations reflects an unmastered relationship to the epidemic and an acting out of cycles of terror, blame, rage, and guilt. Formulation of the epidemic may lead gay men to participate in community work with an entirely new motivation and understanding of themselves. By sorting out psychological issues and moving beyond terror, service work becomes a choice rather than a guilt-motivated demand or a bargain with god. And when one becomes active in efforts against AIDS, balance and moderation are guiding principles, rather than crisis and guilt. Boundaries have been reestablished which allow the individual to distinguish himself as separate from the epidemic. One can choose involvement in caregiving without merging with the role.

Gay men who achieve some psychological balance may find themselves considering a range of specific missions in addition to AIDS work. Two common options involve serving as a witness to the epidemic and working on lesbian and gay community issues. Men feel compelled to share the experience of living through the epidemic and to affirm individual experience and communal history. Witnessing may occur through writing, public speaking, film-making, journalism, and within various cultural forms such as storytelling, comedy, art, and dance. The revival of interest in gay community issues beyond AIDS reflects a mission taken up by many gay men who are forging a tenuous peace with the epidemic. In order to retrieve the attention and energy lost by gay political and social issues that are not directly focused on AIDS, some experience a restored enthusiasm for ending anti-gay violence, pursuing legal protections against job discrimination, and strengthening gay service organizations such as community centers, youth advocacy, and addiction-recovery programs. Because work on lesbian and gay issues was developmentally derailed by the focus of energy, resources, and finances on the epidemic, a resurgence of interest in these non-AIDS concerns reflects a survivor mission aimed at restoring attention to original concerns and ensuring continued progress for a community which continues under siege by both AIDS and societal bigotry.

Over time, AIDS may come to be reconceptualized in a manner similar to that of other complex social issues. Homophobia and anti-gay violence are seen as neither an emergency nor a state of normalcy, and certainly not an acceptable part of life. They are considered complex, urgent issues meriting widescale social and political response. Likewise, the epidemic increasingly is experienced as a complicated and serious threat with profound, far-reaching implications but an overnight solution is no longer the sole focus of community efforts. When the lesbian and gay movement aims to dismantle institutional anti-gay discrimination and violence when it demands an "end" to anti-gay violence, do people actually envision it coming about in the next few years?

Gay men have created a wide range of spaces in which to sculpt formulation of an ongoing epidemic. While religious institutions often are cited as major settings for the search for meaning amidst disaster, gay men have turned to a broad array of networks, social systems, and community institutions for assistance in integrating the epidemic into their lives. Twelve-step programs, service organizations, political activism, and cultural venues provide spaces to struggle with new conceptualizations of the epidemic. Sometimes, however, they encourage men to avoid clear-headed confrontation with the epidemic and instead continue to cycle through denial, rage, and despair. Twelve-step programs, for example, can be sites which encourage gay men to minimize the epidemic's overwhelming impact and adopt a happy-go-lucky attitude which short-circuits the formulation process. Men adopt a perspective which ignores the scope and severity of the epidemic:

> I guess I'm doing okay. My roommate's had to go back into the hospital with PCP, and my best friend was just diagnosed. I've lost so many people to AIDS, that I sometimes think I'm going crazy. But my higher power never gives me more than I can handle, so I guess this is all meant to be as it is. I'm clean and sober today and doing just fine.[16]

Like all disasters and atrocities, AIDS presents barriers to efforts to "make sense" out of it. The struggle for formulation after a discrete, time-focused event such as an avalanche or train wreck is quite different than that which occurs in the midst of ongoing, escalating disaster. An epidemic forces men to attempt to draw meaning from their present circumstances even while the future remains perilous and continues to define itself. This is particularly challenging for HIV-infected gay men, who carry an ever-changing constant barrage of assumptions and predictions about what will happen to their health. Hiroshima survivors faced a similar struggle "to cope with an unmastered past and a threatening future,"[17] because of radiation sickness and other A-bomb illnesses which appeared decades after the war.

Another special challenge to gay men's mastering of the epidemic is posed by the disputed origins of AIDS and the continuing controversy over the role HIV plays in causing AIDS. Atrocities such as the Holocaust or the bombing of Hiroshima caused survivors to engage in internal debate regarding responsibility. Who really was the enemy? In the former situation, the struggle was often to assign differing degrees and kinds of responsibility to Hitler, the Nazis, their followers, the German people, and the rest of the world which stood by while six million were murdered. The challenge in Hiroshima was to distribute blame between Truman, the U.S. people, the A-bomb's inventors, the pilot who pushed the button, and the militarism of Japan's ruling regime.

A plague of contested origins presents challenges to the naming of enemies and assignment of responsibility. Gay men have focused blame in many directions: Presidents Reagan, Bush, and Clinton, gay bathhouse owners, the media, the Radical Right, the homophobic medical and scientific research establishment, our own leadership. Theories of the origin of the epidemic are often thinly masked attempts to assign responsibility for decimation. Conspiracy theories abound, blaming the U.S. government's secret chemical testing program, the Moral Majority, a hepatitis B vaccine campaign, tourism in Africa or Haiti, and the 1980 Mariel boatlift of Cubans. The assumption that someone must be responsible lies behind much of contemporary AIDS literature and politics, and is rarely overtly challenged.

It is worth questioning whether attempts to assign blame for the epidemic are indicative of a refusal to psychologically accept the epidemic's arrival, impact, and continuing toll. AIDS appears not as a medical syndrome or public health challenge but as a form of social injustice. While bigotry, discrimination, and the "banality of evil" clearly continue to feature prominently in the spread of the epidemic, by focusing on these factors, an acceptance of the serendipity of the epidemic is avoided. Does the epidemic have to be anyone's "fault"?

The in-fighting within AIDS and gay organizations and the powerful recurring need to scapegoat leadership may arise out of a similar process of formulation. The various ways gay men struggle to make sense of AIDS reveal psychological, political, and spiritual obstacles to the integration of the epidemic. Taking on the identity of the dead by assuming the goals, life work, or political identity of those who died from AIDS has been common, as if the granting of priority in life to the dead rather than the living provides atonement for sins. Some adopt a "death in life" existence, and are unable to be present in life. The "universal tendency to honor martyrs and resent survivors," which has been documented in Hiroshima reflects psychological resistance to accepting survival and an accompanying need to make reparations to the dead.[18] We sometimes act as if our continuing existence is at the expense of the deceased.

Lifton documented the formation of "guilt community" in the aftermath of the bombing of Hiroshima, which bears resemblance to pockets of gay life in epicenter cities:

A striking feature of the Hiroshima environment is the *communal reinforcement of guilt*–the creation of a "guilty community" in which self-condemnation is "in the air." Indeed, this shared survivor guilt served as an organizing principle around which the hibakusha community originally took shape. . . . We have also seen how this same matrix of death guilt can enmesh and constrict the lives of Hiroshima hibakusha and cause some . . . to feel that they are unable to remain in the city. And whatever symbolically reactivates the survivor experience in general (nuclear testing, for instance) also restimulates this guilt, and places new stress upon the uneasy bonds of the community.[19]

AIDS organizations may become tainted with similar overarching guilt which precludes healthy functioning, appropriate service provision, and functional human relations. When guilt is the predominant force motivating organizational life, community ethics and caring relationships are subverted. Organizational change becomes excruciatingly difficult. Appropriate power relationships and role definitions become blurred. Personnel cling to positions and identities long after they have lost the ability to carry out their functions. At all levels of organizational life–Board, management, staff, volunteers, and clients–AIDS organizations face extraordinary obstacles when unconscious guilt is thick in the air. Rather than acknowledge the "uneasy bonds" of the community, gay men repeatedly trumpet the "unity" and "cohesiveness" of the lesbian and gay community.

The profound differences in formulation which exist between gay men of differing serostatuses present a powerful challenge. HIV-positive gay men and gay men with AIDS may have much to teach uninfected gay men about making peace with the epidemic and regenerating life. An awareness that lifespans may be cut short and a foundation of empowerment that lie at the core of the people-with-AIDS movement allow many gay men with HIV/AIDS to voice determination to keep HIV from dominating their lives. These men insist on balance in life and enjoying "one day at a time." As author and activist Paul Reed wrote:

. . . In the doing, you discover that yes, your world has changed, that indeed life is not what you had planned, but that, in renewed hope, in peace of mind and good spirits, you have achieved an inner balance–serenity.[20]

Some HIV-negative gay men fear social condemnation as they consider reconstructing their lives to include some separation from the epidemic. It is as if leaving professional or volunteer work with people with HIV is equivalent to turning one's back on the cause. Until survivors of the first fifteen years of the epidemic achieve significant progress in recovery from grief and trauma, formulation will continue to be a place of great struggle and internal ambivalence.

VICTIMS OR SURVIVORS?

At an historic summit of people with AIDS and ARC in Colorado in 1983, a set of guidelines and standards were drafted which highlighted basic rights for people with AIDS. The "Denver Principles" provide a succinct rationale for resisting the identity of "victim" or "patient":

> We condemn attempts to label us as "victims," which implies defeat, and we are only occasionally "patients" which implies passivity, helplessness and dependence upon the care of others. We are "people with AIDS."[21]

This insistance of a focus on survival rather than victimization is also reflected in the original "Statement of Purpose" of the National Association of People with AIDS:

> We do not see ourselves as victims. We will not be victimized. We have the right to be treated with respect, dignity, compassion and understanding. We have the right to lead fulfilling, productive lives–to live and die with dignity and compassion.[22]

While politically involved people with AIDS reached consensus early in the epidemic about the varying status slots they preferred to vacate and occupy, other gay men have spent over a dozen years wavering in confusion. Many HIV-positive gay men and uninfected gay men question the necessity of assuming any label for their conditions. Those who have suffered the decimation of the past fifteen years face a stark choice between victimization and survival. While additional statuses may be appropriate to individual men, gay men as a class have been wounded so seriously by the epidemic that any self-conscious step toward survivor status takes on incredible significance. The difference between victim and survivor is a distinction between being passive casualties of the epidemic and being active recreators of life and identity.

It is especially difficult for uninfected gay men to acknowledge that such a choice confronts them. It is common for men to consider themselves as having "gotten off lucky" because, despite sexual histories which outstrip many deceased peers, their bloodstreams do not contain HIV. Uninfected men may discount their own portion of suffering, particularly when they compare their conditions with the daunting issues facing gay men with HIV and AIDS. Some uninfected men see themselves only as witnesses to the epidemic, implying passive observation distanced from emotional or psychological impact.

To breed lilacs, the dead earth must enjoy the benefits of warm spring rains and give way to emergent life. Likewise, to spur regeneration, many gay men make a conscious choice to embrace the role of survivor. Few today would challenge the survivor status claimed by death camp residents and people who lived through the bombing of Hiroshima. After an avalanche or a trainwreck, the deceased are buried, but all are acutely aware that those still standing harbor tremendous need for comfort and support. Yet because of a failure to conceptualize the AIDS epidemic as a catastrophic disaster visited upon very specific and vulnerable populations, gay men who are uninfected are expected to have endured with neither psychological scars nor emotional damage. By underplaying or denying the full range of impact of the epidemic and its power to transfigure emotions, memories, and psyches, the souls of gay men are kept locked in a perpetual winter.

The appeal of victimization and powerlessness in contemporary American culture is tremendous. Many gay men have carved out identities and careers as martyrs to the epidemic. While many have suffered greatly in this epidemic, "pain queens" raise the art of public suffering to a new level. They quantify their losses in a manner reminiscent of competitions over penis size. In a bizarre imitation of ambulance-chasing attorneys, they rush to the bedsides of critically ill people with AIDS who hardly consider them long-standing friends, and force themselves into prominent roles at memorial services. These individuals choose a larger-than-life version of victimization over a humbler, more private survivor status. By doing so, these men keep themselves contained in a continual cycle of drama, panic, and mock grief, and provide the broader community with a role model of crucifixion rather than rejuvenation.

In the AIDS epidemic, victimhood presents an artificial way out for gay men of all antibody statuses. It permits one to relinquish responsibility for one's continuing life and retreat into self-pity, rage, and ennui. It affirms the power of the epidemic and the passivity of gay men and represents neither true defiance nor commitment to life. Some gay men shed the role of victim for the identity of survivor, and revitilization is initiated.

NOTES

1. Robert J. Lifton, *Death in Life: Survivors of Hiroshima* (New York: Random House, 1969), 68.

2. *Ibid.,* 95.

3. Robert S. Root-Bernstein, *Rethinking AIDS: The Tragic Cost of Premature Consensus* (New York: Free Press, 1993), 22.

4. Walt Odets talks about the epidemic as a "permanent form of life." See Walt Odets, "AIDS Education and Harm Reduction for Gay Men: Psychological Approaches for the 21st Century," *AIDS and Public Policy Journal* 9(1) (Spring 1994).

5. Sean Strub, "S.O.S.: Despair to hope. Fear to knowledge," *POZ* I. (1):4 (April/May 1994).

6. Marisa Cardinale, as quoted in "POZ Asks," *POZ* I. (1):13 (April/May 1994).

7. Peter Staley, as quoted in "POZ Asks," *POZ* I. (1):13 (April/May 1994).

8. "We Must Never Accept AIDS," editorial, *Metroline,* April 28, 1994, 11.

9. *Ibid.,* 11.

10. *Ibid.,* 11.

11. American College of Physicians and Infectious Diseases Society of America, "Human Immunodeficiency Virus (HIV) Infection," *Annals of Internal Medicine* 120(4):311 (February 15, 1994).

12. Lifton, *Death in Life,* 367.

13. Donald E. Miller and Lorna Touryan Miller, *Survivors: An Oral History of the Armenian Genocide* (Berkeley and Los Angeles, CA: University of California Press, 1993), 177.

14. George R. Melton, with Wil Garcia, *Beyond AIDS: A Journey into Healing* (Beverly Hills: Brotherhood Press, 1988), 142.

15. Lifton, *Death in Life*, 367-395.

16. Author field notes from an open twelve-step meeting, January 12, 1994.

17. Lifton, *Death in Life,* 4.

18. *Ibid.,* 518.

19. *Ibid.,* 494-495.

20. Paul Reed, *Serenity* (Berkeley: Celestial Arts, 1987), 77.

21. Quoted in Michael Callen, ed. *Surviving and Thriving with AIDS: Hints for the Newly Diagnosed* (New York: People with AIDS Coalition, Inc., 1987), 128.

22. *Ibid.,* 130.

Chapter 9

Community Beyond Suffering

There is hope. There has to be hope. There's always hope.
We just can't go on like this. We can't. . . .

—Ava Gardner, in *On the Beach*

Enough is enough. I can't go on. I can't go on no more.

—Barbra Streisand and Donna Summer,
"Enough is Enough"

Human life is resilient. In the face of mass destruction unleashed
by powerful natural disasters, communities regenerate and nations
rebuild. Following the tragedy of airline crashes, horrors of war,
and desolation of nuclear bombing, regeneration occurs. Hope
springs eternal. Hence it should surprise no one that amidst a tenacious plague causing mass infirmity and death, a revival of life and
community is beginning to occur.

Many times over the past dozen years, gay men gathered around
dinner tables and pondered whether AIDS would bring about the
end of gay male life. Would all of us die? Would gay identity,
culture, and sexuality disappear? If a vaccine or a cure didn't come
our way, would the number of surviving gay men dwindle to just a
handful of bitter old queens, isolated and mad with rage? Would a
panicked government employ coercive measures to corral us into
quarantine camps, or close gay bathhouses, bars, social clubs, and
political organizations?

Little attention focused on anticipating a revival of gay male life
in the face of continuing massive rates of HIV infection. Yet it

seems impossible to block the rebirth of gay culture. Individuals may remain locked in a state of crisis, despair, or panic, but the social order inherently moves forward toward recovery and new balance. As Jewish survivors of the Holocaust emerged committed to the establishment of a Jewish state, and Hiroshima hibakusha became determined to champion the cause of world peace and disarmament, communities of gay men are slowly emerging from an epidemic winter with vision, vitality, and fresh perspectives.

The questions faced now are profound and difficult to answer. If ongoing deaths and continued suffering may be our lot, can we create lives and identities broader than disease and anguish? How can the gay community struggle against the AIDS epidemic and not allow its overwhelming scope to maintain a stranglehold on our spirit or deter an agenda broader than AIDS? At this point in time, do gay men feel ready to contain the epidemic, or will we continue to be contained by it? How are our answers to these questions affected by antibody status?

Before individuals who have suffered greatly can begin a process of healing and recovery, they must fully and honestly face history and themselves, coming to terms with how they have been transformed and who they have become. Likewise, for regeneration to occur at the community level, a collective grappling with the past must take place and the changes wrought by the crisis must be acknowledged. Facing history is central to community trauma recovery and will be essential to the revival of gay community in America.

It is difficult to pinpoint the gay community's self-image at this point in the epidemic. Reflection and analysis have been limited by the reigning emergency mentality and broad perspective on community issues, along with understanding of the epidemic's relationship to movement trends, has been impossible to achieve. The urgency of the epidemic clearly encourages far more action than observation, and, amid a stampede of terror, certain viewpoints regarding AIDS' impact on the gay community have imprinted themselves on the collective mindset. Motivated more by what gay men hope to hear than by a reasoned assessment of reality, the popularized points of view consist of an interconnected series of myths which, while perhaps offering short-term comfort and support, do little to illuminate the contemporary scene or inform our understanding of ourselves. We are in danger of these mythologies being written into history and serving as obstacles to the regeneration of gay communal life.

AIDS AS THE SALVATION OF THE GAY COMMUNITY

In August 1992, *Time* magazine published a cover story on AIDS which shocked activists, service providers, and researchers alike. On newsstands throughout the nation, two-inch high letters declared that we were "LOSING THE BATTLE." The magazine's cover brazenly confronted the despair which had permeated AIDS organizing since 1990, but which few had admitted. Smaller bold letters appeared underneath the main headline to highlight key features: "Mysterious Non-HIV Cases Emerge," "The Search for a Cure Stalls," and "Infection Among Women Grows." Clearly there was no good news here.[1]

Perhaps the most powerful article in the issue focused on the impact of the first decade of the epidemic on the gay community in America. In an essay titled "An Identity Forged In Flames," William A. Henry III reflected upon the conventional wisdom extant throughout the country concerning the ways in which the epidemic had transformed gay male culture. The article's perspective was succinctly summarized in a headline on the essay's first page—"The wildfire of the AIDS epidemic has made gays a community even as it has consumed their lives."

This concept dominates popular analyses of the effects of the epidemic on the gay male population. It is repeated throughout gay and mainstream literature, plays, film, artwork, and music. We are repeatedly barraged with the view that AIDS is to be credited with transforming a self-indulgent, pleasure-seeking clan of party boys into responsible, mature citizens who must now make restitution to society for their wanton youth. Selfishness and decadence have been melded into "community" and a sophisticated political powerhouse has been created from an inchoate, idealistic mass.

The *Time* essay clearly gives voice to a moralistic interpretation of the epidemic's effects on homosexual men:

The crisis turned an often hedonistic male subculture of bar hopping, promiscuity and abundant "recreational" drugs–an endless party centered on the young and the restless–into a true community, rich in social services and political lobbies, in volunteerism and civic spirit. . . . Says Eric Marcus, of San Francisco, author of *Making History: The Struggle for Gay and Lesbian Equal Rights,* a new oral history of the movement: "In the mature sense of the word community, you can make a case that there really wasn't much of one for a great many gays before AIDS." Thus it has become almost an incantatory mantra within gay circles to say the catastrophe "has not been without its gifts."[2]

When I hear someone say, "AIDS is the best thing that ever happened to the gay community," a statement frequently echoed in the worlds I have inhabited, I want to scream. Nothing pushes my buttons quicker than talk of the "special gifts" or the "silver lining" of the AIDS epidemic. Such a cavalier perspective seems not only to minimize and distort the horrors we have suffered, but inevitably lead to a grotesque rewriting of history which simplifies and mythologizes recent developments in gay communities. Just as current discourse on gay male sexuality reflects a disturbingly smug and conservative look back at sex in the 1970s, the "silver-lining" precepts of the epidemic represent a profound violation of what we've been, what we are, and what we are becoming. As I listen to gay men parroting this notion, I hear a subtext quietly murmured in my ear: "On one hand, we've lost 200,000 gay men. On the other hand, we've repented our ways, finally grown up, and been willing to assume the responsibility and value of *true* brotherhood. I guess that's a fair exchange."

It is common, following disasters, for hope to masquerade in this particular guise. In an effort to boost flagging spirits, earthquake survivors discuss the benefits reaped from new homes, strengthened roads, a unified neighborhood spirit. Many people need to take from catastrophe a little bit of knowledge or improvement for the world, as if to say, "Well, if people had to die, at least let's make something positive from this experience." Such self-conscious optimism becomes part of the "post-disaster utopia" which follows disaster and represents a swift and incomplete attempt to make sense out of the senseless and provide compensation for tremendous losses which have occurred.

It would feel gruesome to most people to initiate discussion of the "good things" which came out of the Holocaust, or the "special gifts" gained by the Japanese out of the bombing of Hiroshima and Nagasaki. The survivor missions which arose from these atrocities focused on ensuring that similar events were never again allowed to occur. Because the Jews and Japanese so clearly were assaulted by a force of overwhelming evil, few place the blame for decimation and genocide at their doormat. Retrospective talk about the "wisdom" gained would seem insulting. Attempts to blame the victim–claiming Jewish "passivity," a supposed refusal to fight back, and Jews knowingly marching like sheep to their slaughter–are confronted, challenged, and vigorously denounced. While certain extreme historical events appear too daunting to allow for public discussion of a silver lining, AIDS apparently is not one of them.

Rarely has the gay community, in a powerful and unified voice, disputed myths imposed by homophobic formulations of the epidemic. The view that AIDS miraculously created community out of an anarchic mass of sex-crazed queens arises out of a deep sense of shame and self-disgust running through the surviving gay population. The belief that the decade following Stonewall was void of authenticity, fellowship, and value disparages the pioneering networks of gay liberation, many which triumphantly continue into the present. I can recall passionate debate during the 1970s among collective members at *Gay Community News* about the meaning of "community," and whether lesbians and gay men were a singular community or a series of autonomous communities, but my experience runs counter to some individuals' need to write off those years as mindless and without valuable, lasting connections. A distinctly Christian worldview seems to have been imposed on gay male life which creates from the complexity of our communal lives a three act play limited to fall-from grace, crucifixion, and resurrection.

Occurring at the same time is a mass tendency to attribute everything which has happened to gay men in the past fifteen years directly and solely to the epidemic. The inherent developmental process attached to community and political organizing is discounted as the gay movement is relegated to a secondary position, as an adjunct or afterthought of AIDS. The epidemic variously is credited with making the gay community politically stronger, increasingly visible, and tactically sophisticated. Pundits see AIDS as the source of what they call the "new spirit" of grass-roots activism, a reason for the growth and institutionalization of gay organizations, and the healer of a wide range of community rifts.

This has been allowed to happen–indeed been encouraged to happen–in some sectors of the gay community by guilt bubbling through the gay male population, buttressed by a lack of sincere interest or knowledge about pre-epidemic community life. The immense scope of the health crisis and the human predilection to merge with catastrophic experience in the midst of disaster, makes many unable to see beyond AIDS. The epidemic becomes not solely a major influence on gay community development, but the *only* influence.

Two particular myths exemplify this common failure to grasp the interplay of factors which shape the communal life of a diverse and fragmented population. The first myth exemplifies three hazards of political science–hyperbole, fallacy, and gross simplification. It states that AIDS is responsible for the development of a new and exciting brand of gay activism, and portrays the movement of the 1970s as tame, uninspired, and lacking in mass participation. ACT-UP and Queer Nation's politics, tactics, and organizational cultures are seen as entirely new features to gay organizing. This myth celebrates that homosexual politics finally has privileged urgency over civility, integrity over compromise, and mass consensus over "self-appointed" leadership.

It is difficult to disentangle the recent history of gay and lesbian political organizing from community response to the AIDS epidemic. We will never know how the movement would have developed without the interruption of AIDS. In the 1980s, AIDS was widely accused of draining attention and resources from non-AIDS focused activism. Ironically, by the 1990s, things shifted and many attributed the increased visibility and respectability of gay rights efforts to the epidemic. Whether gay and lesbian organizing advances or wanes, the AIDS epidemic receives the credit or the blame. Hence it is difficult to refute claims that the increasing sophistication, visibility, and access to power of the gay and lesbian movement is a result of the skills and experience garnered from AIDS organizing.

A review of the history of modern American social change movements, however, may lead one to conclude that gay organizing would have expanded in scope and sophistication in the 1980s even without the intervention of an epidemic. Efforts of the 1970s created a tremendous foundation of cutting-edge analysis, organizing experience, and collective wisdom which would have borne fruit in the 1980s and 1990s, even without AIDS. It might be more appropriate to say that a dynamic, synergistic relationship has existed between AIDS activism and gay organizing since the early 1980s which has resulted in a cross-fertilization of strategies and tactics.

Specific tangents to the theory that links gay community progress to AIDS should also be challenged. Many claim that AIDS is the primary factor bringing increasing numbers of lesbians, gay men, and bisexuals out of the closet. Yet as the post-Stonewall movement coalesced and chipped away at systemic homophobia in American culture, a variety of shifts occurred which inspired the coming out of increasing numbers of people: anti-discrimination protections were established, community centers became institutionalized, the quality of communal life improved, media coverage increased and broadened, peer support resulted in greater self-acceptance, and our identities were constantly shifting. The gay community was on a steady path of increased visibility before the first cases of AIDS were diagnosed, although we will never know where this path would have taken the community without the intervention of AIDS.

Some believe that gay militancy began with ACT-UP and Queer Nation. While the movement of the late 1970s and early 1980s was dominated by assimilationist objectives and moderate strategies aimed at mollifying the status quo, the initial post-Stonewall years teemed with radical grass-roots activism. The street actions, zaps, and graphically inspired posters and leaflets of contemporary activism draw on a rich tradition of similar tactics developed during the early days of gay liberation and women's liberation. Militancy migrates in and out of American social change movements; it would be a simplification of historical fact to credit the invention of grassroots activism to any single source–especially contemporary AIDS activism.

The appearance of AIDS in the early 1980s seriously derailed the developmental process of the gay and lesbian movement as talent, energy, and resources flowed in many directions. By the late 1980s, the powerful rage which had erupted and was directed into AIDS militancy linked up with a renewed spirit of movement building and empowerment-based politics in the gay and lesbian community. AIDS certainly has been an important catalyst for renewed gay rights and gay liberation efforts, but a wide range of other factors have also made their contribution to revived activism, including the culture and concerns of Generation X, evolving limitations on identity politics, and the increased repression and economic injustices of the Reagan-Bush-Gingrich years.

The second myth meriting debunking involves the perception that relations between gay men and lesbians have undergone a sea-change as a result of unified work against the epidemic. *Time* magazine asserted a viewpoint commonly heard among gay men: "AIDS has advanced lesbians to positions of leadership, in part because so many of the erstwhile male leaders are dead or dying."[3]

This theory posits that AIDS has healed the great divide between lesbians and gay men, caused lesbian-feminists to finally value their friendships with men, and promoted the creation of a truly cosexual community. In essay after essay and speech after speech, men trumpet the vast heroism of lesbians who, in the face of the scourge, supposedly were willing to let go of earlier animosities and become altruistic caregivers for gay men. With little insight into the roots of historical tensions between lesbians and gay men, and even less sincere interest in specific details of a women's health agenda, gay men fall over each other in attempting to tout publicly the contributions of lesbian caregivers.

Lesbian leadership of the mixed gay movement predates the epidemic. Countless women have leadership careers collaborating with gay men which span several decades.[4] To see an increasing prevalence of lesbian leadership primarily in terms of AIDS killing off gay men and leaving vacancies to be filled by "lesbian affirmative action," is to deny the tremendous organizational skills women have earned through years of education, multi-movement organizing experience, and political grunt work. Women have the qualifications to be leaders of a mixed movement–whether or not large numbers of gay men are in the applicant pool–and the idea that lesbians have moved into positions of power primarily by stepping over the corpses of gay men implies that, in the absence of AIDS, all things being equal, men would continue to win these jobs. In an ironic replay of World War II's Rosie the Riveter, some imagine that women are simply "filling in" for men who went off to war. If the war ends, will lesbians be expected to return quietly to their previous positions of support and deference to gay men?

This myth assumes that relations between lesbians and gay men in AIDS organizations are cooperative and collegial and that women leaders in the mixed gay movement are accepted with open arms by men. Simply by acknowledging the contributions of lesbians to the fight against AIDS, gay men think they have done what is necessary to become great boosters of women's leadership. Indeed female leadership in both the mixed gay movement and AIDS system continues to experience signficant sexism, overt and covert discrimination, and a trivialization of woman-centered concerns.[5] In local communities throughout the nation, lip service given by men concerning lesbian efforts against AIDS is often a foil for an intense undermining of lesbian leaders. Public statements that paint the community as one big happy family are belied by private derogatory comments, sexist jokes and gossip about women, a failure to include women's issues as an integral and proportional part of a movement agenda, and an overt hostility toward assertive dykes. Rather than "heal the rift" between women and men, the epidemic may have brought about a superficial appearance of cosexual collaboration in the community and an increase in men's misogyny. The overwhelming agenda and finances of "mixed" gay groups continue to focus on male-oriented and male-defined issues despite frequent female leadership at the top. Gay men who are sincerely commited to giving up power, financial resources, and authority have a great deal of work ahead.

It needs to be said: the AIDS epidemic has *not* been the salvation of the gay community. Whatever gains have been made in the past dozen years have grown as much out of the natural developmental process of gay movement organizing as from its synergy with AIDS

efforts. Certainly AIDS influences the trajectory of the gay movement–helping to expedite some things, and block others–but a
search for the silver lining in this disaster commonly results in
closing one's eyes to what we have lost or denigrating our pre-
AIDS community potential.

AIDS has decimated communities of gay men throughout America, leaving many surviving men in various states of isolation, disinterest, alienation, and hostility toward the gay community. The
friends and lovers with whom we'd expected to go through life are
dead, dying, or slowly going mad. Social networks and friendship
groups have often been whittled away, fragmented, or smashed to
pieces. Life goes on and the remaining institutions of community
life have continued to function, but it is absurd and insulting to
believe that community came to exist for gay men only when the
epidemic gave us the opportunity to change each others' diapers
and scatter each others' ashes.

Gay community life in the 1990s is complex. In large cities,
inhabited by tens of thousands of gay men, lesbians, and bisexuals,
individuals courageously summon up the energy and hope to create
new cohort groups in an attempt to generate the comfort and support
needed to go forward. An increasing number of subpopulations are
seizing the word "community," making it their own, and defining
the boundaries of their particular turf. Among gay, lesbian, and bisexual people, we now have the sports community, the leather community, the drag community, the black gay community, the gay Left
community, the gay conservative community, the AIDS community,
the deaf leather community. In increasingly small parcels carved out
of the greater terrain of contemporary gay life, people are eagerly
mapping sites from which to initiate work to rebuild community.

REGENERATING GAY COMMUNITY IN AMERICA

A group of gay male education leaders in San Francisco came
together in 1992 to attempt to understand the causes of increased
infections among local gay and bisexual men. Under the leadership
of Dana Van Gorder and Mark Cloutier, two respected organizers,
the group spent nine months perusing research, reviewing transcripts of focus groups, and analyzing statistical information. In

November, 1993, they issued a report, titled "A Call for a New Generation of AIDS Prevention for Gay and Bisexual Men in San Francisco."[6]

The report focused on fourteen recommendations for reducing the spread of HIV among gay and bisexual men, including "Making condoms more available," "Building a greater sense of responsibility for safe sex," and "Making it clear that 'tops' can become HIV positive." Near the head of the list, embedded in a recommendation titled "Self-esteem, Community and Future: Addressing Emotional and Psychological Issues Interfering with Safe Sex," the report raises a crucial question about community life for gay men in the 1990s:

> This effort should make use of a variety of strategies that increase resolve to survive the epidemic by recognizing and valuing the experience of gay and bisexual men dealing with this epidemic, building self-esteem, strengthening ties to the community, building a future and creating a stronger identity for the community apart from the epidemic.[7]

A dynamic interplay always exists between the individual and the community. One cannot "get better" without the other also experiencing improvement in some small way. The successful regeneration of individual gay men will inspire changes at the community level. Likewise, the failure of the broader community to revive will limit the potential progress of individual gay men. In earlier sections of this book, I have suggested specific ways in which individual gay men might work to revive traumatized psyches and reclaim their erotic lives. Such work must be accompanied by parallel interventions at the community level.

We must think about both self-improvement and community development; our concern and care must focus on ourselves as well as the social networks we inhabit, the organizations in which we participate, the communities in which we live. If we hope to see the reemergence of gay communities as powerful, living, vital entities offering authentic sustenance and support and providing purpose and meaning in life, significant attention and resources must be devoted to community-wide revival.

This is one of the key messages I find in the "Call for a New Generation of AIDS Prevention in San Francisco." Beyond the recommendations, analyses, and suggestions, there is a clarion call insistently proclaiming that prevention is not enough. AIDS is not enough. Meaning in life cannot emerge from an epidemic without context. Community cannot be defined by disease. People need more and want more. As long as gay men continue to be defined primarily in relationship to HIV, our collective lives will remain in a frozen, petrified state, lacking vitality and vision. In the short-term, AIDS provided gay men with direction and purpose, but as the epidemic proved wider and more tenacious than expected, gay male identity, community, and humanity began to merge with a syndrome of viral infection and opportunistic diseases. Life narrowed incredibly, until the self-images of individual gay men were defined in large part by the presence or absence of a microscopic virus in our bloodstream.

This is no way to build a movement. It is no way to live a life. For gay men to begin what will probably be a multigenerational shift into fewer infections, we must begin now to offer a vision of community that neither denies the realities of the epidemic nor is held hostage to its demands. We have moved from denial about AIDS into merging with AIDS; it is time to place AIDS in a position of balance in gay community life. The lives of gay men must integrate the realities of an ongoing epidemic, while providing a broader, more comprehensive, and life-affirming agenda. Survival itself offers gay men an opportunity to affirm life, sexuality, and identity beyond the narrow confines of the AIDS epidemic.

The following suggestions are offered as an initial blueprint toward the reconstruction of community for gay and bisexual men throughout America. While the list is neither definitive nor complete, it includes a wide range of recommendations which will enhance both the ability of individual gay men to reconnect with community and the potential of gay community life to move toward a fuller and more life-affirming state.

RECOMMENDATIONS

1. We Must De-AIDS Gay Identity, Community, and Culture

Gay men are not a disease, yet AIDS has tainted us in a variety of ways which prove difficult to leave behind. Every play or movie about the lives of contemporary gay men does not need to climax with an AIDS death. Every novel, poem, or piece of music about gay men need not focus on doom, death, and destruction. There are other aspects of gay male life and identity which merit cultural exploration. Gay men have much to offer the world in addition to our experience in the epidemic. While I do not encourage denial of the continuing march HIV disease makes through gay communities, I believe the merging of AIDS into gay identity is one of the root causes of continuing infections. At this particular juncture, the costs of gay men psychologically equating AIDS with gay identity far outweigh the benefits. When newly infected gay men–including young gay men–report that HIV infection confers a "red badge of courage" and makes one "much gayer," it is time to find a way *as a community* to begin to lift the imprint of AIDS off of gayness.[8]

This realization is not a new one for many of the gay men who have discovered that they are HIV positive. Once infected or diagnosed, many have committed themselves to living a life broader than their infection. This does not mean denying it or not treating HIV infection; it *does* mean not making the infection the center of one's existence and identity. Under the strain of infection, Marlon Riggs produced pioneering films exploring black gay men's identities and relationships.[9] Paul Monette not only wrote memoirs and novels about life in the epidemic, but authored a masterpiece about growing up gay.[10] Randy Shilts researched and wrote a powerful tome on anti-gay discrimination in the military, after he was diagnosed with AIDS.[11] The ability of these men to see AIDS as part of their identity, but not as the entirety of their life's work serves as an example to the broader gay male community.

Survivors of extreme historical events have had to struggle with parallel questions about disaster and identity. Holocaust survivors who told nothing about their lives in death camps and refused to answer questions about their wartime experiences, tainted their children with the power of the epidemic. Likewise, individuals who, after liberation, continued to live in a state of captivity, and defined their lives and identities solely as Holocaust survivors, often failed to achieve a broader engagement with life. Only those able to find a way to forge some kind of peace with the horrors of the Holocaust have gotten on with the business of living and de-

fined their lives, humanity, and Jewish identities in rich, life-affirming ways. Is forging peace possible for HIV-infected gay men? For
uninfected gay men?

2. The Gay Political Movement Must Prioritize a Broad Agenda

Throughout the nation, local gay community groups which maintain a mission distinct from AIDS, have received less stature and
fewer contributions and volunteers than AIDS organizations. For
the first decade of the epidemic, this reflected a narrowing of the
community's agenda. While individual men can argue whether this
was appropriate or not, after 1990, it seemed to become politically
impossible for almost any group to sustain a single-issue agenda
any longer. Other pressing gay issues forced themselves onto lists
of organizational agendas: gays in the military, anti-gay violence,
domestic partners and gay marriage, religious extremist attacks on
gay rights, media coverage of gay issues. This has made some gay
men quite unhappy:

> A couple of years ago, in the throes of Clintonmania, there
> was a palpable sigh of relief: finally the AIDS crisis was over
> (sort of). Marriage and the military became hot issues. By
> changing priorities, gay leaders implicitly granted permission
> to HIV-negative men to start throwing away their condoms.
> Fifty years from now, "queer" historians might rate this as a
> moral betrayal of monstrous proportions.[12]

I believe the broadening of the agenda is a healthy reflection of a
community emerging from a stage of intense captivity to AIDS, and
should be supported. The rebirth of gay community will only occur
when a gay agenda autonomous from the epidemic is embraced by
masses of gay men as their birthright. Other health issues—including
alcoholism and addiction, cancer, mental health, anti-gay violence,
and a broad range of sexually transmitted diseases—must join AIDS
as cornerstones of a gay men's health agenda aimed at improving
the quality of life and the well-being of the body politic. Gay men
working in a cosexual movement must begin to seriously consider
and work toward a lesbian health agenda beyond AIDS, including
cancer, alcoholism and addiction, chronic fatigue/immune dysfunc-

tion syndrome, violence against women, reproductive health, and mental health.

3. The Community Must Begin to Discuss Sex

The world imagines that gay men talk about and participate in sex twenty-four hours a day. Our discussions are thought to be candid, analytical, and empowering. Many believe that gay men as a class have an unusual ability to disclose sexual activities to one another, and to engage in thoughtful, probing dialogue about erotic desire. Gay men are expected easily to transform sexual decision making and thinking into conduct.

Gay men's sex discourse has been neither extensive nor sophisticated during the epidemic. Safe sex education has displaced the articulation of erotic desires and open discussion of sex. We have all learned the lingo of HIV prevention, and we employ it in the clinch with sex partners and around dinner tables with friends, but this kind of talk is different from honest, probing discussion of sexual issues. Our primary venues for sexual conversations are gossip, HIV education, and therapy. Few gay men are comfortable with discussions about the meaning sex has to our lives, and many fail to disclose–even to close friends–the activities and desires we enjoy.

This becomes immediately apparent when discussion about sex issues occurs at the community level. In public forums, letters to the editors, opinion pieces, and through political action organizations, discourse quickly becomes polarized, fueled by fear and rage, and riddled with guilt, shame, judgment, and denial. Our articulation of sex issues mirrors the state of our community. Complexities of sexual desire are often ignored, and men's motivation to engage in specific acts is simplistically explained. Some men articulate a public political position about sex which they personally violate weekly.

In the 1970s, the gay men's community began a conversation about sex which probed a wide range of issues which are relevant to gay male sexuality in the 1990s: the relationship of masculinity to sexuality; sex roles and fantasy; monogomy, polygamy, and promiscuity; the reclamation of post-colonial men's bodies; and issues of power, trust, and sexual relations. The discussion wasn't complete and had many failings, but it offered an intial attempt to expand men's consciousness about their erotic lives. AIDS interrupted this conversation, as gay men were subtly told what was proper and improper to state publicly, and which of our desires and activities were now forbidden.

Many men seem to base their thinking about sex solely on personal experiences. They extrapolate from their own encounters and draw conclusions about the entirety of gay men's sexuality. Research and statistics are devalued, assumptions are made about other men which may not be accurate. Hence when men speak about controversial issues such as bathhouses, sex clubs, "public" sex, promiscuity, and S/M, they frequently give voice to their own fears, preferences, and prior experiences rather than a thoughtfully constructed policy position based on a measured review of available information.

Opening a dialogue on sex among gay men will be an important step toward community rejuvenation. It will be an indication that gay sex is surviving the epidemic, and that there are many sexual issues that merit discussion for reasons besides HIV prevention. Furthermore, because balanced conversation can only occur once men have started to work through issues of sexual guilt and shame, healthy public discourse will be a sign that gay men are stepping back into the land of the living, and reclaiming gay sexuality.

4. Support Both Separate and Mixed Spaces for HIV-Positive and HIV-Negative Men

Few people deny that HIV-infected gay men and people with AIDS need venues for support and discussion with men who share their status. From the early days of the epidemic, a peer model of emotional support has developed and entire organizations and networks of people with HIV and AIDS have coalesced around the need for shared wisdom to emerge out of a convocation of peers. In epicenter cities, social organizations, mental health support groups, and even dating services have been established focused on the needs of HIV-positive gay men.

Parallel organizing by uninfected men has met a great deal of resistance, but not always from HIV-infected men. Support groups for HIV-negative gay men have been discounted, mocked, and derided. Social programs which can fill a wide range of needs of uninfected men have been accused of "viral apartheid."[13] In one midwestern city, local activists protested the creation of services for HIV-negative gay men, taking out an advertisement in the local media demanding that not one cent of AIDS-related funding be used to support these efforts.[14] One therapist's proposal to convene a workshop for HIV-negative men at a national gay conference was met with derision. "Isn't that like Germans getting together after World War II to congratulate each other on not being Jews?" he was asked.[15]

Survival is a critical issue for the gay men's community at this point in its development. It is a matter which deserves to be on the mind and lips of every gay man, regardless of antibody status. People with HIV disease need to discuss long-term survival issues, treatment strategies, sex matters, and the natural history of HIV disease, as well as the torrent of feelings which accompany living with a life-threatening illness. HIV-negative gay men need to discuss long-term survival issues, sex matters, and the impact of the epidemic on their psyches. Both of these discussions are valuable and both need to occur among peers of similar antibody status. By shaming uninfected men away from creating community with one another, a powerful message is delivered: you must be infected to merit attention and concern in this community.

Offering separate services and venues for gay men of differing antibody statuses does not preclude a commitment to dialogue between men with HIV disease and uninfected men. In fact, such dialogue is essential for continued community building. While some have concluded that the gay community has become fractured along antibody status lines, my own experience with gay men throughout the nation reveals a vast number of men of differing statuses in relationship together–either romantic, sexual, friendship, political, or professional. Few men have carved out lives entirely with men of the same antibody status.

In an ongoing epidemic, we need spaces to come together and spaces to be apart. Individual men will find that at certain times they will need to speak with others in similar situations to their own, and at other times need to speak to a broader, more diverse group. For any community to fulfill its function as a place of support and sustenance amidst a continuing avalanche of loss, these differing needs unabashedly must be affirmed and supported.

5. Support Gay Men's Involvement with Children and Youth

A common response to mass catastrophe which brings about loss of life and causes survivors to experience great amounts of infirmity and death, is to focus on affirming life through the reproduction of the species. After Hiroshima, Japanese culture experienced a fierce—almost obsessive—focus on reproduction, child-rearing, and the creation of the next generation of Japanese.[16] Many populations which have suffered genocide during the twentieth century have emerged from the experience determined to replenish their ranks and ensure their population's survival in the face of decimation.[17]

It should not surprise observers of community response to catastrophe to note increased gay male interest and participation in becoming fathers, working with children and teenagers, and serving as sperm donors for lesbians. Gay men's interactions with children and youth have long been considered controversial due to the stigma of child molestation which society confers on gay men. Despite progress made by the gay movement, recent sex panics surrounding adult-child sex issues (charges against Michael Jackson, the Jeffrey Dahmer murders, North American Man/Boy Love Association controversies) may have strengthened the linkage between gay men and pedophilia in the public mind. Homosexual men have been involved in the lives of children for a long time—as child advocates, teachers, school administrators, social workers, children's book authors, and leaders of social, fraternal, and athletic networks—yet the majority of gay men in these professions have remained closeted. Today, gay men working with children wrestle with overt discrimination and whispered allegations which arise when the relationship between children and gay men enters the public sphere.

The involvement of gay men with children has changed dramatically since the start of the epidemic and may reflect both the natural developmental course of gay liberation and a response to gay men's premature and overwhelming experience with death. Gay men's increased involvement with fatherhood—as sperm donors, co-parents, adoptive parents, and full-time fathers—has been commented upon extensively in the popular media which have cited in particular gay men's roles in the continuing "lesbian baby boom" of the

1980s and 1990s."[18] Less visible has been the increased participation by gay men in the creation and development of a wide range of educational, social, and health-oriented services focused on gay, lesbian, bisexual, transgender, and questioning youth.[19]

How can we explain the sudden increased involvement with children and youth by gay men? Certainly many factors contribute to the situation, including a determination voiced by some gay men to provide gay youth with opportunities for affirmation and peer support unavailable twenty-five years ago. One AIDS journal suggested a connection between the epidemic and gay men's increased interest in child-rearing:

> Robert Lifton identified having children as a strategy that people use to deny mortality. It is no coincidence that in these uncertain times—when youth and beauty fail in the face of such epidemic decline and death—that gay men and lesbians are claiming the right to have children.[20]

An article on HIV-negative gay men in the *Los Angeles Times* makes a similar connection between the epidemic and the current baby boom:

> For some gay men and lesbians, surviving the epidemic has led to the ultimate affirmation of life: having children.
> Cedric Yap, 32, a mortgage banker in San Francisco, and his gay lover took the test largely to determine whether one or the other could safely father a child. "Testing negative strengthened our resolve," Yap said.[21]

Lesbian and gay community support for children and youth is likely to continue as the epidemic deepens. Yet the stake which lesbians and gay men have in these concerns appears to be distinct from that of certain ethnic, religious, and racial groups whose bloodline is threatened by genocidal action. Because lesbians, gay men, and bisexuals need to neither reproduce nor "recruit" to ensure the survival of the queer tribe, the fear that AIDS will wipe out future gay male life seems difficult to substantiate. Efforts aimed at fostering the health and well-being of future generations of queer youth focus less on reproducing the species and more on altering key institutions–schools, family, media, Boy Scouts, military, organized religion–which exert a powerful influence over the self-image and self-esteem of sexual minority youth. The increased attention and resources devoted to these matters in recent years represents an affirmation of life and a commitment to the future of the community.

6. Encourage the Celebration of Life

During recent years, concerns have surfaced amongst the leadership of gay organizations and on the pages of the gay press about the penchant which lesbians and gay men appear to have for parties, festivals, and mass celebrations. This is not a new debate. For many years, annual events marking Lesbian and Gay Pride Week were the subject of fierce debate about whether the convergence of the masses was to focus on either a "march" or a "parade," a "demonstration" or a "festival." While often the overt discussion focused upon politics versus culture, the conversation's subtext concerned the increasing commercialization of gay culture, the relationship of the movement to traditional American social change movements, and judgments about gay male culture's focus on sex, costumes, and genderplay. The political status quo of the gay community has long harbored conflicted feelings about celebration.[22]

The March on Washington in 1993 raised this debate to an entirely different level. As the national lesbian and gay community was placed center stage during a brief period of unprecedented media visibility, several factors caused leaders of established organizations to question the "propriety" and usefulness of aspects of the weekend's events. C-SPAN's uninterrupted coverage of the rally at the U.S. Capitol exposed to millions of viewers barebreasted lesbians, flagrantly sexual gay men, and one lesbian comic's declaration of desire for the First Lady. Religious extremists unveiled and mass-distributed controversial videotapes such as *Gay Rights, Special Rights,* and *The Gay Agenda,* which included footage of local and national marches with special focus on controversial segments of the community (leatherfolk, sadomasochists, NAMBLA, clubkids).[23]

Perhaps the strongest reason for escalating criticism of community partying is the increasing frustration felt by community organizations at their limited budgets and memberships. When they see a million people marching on Washington, and national groups tally memberships in only the tens of thousands, a certain kind of envy sets in. If gay men are willing to drop thousands of dollars on a week at Club Med and spend their vacations shuttling between International Mr. Leather, Hotlanta, Hellfire Inferno, Mr. Drummer, Labor Day/Los Angeles, and the Saint's White Party, and some lesbians throw similar sums at Olivia cruises, and Dinah Shore Golf Tournament weekends, why can't our political groups receive better funding?

Another underlying reason for internal conflict about celebration may be connected to mass survivor guilt extant in the community. If so many friends and colleagues have died, isn't there something obscene about those remaining behind choosing to dance the night away? The *Los Angeles Times* noted this internal conflict after interviewing gay historian Allan Bérubé:

> To celebrate his antibody-negative status would be unseemly, said historian Bérubé, whose lover of four years, a British-born biochemist, died last year. "It would be like rich people celebrating around the homeless," Bérubé said.[24]

While critiquing the focus, position, and public relations of gay community parties and celebrations is merited, leaders should resist any temptation to excoriate celebration from its central position in the movement. Every oppressed group has created social and cultural outlets which affirm life and community values, even in the midst of extreme historical cataclysms. Amy Tan, in *The Joy Luck Club,* provides rationale for celebration through the powerful voice of one of her central characters who struggled to survive the Cultural Revolution in China:

> People thought we were wrong to serve banquets every week while many people in the city were starving, eating rats and, later, the garbage that the poorest rats used to feed on. Others thought we were possessed by demons–to celebrate when even within our own families we had lost generations, had lost homes and fortunes, and were separated, husband from wife, brother from sister, daughter from mother. Hnnnh! How could we laugh, people asked.

It's not that we had no heart or eyes for pain. We were all afraid. We all had our miseries. But to despair was to wish back for something already lost. Or to prolong what was already unbearable. How much can you wish for a favorite warm coat that hangs in the closet of a house that burned down with your mother and father inside of it? How long can you see in your mind arms and legs hanging from telephone wires and starving dogs running down the streets with half-chewed hands dangling from their jaws? What was worse, we asked among ourselves, to sit and wait for our own deaths with proper somber faces? Or to choose our own happiness?[25]

While it might seem to some like a bizarre transmutation of reality to witness huge dance parties, upbeat street fairs, and endless parades of community celebrants while the epidemic rages among us, gay men need not harbor any feelings of guilt about celebrating life when we are immersed in so much death. Rather than a denial of the ugliness and sorrow which intrude upon our daily lives, mass celebrations may affirm commitment to community and life, and offer a vision of ourselves broader than our illnesses and victimization. Gay men are caregivers, but more than caregivers; we suffer tremendous pain, but our pain is not all of who we are; we are surviving, but for our communal lives to have meaning, we must find ways to be more than survivors.

7. Encourage Gay Men to Seek Spiritual Outlets

Many have attributed the rapid expansion of gay religious organizations over the past decade to the epidemic. In times of overwhelming, unexplainable loss, religion has historically been credited with offering widespread support and encouragement for developing an understanding and acceptance of what has occurred. Despite continuing entrenched homophobia and sexism in most major religious denominations–and an apparent and shameful escalation in bigotry towards gay people by the Catholic Church–traditional concepts of divinity and faith have been revisited by increasing numbers of gay men and lesbians who are seeking succor from incredible pain and loss.[26]

Gay men's spiritual quest for meaning during the epidemic has not limited its focus to traditional religions. A host of additional resources have been explored by large numbers of gay men as they attempt to find an explanation for what seems to be unexplainable and come to terms with what seems unacceptable. While increased lesbian, gay, and bisexual involvement has been observed in traditional mainstream religions as well as gay-focused denominations and groups such as Metropolitan Community (MMC) Church, Dignity, Integrity, and gay-oriented synagogues, less noted has been the influx of gay people into New Age groups, gay-positive black churches and Latino spiritual communities, the Radical Faeries, Buddhist sects and twelve-step programs. Whether singing spirituals in a church choir, participating in a solstice ritual, convening a healing circle, or attending an Alcoholics Anonymous meeting, gay men are using all available resources in an attempt to find peace.

Gay men's energy directed toward these programs deserves respect from the broader gay and lesbian community, yet such appreciation is rarely forthcoming. Often MCC churches, gay twelve-step roundups or Course in Miracles workshops receive condescending, grudging acceptance by political activists, intellectuals, and service providers. In part, this is due to contemporary societal disdain for and devaluing of anything resembling the spiritual. Many prefer to grapple with the epidemic through explicitly political venues only, and other gay men's needs for alternate paths which address existential and spiritual questions are mocked. Some consider these spiritual resources as obstacles to successful formulation, claiming that faith in a "higher power" or "owning responsibility for one's disease" avoids the medical and political realities of HIV and promotes denial. Whatever one's personal experiences with spirituality or organized religion, the burgeoning need of gay men to sort things out spiritually should not be suppressed for political ends. Individual men must be trusted to observe, evaluate, and hold accountable spiritual and religious programs for adequately meeting the needs of a community which continues to face profound and difficult questions.

8. Gay Men Must Find Opportunities for Witnessing

Surviving gay men have a desperate need to share their experiences in the epidemic and receive affirmation and support for our suffering. In an epidemic which is continuing, and no doubt will see additional surprising turns in the future (moments of hope, periods of despair, even real progress), gay men need both public and private outlets for communal exchange and witnessing.

Cultural venues are often primary sources for sharing experiences of mass cataclysm. Mainstream and community-based arts provide opportunities for the ritualization of stages of epidemic response. Literature, art, performance, theater, and music all can serve this function. The Names Project AIDS Memorial Quilt provides a large-scale experience of mourning and serves as a tangible representation of collective loss. Annual candlelight marches, as well as local memorial services and funerals occurring more frequently, offer opportunities for collective grief and mass participation in memorializing the dead.

Perhaps the greatest obstacle faced by gay men who seek to provide testimony about their lives is the often unspoken division between "acceptable" and "unacceptable" experiences of the epidemic. While many people might find comfort in the belief that all gay men share a common experience and common reaction to the epidemic, this concept is untrue. Furthermore, some gay men's observations and opinions seem alarming to others and are pathologized or labelled "unacceptable" or "incorrect." Men must be permitted to experience *whatever they are experiencing,* and provide whatever testimony they find appropriate, throughout the epidemic. Shaming and repression will assist no one. Suppressing feelings or denying emotion for the sake of political strategy must be considered carefully and approached with great caution. Gay men not only come from varied backgrounds and histories but have extremely diverse experiences of the epidemic. Differing reactions and varied formulations should be expected from gay men.

Historical calamities have produced vast bodies of literature and art which document the complex processes of formulation experienced by affected communities. A similar canon of AIDS literature and art is being created which represents gay men's quirky and variegated attempts to come to grips with an ongoing epidemic and to communicate to the world all we have experienced.

9. Encourage the Rebirth of Gay Identities

Various socially constructed gay identities have been markedly transformed by the epidemic. Identities which prior to the epidemic emerged out of confrontation with gender roles, social power, friendship, and sex, have been stamped with the powerful imprint of sickness and death. How have our identities as gay men been changed by AIDS? What venues are available to us as we attempt to discover and define gay identity after the arrival of AIDS? How has gay masculinity been changed? What does it mean to be a gay man in varying American cultures today? What kinds of identities are emerging among queer men and gay teenagers?

These difficult questions merit examination. Because group identities are mutable and ever changing, they shift through time and circumstance to reflect issues impacting the population. Gay men are often said to have become more caring, loving, and empathetic due to the epidemic, but the real changes may be more complicated and difficult to define. It may be easier to identify changes in gay male identity through the continual emergence of new generations of gay men from varying class and cultural backgrounds constructing identities and lives amid an ever-shifting epidemic environment.

Identity is a precious thing to gay men who went for so long without self-affirmation or the context of a community. In encouraging the regeneration of gay life, thoughtful critical analysis and discourse should be encouraged which explores postepidemic formations of gay identity.

10. Explore Multiple Identities

Anecdotal evidence indicates that men's conceptualization of and relationship to gay community and identity produce vastly different experiences in the epidemic. While many men who have sex with men have experienced the deaths of friends and lovers, men who publicly and closely identify as gay men, and spend much of their lives in gay social networks or participate in gay functions, political organizations, and religious institutions may suffer powerful, nontangible losses from which men who are at once neither closeted nor powerfully gay-identified are shielded. Men whose gayness does not provide primary definition to their lives and social circumstances, men who may have been closeted to some extent in their pre-epidemic professional and social lives, and men who maintain strong connections to their ethnic, racial, religious, and class roots may experience the epidemic differently than men whose primary long-term identification has been with gay community.

As long as gay identity and AIDS continue to be merged in the mind of America, it may be helpful to explore the promotion among homosexual men of other identities in addition to gay identity. Does a black gay man who is more identified with his African-American heritage and the local black community feel less pull to immerse himself in the AIDS crisis? Do gay men who have strong working-class consciousness and who inhabit primarily non-gay working class spaces (workplaces, social and sports venues, neighborhoods) have a buffer against the epidemic? Do Jewish gay men who feel equal commitment to a Jewish community (which has long placed emphasis on survival) and to the gay community, have stronger resolve to remain uninfected? How does a strong professional identity influence gay men's experience of the epidemic?

These questions are difficult to answer, as research into dual- and triple-identity lives has only begun to emerge. During a time when Irish gay, lesbian, and bisexual activists are insisting on equal participation in St. Patrick's Day parades, and queers of other ethnic identities (Puerto Rican, Japanese, Chinese, Italian, Jewish) are making similar inroads in their communities-of-origin, it may be valuable to consider encouragement of strong, multiple identities. Not only would additional group identities offer an alternative to some men's exodus from gay identity and community, but they might provide fertile ground for meaningful coalition-building beyond the limits of traditional identity politics.

It is not clear whether the development of strong multiple identities will deter, promote, or do nothing about HIV transmission among homosexual men, but it is certainly worth exploring. Some racial and ethnic groups–particularly African Americans and many Latino populations–are disproportionately represented in statistics of American people with AIDS, and hence further suggest a need for research and close analysis of this theory.[27]

11. Community Commitment to Combatting AIDS Must Continue

Edward King encourages "Re-gaying AIDS" in *Safety in Numbers*.[28] King argues that "community ownership" of AIDS is necessary for prevention to successfully occur. His arguments are compelling and powerful. I find myself alternately agreeing and disagreeing with his proposals.

I have written extensively about the premature and homophobic de-gaying of AIDS in the mid-1980s.[29] Ultimately, I believe more attention has gone toward de-gaying AIDS than de-AIDS-ing gays. I do not believe the two operate as one or that removing much of the imprint AIDS has placed on gay identity and culture results in the gay community turning its back on AIDS efforts. I believe that an effective escalation of community efforts will only come about when HIV's stranglehold on our communal consciousness is loosened.

Even after gay men are no longer the majority of new AIDS diagnoses in the nation, there is compelling reason for AIDS to remain as a top priority on the gay community's agenda. King encourages "cataloguing the neglect," "assessing need," and "biting the bullet" on resource allocation. His section titled "Gay Men Fighting AIDS" provides one example of current efforts to reinvigorate activism amid an ongoing epidemic. While some believe we should fully de-gay AIDS, I believe such a move would have considerable long-term consequences for both HIV-positive and as yet uninfected gay men.[30]

12. Love Between Men Must Be Treasured and Promoted

It is easy to forget or discount the value of loving relationships in assisting individuals and communities as they navigate through extreme crisis. Loving relationships–which may take the form of primary relationships, friendship networks, family members, neighbors, or colleagues–can offer a great deal of affirmation, comfort, and concrete support to a person struggling against despair, hopelessness, and terror. One insightful journalist has written:

> Our best chance of keeping our courage up in an era of holocaust lies in enhancing our skills at sharing love and emo-

tional support. This is one basis of gay and lesbian radicalism in the '90s: to feel all of our feelings, including grief and loss, and to turn them into service in activities that are meaningful to each of us.[31]

The barriers which keep gay men from establishing loving, trusting relationships often have gone unexamined. Much has been written about gay men's ability to develop individual friendships with women and other gay men.[32] Yet some gay men express discomfort and alienation in one-on-one and group situations and lack social skills to smooth the rough edges. Some have long found it difficult to forge nurturing friendships, particularly with other gay men, because of limitations linked to masculinity. They are reluctant to express feelings, unable to offer or ask for emotional support, and live in the intellect or the body rather than the heart. While gay male culture's privileging of friendship networks and social groups over the nuclear family and the monogamous couple has failed to receive deserved recognition as a critical strength of communal response to the epidemic, the gay community has done little to confront real barriers facing many gay men as they struggle to establish loving, interpersonal relations.

Gay men's need for love, comfort, and affirmation is likely to have increased over the past dozen years, yet ironically, AIDS constructs specific barriers to the creation of loving relationships between men. After losing many gay male friends to AIDS, some hesitate emotionally to invest in new friendships with gay men. Psychic decomposition makes many men moody, erratic, and unreliable; strong ambivalent vibes are put out revealing inner conflict. Social networks are often fraught with drama, conflict, and internecine warfare, as many gay social networks may have been destroyed by interpersonal tensions as by deaths. Although the community's public line has been that we have "taken care of our own" despite public disinterest and governmental neglect, those on the inside of gay community groups are aware that accompanying the epidemic are the cannibalism of leadership, endless griping, and profound misgivings concerning gay men's interpersonal relationships with one another.

Love is rarely placed prominently on the formal agenda of the gay community. Yet at this time it would prove worthwhile to consider ways to support and promote love in the community–not a romanticized, sentimentalized, or politicized love–but authentic, honest interaction, support, and affection between men. While catastrophe presents formidable obstacles to loving relationships, many gay men have managed to embark on new relationships, created social networks to replace those destroyed or thinned by the epidemic, and joined caregiving networks motivated by honesty and love rather than denial and guilt.

Relationships between HIV-positive and HIV-negative men merit particular attention. While the media at times has featured articles exaggerating the divide between the two groups, the complicated ways antibody status affects contemporary gay men's relationships should not be ignored. Many find it easy to rush to judge the decisions or conduct of individual men in this area. If a man has buried two lovers, is he wrong to place a personal ad looking for an HIV-negative gay man? If an infected man seeks a peer who struggles with similar health concerns, is he wrong to attend a single's brunch for HIV positives only? Gay men's relationship to their own antibody status and that of potential friends and lovers is complex and everchanging. A man who seeks only HIV-positive friends this year, might seek HIV-negative friends next year. As one's experience in the epidemic shifts, needs shift as well. The community must give each man space to make his own decisions and steer his way through this minefield to the best of his ability.

Promoting love between men can take many forms. New venues for single men to meet other single men might be conceptualized and created, as well as workshops, dinner parties, and social groups which address difficult issues facing male couples. Rituals and traditions which promote connection between individuals and form long-standing bonds between friends might be articulated. While community attention seems riveted upon domestic partners' benefits and gay marriage, equally important to many gay men is the creation of networks and social organizations of ethnic and culturally specific gay men, sports teams and cultural groups, and neighborhood associations of lesbians, gay men, and bisexuals.

BEYOND THE MASS CULTURE OF CRISIS

During a period when many gay men experience feelings of isolation and alienation, increasing effort might be focused on community building. Gay men do not need additional pseudocommunities which tell us what to say, how to feel, and whom to be, or promote a false sense of connection based on limited identity constructs or disjointed sexual politics. We need small, accessible networks which offer safe opportunities for intimate exchange of real feelings, and provide the support and shared pleasures out of which grow true community.

Gay men will survive AIDS. Gay sex will continue during an ongoing epidemic, and gay identities will continue to emerge, transmute, and reemerge. Some men will concentrate their efforts on ensuring individual and collective survival, while others will continually critique the gay cultures and communities which serve as the foundation for ongoing communal life. If gay men are to have lives which they believe are worth living, and if gay community is to be more than a commercialized, mass culture of crisis, a concerted effort to redesign and reconfigure collective life must be initiated.

NOTES

1. *Time*, August 3, 1992.
2. William A. Henry III., "An Identity Forged in Flames," *Time*, August 3, 1992, 36.
3. *Ibid.*, 37.
4. To name only a few of the lesbians who have worked with gay men since the 1970s: Virginia Apuzzo, Elaine Noble, Barbara Gittings, Betty Powell, Roberta Achtenberg, Jean O'Leary, Amy Hoffman, Robin Tyler, Joyce Hunter, Carole Migden, Meryl Friedman, Vivian Shapiro, Leslie Cagen, Pat Norman, Ann Maguire, JoAnn DiOrio, Betty Berzon, Rose Walton, Karla Jay, Gayle Rubin, Deborah Johnson-Rolon, Pat Califia, Arline Isaacson.
5. For two differing perspectives on these issues see Torie Osborn, "Lesbian Nation," *The Advocate*, May 31, 1994, 80, and gay press coverage of the 1994 NOW conference in San Francisco where some "were more vocal than ever about sexism in the gay community." See Doug Seto, "Sexism and Homophobia: NOW Conference Raises Issues," *Bay Area Reporter*, May 19, 1994, 11.

6. *A Call for a New Generation of AIDS Prevention for Gay and Bisexual Men in San Francisco,* ed. Dana Van Gorder (San Francisco Dept. of Public Health, August 1993).

7. *Ibid.,* 8.

8. Jane Gross, "Second Wave of AIDS Feared by Officials in San Francisco," *The New York Times,* December 11, 1993, 8.

9. Riggs produced the Emmy Award winning *Ethnic Notions* and *Tongues-Untied,* which won best documentary at the Berlin International Film Festival. See "Marlon Riggs–Documentary Filmmaker," obituary, *San Francisco Examiner,* April 6, 1994, A-15.

10. Paul Monette, *Becoming a Man: Half a Life Story* (New York: Harcourt, Brace, Jovanovitch, 1992).

11. Randy Shilts, *Conduct Unbecoming: Lesbians and Gays in the U.S. Military, Vietnam to the Persian Gulf* (New York: St. Martin's, 1993).

12. Robin Hardy, "Accentuate the Positive," letter to the editor, *Village Voice,* March 21, 1995, 6.

13. See Tim Farrell, "Viral Apartheid," *Bay Area Reporter,* January 7, 1993; also Michael Botkin, "Viral Apartheid," *Bay Area Reporter,* February 23, 1995, 24; Andrew Coile, "Polarized into 'Positives' and 'Negatives,'" *Washington Blade* 24(4), 39; "Blood Brothers New Club Targets HIV-Positive Men,"*QW* August 30, 1992, 12. For a view supportive of HIV-negative gay men's organizing from an HIV-positive journalist see Connie Norman, "Tribal Writes," *San Diego Update,* December, 29, 1993, A-11.

14. Jon D. Barnett, "HIV Negative Support Group Formed," *St. Louis News-Telegraph,* February 11-24, 1994, 5.

15. Tom Moon, conversation with author, January 15, 1994.

16. Robert J. Lifton, *Death in Life: Survivors of Hiroshima* (New York, Random House, 1969), 117. Lifton discusses "survivors' particularly strong need to reassert the continuity of life through marriage and children," following the bombing of Hiroshima.

17. See, for example, Mireya Navarro, "Holocaust Survivors' Emphasis is on Life," *The New York Times,* February 19, 1995, 12.

18. Robert L. Barret and Bryan E. Robinson, *Gay Fathers* (Lexington, MA, Lexington Books, 1990); also April Martin, *The Lesbian and Gay Parenting Handbook* (New York, Harper Collins, 1993), 95-101.

19. See Gilbert Herdt and Andrew Boxer, *Children of Horizons* (Boston, Beacon, 1993).

20. Herman Kaals, "Grief Counseling for Gay Men," *Focus: A Guide to AIDS Research and Counseling* 7(7) (June 1992):2. Kaal references R.J. Lifton, "The Sense of Immortality: On Death and the Continuity of Life," in H. Feifel, ed. *New Meanings of Death* (New York, McGraw-Hill, 1977).

21. Victor F. Zonana, "AIDS Takes Toll on Ones Left Behind," *Los Angeles Times,* May 6, 1989, 24.

22. See "Stonewall 25: Let's PARTY!," editorial, *Bay Windows,* April 14, 1994, 6; "Party On," editorial, *Out Now,* May 3, 1994, 12; Marvin Liebman, "It's

Time to Grow Up and Accept Responsibility," *Washington Blade,* March 17, 1995, 53; William J. Mann, "Fete Accompli," *San Francisco Frontiers,* February 16, 1995, 15-19.

23. See the following videocassettes: *The Gay Agenda.* 1992. Lancaster, CA: Spring of Life Ministries; *The Gay Agenda in Public Education.* 1993. Lancaster, CA: Spring of Life Ministries; *Gay Rights: Special Rights.* 1993. Anaheim, CA: Jeremiah Films.

24. Zonana, "AIDS Takes Toll on Ones Left Behind," 24.

25. Amy Tan, *The Joy Luck Club* (New York, Putnam, 1989), 24-25.

26. For a thoughtful analysis of the relationship between the gay and lesbian community and the Catholic Church see Richard L. Smith, *AIDS, Gays, and the American Catholic Church* (Cleveland, Pilgrim Press, 1994).

27. Centers for Disease Control, *HIV/AIDS Surveillance Report,* 5(1) (Atlanta: May 1993); National Commission on AIDS, *The Challenge of HIV/AIDS in Communities of Color: Ninth Interim Report* (Washington, DC: 1992); National Minority AIDS Council, *The Impact of HIV on Communities of Color: A Blueprint for the Nineties (Washington,* DC: 1992).

28. Edward King, *Safety in Numbers: Safer Sex and Gay Men* (New York: Routledge, 1993), 254-277.

29. Eric E. Rofes, "Gay Groups Vs. AIDS Groups: Averting Civil War in the 1990s," *Out/Look* 8 (Spring 1990):8-17.

30. For an alternate view to my own, see Nik Trendowski, "Bound and Gagged by Red Ribbons–Homosexual Activists Perpetuate Misnomer of AIDS as Gay Plague," *Daily Trojan* (University of Southern California), March 24, 1995, 4.

31. Terence K. Huwe, "On Grief and Service: Communal and Personal Responses to AIDS," *San Francisco Sentinel,* November 5, 1992, 22.

32. Friendships among gay men have been discussed by H.W. Seng, "Loving Friendship," and Joseph R. Demarco, "The Care and Feeding of a Friendship Network," in Eric Rofes, ed. *Gay Life: Leisure, Love, and Living for the Contemporary Gay Male* (Garden City, NY, Doubleday, 1986), 145-148, 135-144. Friendships between gay men and heterosexual women are analyzed in John Malone, *Straight Women/Gay Men: A Special Relationship* (New York, Dial Press, 1980). For relationships between lesbians and gay men see: Joan Nestle and John Preston (Eds.), *Sister and Brother: Lesbians and Gay Men Write About Their Lives Together* (San Francisco: Harper San Francisco, 1994).

Epilogue:
Discovering the Invincible Summer

In the depth of winter, I finally learned that within me there lay
an invincible summer.

–Albert Camus
Summer

I'm coming out . . .
I want the world to know,
got to let it show!

–Diana Ross, "I'm Coming Out"

Over the past year, I have traveled throughout America, searching. I haven't always been clear about what I've been looking for,
but internal forces within me were crying out for something. At first
I thought my migrations were motivated by the difficulties I'd
experienced at home in San Francisco. I felt uncomfortable in my
own neighborhood as a result of my public fall from grace and I
assumed this made me search for relief in locales where I could be
anonymous. As I traveled throughout the nation–to Virginia and
North Carolina, Louisiana and Texas, Massachusetts and New
York, Oregon and Washington, Wisconsin and Illinois–my self-
awareness increased and I grew to consider my travels neither as
vacation nor retreat, but as a very special kind of quest.

It was during a warm November weekend in Durham, North
Carolina, that I first suspected my travels were motivated by a
special mission. I was attending Creating Change, the annual move-
ment-building convention of the National Gay and Lesbian Task
Force (NGLTF), along with 1,000 other activists from throughout

the nation. The four-day conference was jam-packed with speeches, workshops, exhibits, and performances. I dashed in and out of conference rooms, hurtling between "National Overview of Right Wing Activity," "Advancing a 'Gay Agenda' on Campus," and "Access to Power: Whose Access? Whose Power?" Friends and colleagues pulled me aside to chat, I winked at handsome guys, and vendors lured me to consider purchasing t-shirts, bumper stickers, and magazines.

This conference is special to me and I annually make it a point to attend, even when funds are tight and my schedule is overburdened. Each year, amid the chaos and anarchy of Creating Change, I manage to imbibe a large dose of energy and optimism from fellow activists. While I exit most conferences feeling overwhelmed, disheartened, or simply spent, Creating Change leaves me refueled and ready to continue working for the things in which I believe. This year was no different.

As a Board member of NGLTF at the time, certain duties were heaped onto my plate at the conference–I was expected to schmooze donors, attend a meeting with NGLTF members, and organize a few workshops and panels. This year, I was happy to be invited to organize a day of discussions focused on sex. The four panels I developed were "Cutting-Edge Issues Impacting Sex and Sexuality," "Talking About Sex Across Two Gay Generations," "Objectification and Intimacy: The Impact of Porn Culture on Our Sex Lives," and "What Is Sex Like For Us in an Age of AIDS?" About 200 people filtered in and out of this day-long intensive workshop and I was fascinated by the powerful participation of lesbians, gay men, and bisexuals in their teens and early twenties. People talked with great candor about their sex lives, and many felt comfortable thinking aloud as they struggled to find words to capture and convey the details and meanings of erotic desires.

During a break between two of the workshops, a tall, thin man approached and engaged me in animated conversation. Passionately concerned about HIV infection among gay men, this thirtysomething graduate student from Atlanta seemed quite agitated about the discussion in the last workshop. He couldn't understand how the participants could discuss sexual issues for an hour and a half and not discuss AIDS. "How can so many intelligent people be talking about promiscuity, kinky sex, and certain high-risk sexual activities, and not even mention HIV prevention?" he asked increduously. "Isn't this serious evidence of the denial of the community?"

Until he raised the matter, I hadn't realized that I'd participated in a ninety-minute conversation with a room full of all kinds of queers and we'd talked about a wide range of sex issues without the intrusion of HIV. Immediately I felt ripples of guilt ooze through my veins. How could I allow this to occur? Would this gentleman believe that a topic as enormous as AIDS could be omitted through oversight? And why hadn't any of us even noticed that such an omission had occurred?

As I fumbled with my thoughts and over-inflated sense of responsibility, another person approached. A twenty-three-year-old, self-identified "femme-lesbian" who worked as a safe sex educator in Los Angeles, waited patiently while the gentleman from Atlanta and I sorted through our thoughts together. When we finished and he exited the room, she smiled sheepishly. "I couldn't help overhearing your discussion," she confessed to me. "And I had come up to talk with you about the same matter, but from an entirely different perspective."

She continued, "I wanted to say how happy I was that a group of men and women could talk about sex issues together for a long period of time and not have the discussion railroaded into AIDS. It felt so exhilarating to me to feel the freedom once again to consider sex as a matter worthy of discussion—not in reaction to pregnancy, abortion, birth control, or AIDS—but as a valuable topic itself."

I listened to her closely. "What's important to me," she continued, "is that we not let anyone reduce our erotic desires to simple products of HIV discourse. What I mean by that is that I don't want to feel that thinking or talking about sex always has to be focused on AIDS. As an HIV educator, I certainly see the value in encouraging queers to discuss HIV prevention and our sex lives. But I also see the value of celebrating our sexualities as goddess-given gifts that are valuable, healthy, and vital to our survival. And that's what the discussion felt like to me—a constructive, empowering articulation of the power of queer sex."

My head was spinning. As much as her words made sense to me and affirmed my own unconscious need for space apart from the epidemic, I felt conflicted about the absence of AIDS from the discussion. What was this about? While the final workshop of the day was focused on the epidemic's powerful impact on our sex lives, didn't I have a responsibility—as the convener and as a Board member of the National Gay and Lesbian Task Force—to do more?

I pondered these questions throughout my time in Durham. The final workshop of that day was focused on sexuality and HIV and the room was electric with the powerful feelings which emerge when a roomful of strangers talk about controversial matters. Yet when all was said and done, I didn't feel resolved about the position AIDS played in the day-long conversation, and in my head, I wrestled with questions. Does AIDS have to be center stage in all gay discussions until we've found a way to bring the epidemic to an end? Is it okay to consider gay male sexual issues beyond HIV prevention—to talk about intimacy, roles, power exchange, meaning, promiscuity, and monogomy—like we tried to do before the advent of AIDS? Or is such discussion simply a retreat into denial? Do I sometimes need to pretend that the epidemic hasn't happened?

Some clarity about these questions came over me later in the weekend, but not through a workshop or plenary speech. As I sat in the hotel lounge, thumbing through the conference book, I felt a surge of excitement run through me. A broad, multi-layered community agenda spread throughout the weekend—lesbian mothers, gays in the military, fight the Right, media advocacy, queer youth, organizing in the workplace, countering racism in the community, domestic partners, erotic desire, sodomy law reform, international issues. Sure, AIDS was a part of it, in workshops titled "AIDS Prevention Issues," "Promoting Our Research Agenda," "AIDS and Sexuality," but that single topic no longer eclipsed the entire agenda of lesbians, gay men, and bisexuals.

I thought back just a few years ago—to the mid 1980s—when I was executive director of the Los Angeles Gay and Lesbian Community Services Center. I recalled the frustration I felt because, even though we were doing cutting-edge work on a critical range of health care issues—suicide and mental health, alcoholism and drug addiction, sexually transmitted diseases, domestic violence—all anyone wanted to talk about or fund was AIDS. Our applications for government grants for support groups for gay youth had to be presented as HIV-prevention efforts. When public officials visited the Center, they breezed past the lesbian resource room and the youth jobs program. They wanted to see the AIDS clinic. Legal advocacy for men who were entrapped in public parks or lesbians who lost custody of their children was considered neither important nor sexy; advocacy for people with AIDS who'd been fired from their jobs or discriminated against by the health insurance industry was where interest focused.

In those days, it seemed that lesbians and gay men only merited attention and support when we were struggling with AIDS. How I raged against this! Whereas Hollywood stars had started to fall over one another to appear at benefits for AIDS Project Los Angeles and other AIDS organizations, it was impossible to get celebrities to appear at the annual dinner of a gay community center. In the mind of America, AIDS brought with it the dignity of victimization: it was okay to help gay men, as long as we were dying. Gay advocacy work brought with it a defiance of victimization: it was all about politics, empowerment, and liberation. Few people–including few gay men–believed that gay health issues other than AIDS were worth funding.

As my mind refocused once again into 1994, I realized just how far we had come. Not only have lesbian and gay issues started to receive serious attention in many sectors, but it was no longer necessary to fill a queer conference with AIDS-focused workshops in order to ensure mass participation. While people had been hungry to participate in AIDS volunteerism and political advocacy in the latter part of the 1980s, by the 1990s, people were energized as well by the thirst for civil rights, freedom, and liberation. AIDS no longer inherently means consumption of total energies, interruption of all gay men's lives, or derailment of a broader community agenda. Instead, because so many continue to be infected and ill, AIDS has been integrated into the community's political and health care work, and a broad agenda is moving full steam ahead.

A QUEST FOR RENEWAL

It was as I flew home to San Francisco from the conference that I realized I was on a quest to discover indications that regeneration was beginning to occur for gay men in America, however subtle and tentative the signs might be. All of a sudden my eyes were opened full-wide, as I searched the pages of gay newspapers, packets of organizational information which appeared daily in my mailbox, and the streets of gay neighborhoods. But, more than anything, I looked to the lives of other gay men for signs of new life emerging.

I began to attend large-scale community events in various parts of the country to seek evidence of revival among the various queer subcultures. During President's Day weekend, I joined 400 "bears" (big, hairy, bearded guys) at the "National Bear Expo" held at a large hotel in San Francisco. A few weeks later I flew to Florida, to attend the "Florida Roundup," a convention of over 1,000 clean and sober queers who participated in twelve-step recovery programs. In May, I made my way to Chicago to check out International Mr. Leather weekend—over 4,000 kinky gay men converging on the Windy City for a Memorial Day weekend of parties, workshops, and social events.

What I discovered on my travels was that the epidemic winter suffered by the nation's gay population had begun to melt into springtime. Don't get me wrong: none of these events ignored or downplayed AIDS. Men walking with canes or transported in wheelchairs were in evidence everywhere. Workshops and special caucuses were held at every event focused on providing support for HIV-positive people. Contestant after contestant in the International Mr. Leather Contest proclaimed his commitment to the fight against AIDS and listed credentials as AIDS educators, fundraisers, and members of ACT-UP. What had changed was that the community was no longer tightly confined, held hostage-like, in the bondage of AIDS. Somehow, it had struggled free from the handcuffs, shrugged off the chains, and stood tall again, ready to take on life itself.

I sat in a workshop at the Florida Roundup and listened to speaker after speaker tell of the struggle to reclaim sexuality amid a world of increasing danger and disgust for gay men's sex lives. Sure, some men first had to spit out their statements of shame, and guilt, and remorse. One man unabashedly told his peers, "Dating in this program is like fishing in the Atlantic Ocean. You might catch something, but would you eat it?" But other men spoke of the naturalness of gay sex, the connections between desire and love, and the moral principles they tried to follow in their erotic relationships.

After the workshop convener shared his own story and spoke defiantly against contemporary forces attempting to rein in male sexuality ("It is entirely natural for me to have gay sex. It is an expression of my love and god-given nature . . . ") the dam came down and the room took on the spirit of a testimonial meeting. One young gay man shared the joy he found as he broke through barriers and began to kiss men for the first time in his life. A man whose lover had died of AIDS spoke of his excitement in dating, and of the thrills he found in rediscovering gay men's sex cultures after a decade apart from it.

In Chicago, amid the heightened erotic energy of International Mr. Leather weekend, I found myself having lunch one afternoon with a short, fit, masculine man from Iowa. We had eyed one another in the hallways of the hotel and, when he entered the restaurant and was told that all tables were full and he'd have to wait to be seated, I signaled him to join me. After ordering lunch (three hamburgers and nothing else), he began to speak to me enthusiastically about his experiences over the weekend. His eyes sparkled as he spoke of the men with whom he'd conversed, danced, dined, and enjoyed sex. He told me of his amazement at seeing such a diverse group of men from so many different parts of the world, who were friendly, hospitable, and "without the attitude you run into all the time when gay guys get together." He regaled me with stories about his sexual escapades, his excitement at experiencing some long-held fantasies, and the reunion he'd had with an ex-lover from twenty years ago whom he hadn't seen in all that time.

Jack's candor and spunk made me comfortable enough to ask questions and, when there was a natural break in his stories, I commented upon his enthusiasm (I think I told him that he sounded like a "pig in shit") and asked him if this were the first time he'd attended an event like this. Because of his wide-eyed excitement and the ingenuous perspective he brought to his observations, I guessed that he had just come out of the leather closet. But he shook his head and said no. In fact, he attended this same event half a dozen times over recent years. I told him that his extreme pleasure in the event and the thrill which he conveyed as he discussed the weekend made me think that he was a "newcomer" to this kind of adventure.

Jack grew quiet for a moment and I watched his thoughts turn inward. He chomped on one of those burgers, then cleared his throat and his voice took on a serious tone. "It surprises me to hear you say that I sound like a kid comin' out for the first time," he said, "but then again it doesn't really surprise me at all. If you'd been at this weekend a year ago, and had the bad luck to invite me to have lunch with you then, you would have had a very different experience. You probably would never had let me join you for a meal again.

"You see, a year ago I was still very caught up in the news that I had AIDS. I'd been diagnosed back in 1989, and I spent about four years feeling sorry for myself and waiting to die. AIDS controlled my moods and my spirit. It told me what to do and when to do it. I felt bitter about my wasted life and angry at everyone—gay or straight, with AIDS or without. I wasn't very pleasant to be around.

"I don't know why I'd come to party weekends like this . . . probably just to sit around and rain on everyone else's parade. I didn't enjoy myself. If I had sex, I complained about it afterwards to anyone who would listen, and if I didn't, I complained then too. I griped about the contest, the men, the weather—everything except the food. I hated men who were having a good time and I sought out the guys who were as depressed and self-pitying as myself. It wasn't attractive.

"Something changed last summer and I still can't explain why or how it happened. But, all of a sudden, I wanted to live again. I quit the job I'd had for ten years and went out on disability. I made a list of all the things I'd wanted to do in my lifetime—see the Grand Canyon, bowl a perfect game, swim in the Carribean, parachute out of an airplane . . . these kinds of things. And then I threw a tent, sleeping bag, and my gear in the back of my pickup truck, and drove off to do as many of these things as God would allow me to do before I died.

"It's been quite a year," he confided. "When it came down to it, I didn't have the nerve to jump out of an airplane, but I did take a balloon ride in Arizona, and I rafted through Grand Canyon, and I visited the reservation where my grandfather was raised. I've been to Hollywood and Alaska, and even Disneyland. And do you know what? I haven't been sick one day this entire year. Sure, I still have to take my medication, and my immune system is still pretty screwed up so I've had all these weird rashes and my mouth fills with thrush every night. But as I picked myself out of the toilet I'd been living in since I was diagnosed and became determined to have a good time, my life changed entirely.

"I have no illusions," he said quietly. "I know some guys think they are going to survive AIDS, but I'm not one of them. This disease is gonna get me, in a few months or a few years. But I'm not gonna sit around and wait. I've made more lists of things I want to do, people I want to see, adventures that await me every day. And the only thing that's gonna stop me will be HIV.

"So, I'm sorry to yack and yack about all of this to you," he chuckled. "I'm sure you didn't invite me to sit with you to hear my long, sad story. But, if you hear enthusiasm in my voice or notice that I seem to enjoy everything that happens, it's because you're talking with a man who is eager to enjoy each day, no matter what happens. If I cruise a hot-looking guy in the elevator and he's not interested, it doesn't get to me anymore. I trust other things are meant for me, and I can't waste my energy on the opportunities I don't have. My focus is entirely on the things that I do get to do." With that as his concluding remark, he pushed back his plate of burgers, signaled the waiter for some iced tea, and sat back and looked at me.

I felt gears shift within my head. Surviving for four years with an AIDS diagnosis left this man with a desire to live a very full life. He wasn't dead yet, and he was damned sure that he was going to embrace all that the world had to offer before the Grim Reaper got him. Why didn't I feel this same calling?

As I traveled and talked with gay and bisexual men throughout different parts of the nation, I saw the greatest determination to reengage with life from men who were infected with HIV. Something about this stage of the epidemic was motivating increasing numbers of men who struggled with the threat of an AIDS diagnosis to seize the day. Uninfected men seemed to be in a vastly different place—still frozen, shut down, chained in the trenches of shell-shocked warfare. One man I spoke with in Louisiana told me that he was determined to wear a red ribbon everywhere he went until the epidemic was over. As he told me more about himself, it became clear to me that this man was bringing AIDS with him wherever he went. Though he was HIV negative, he believed that AIDS had to be brought into every aspect of his life and every aspect of gay community life, if we were ever going to find the cure. In short, he made sure that a disease which wasn't flowing through his bloodstream, was flooding every other part of his life.

My quest to find signs of rejuvenation in the lives of other gay men was a significant component of my return to the land of the living. As I came upon men who were building houses, starting new relationships, adopting children, pursuing career dreams–creating a future for themselves and for future gay men–my own eyes began to look again toward a future. My lover and I began the process of finding a house to buy. I applied and was accepted to graduate school and–unlike the other times I applied during the past dozen years–this time I didn't use the epidemic as my excuse to defer admission; I actually enrolled in a program and began classes. Over a period of many months, I felt the dense shell which had come over me and thickly encapsulated my spirit, begin to weaken, crack, and drop away.

THE MUSIC COMES ALIVE AGAIN

It was in Florida, at a poolside dance party with thousands of clean and sober gay people that my reentry to life occurred. I had traveled to the event by myself, hoping I would find acquaintances with whom I could socialize. Sure enough, my old friend Jim from Provincetown was there. He had been one of a quartet of mentors I had during my late twenties, men who lived on Cape Cod, were openly gay, and led lives which I only dreamed of having. By 1990, Don, Paul, and Stephen–the other three–were dead, and Jim was HIV positive. We hadn't spent much time together over recent years, but we instantly reestablished our connection and filled one another in on the changes in our lives during the intervening years.

I believe the catalyst which reunited me with myself was sent to me that weekend in the person of Jim. Not only was he an example to me of a man who put energy into maintaining health and participating in educational and political efforts of the gay community, but he was alive with life, resilient, and able to integrate sadness and fears into his general profile of cheerfulness, service, and faith. He took me on car rides to South Beach, introduced me to interesting people, and gave me endless advice on my attire. Something about being with Jim—remembering who we were and confronting what we had become—and the spring break atmosphere of Miami Beach, combined to ignite a spark inside me which had dimmed many years ago.

Jim and I attended an "Ice Cream Social" one evening, around the hotel's massive pool, under a clear sky filled with twinkling stars and a full moon. We were first in line for the treats, and I filled my plastic cup with scoops of ice cream and sorbet and topped them with M&M's, butterscotch sauce, and a thick goo of pecans. As we stood on the sidelines and the disc jockey began spinning tunes, we were surprised to discover that he was focusing on the music of our earlier years: Sylvester, Diana Ross, the Village People, Grace Jones, Thelma Houston, Patti Labelle, Laura Branigan, Donna Summer.

We moved onto the dance floor, as the beat of the music combined with the sugar pumping into my veins and the warm night air to open up some of the padlocked vessels inside of me. Somehow my feet were able to dance to the music, connect with its rhythms in a way they'd rebelled against over the past few years. My memory returned to me, not as a source of sentimentality or regret, but as a part of myself which was able to function again and provide me with the gift of remembering who I was and informing me of whom I could be once again. The heart that I thought was lost forever, shattered a dozen times by the epidemic and then broken again, began to throb along with the beat of the music, and once again it opened wide inside of me.

Under those tall palm trees amid the balmy breezes, the music came alive for me again, as Jim and I danced to the familiar melodies of the past: "I'm a victim of the very song I sing . . . ," "Too many broken hearts in the world . . . ," "Love taught me who was the boss. . . . " His eyes connected with mine when the Abba medley started and I'm sure our thoughts were on similar souls when Dream Factory sang out:

> We'll always be together, however far it seems.
> Love never ends: We'll always be together
> Together in Electric Dreams.

But it was when Patrick Hernandez's deep voice boomed over the speakers singing "Born to be Alive," that I lit up—fully alive for the first time in a dozen years. I could tell myself finally that awful things had happened, the men the music sparked me to remember were now dead, and the dreams I once had had been mutilated beyond recognition. But I was alive and it was Spring Break in Miami Beach, and the music was wonderful, and the friendship inspiring. I felt myself reentering my body and my life, as if returning after being beamed up to a UFO and psychically possessed for a dozen years. It was then that spirit once again filled me, and the legacy available to all survivors of disasters–the return of the possibility of again living and thriving–came to me, like a wave of salty sea water wildly washing over me, giving me a moment to catch my breath, then rolling over me again.

Once the music had come alive for me again, I began to notice signs of community-wide regeneration everywhere I went. Rebirth was affirmed by the incredible eruption of organizing among subpopulations within the gay community–queer youth, Bears, African-American lesbians and gay men, bisexual activists. As I sorted through the flood of cultural work produced by lesbians, gay men, and bisexuals, attending films and plays, art exhibitions and literary readings, I found evidence of the rebirth of community life beyond suffering and beyond AIDS. I was peering at the world through new lenses, and I liked what I saw.

My search for intelligent life took the form of travels outside my hometown because I thought that the vast toll the epidemic had taken on San Francisco ensured that the City would be the last place to experience a revival of gay life. Perhaps my personal circumstances dictated my worldview, but I viewed the city–and particularly the gay neighborhood in which I lived, the Castro–as bleak, depressed, and weighted down by the decimation of the epidemic.

Yet a visit from my dear friend Tom opened my eyes to a different vision. Tom is an openly gay high-level appointee in the Clinton Administration. The day he was slated to begin his job was the day his partner–the love of his life–died of AIDS. He'd suffered the loss terribly. After the funeral was over, possessions sorted through, and initial days of mourning were completed, Tom threw himself into an intense work schedule, spending the week in high-level meetings in Washington and the weekends touring the nation giving speeches.

His travels brought him to San Francisco about a year after his lover's death and we carved out an afternoon and evening to spend together, catching up and touring through the Castro. We walked up and down Market Street on a hot May afternoon, cruising, joking, and sharing mundane details of our current lives on separate coasts. It was only when we stopped for cold glasses of iced tea at a sidewalk café that Tom reflected on the city he hadn't really seen in about five years.

"It's really changed," he declared. "The last time I was here was in 1989, right after you moved to the Castro. I remember how sad everything seemed–dirty, decadent, depressed. It was like walking the grounds of an asylum, or the halls of a hospital after an airplane crash. Everyone seemed sullen, lots of stores were vacant, and the whole spirit of the place alternated between solemn and funereal or manic and drunk. I hated being here and couldn't understand how you could live in this neighborhood and work at an AIDS organization in this city. But now it feels so different, as if someone has lifted a thick curtain off the neighborhood and allowed the sun to shine again. It feels like summertime has arrived after a very long and cold winter."

We stood at the crossroads of Market and Castro in the late afternoon sun. I gazed down the Castro Street hill toward 18th Street. Tom was right: the neighborhood *had* come alive again. While the streets never stopped teeming with men, the energy had gone through the series of unsettling shifts that he had described. Now it felt upbeat again but not crazed or manic. The district was filled with bookstores, New Age shops, burger joints, and queer clothing markets. Almost a dozen coffee shops had emerged in recent years, replacing bars and discos as the primary site for rendezvous and flirtations. The lesbian owner of a company offering walking tours of gay San Francisco passed by, leading a half dozen tourists wearing pink triangle shirts and carrying disposable cameras.

The Board of Supervisors had just voted to allow the Bank of America building, a massive landmark which served as the centerpiece of the neighborhood, to be converted into "The Life Center," a multi-organizational AIDS service center which would also house a franchise of a local bagel chain. While major opposition to the project was vocalized by competing merchants, I heard plenty of grumbling about placing a monument which screamed out "People are dying!" in the middle of the Castro. Would it attract more homeless and poor people? Do we want the neighborhood and our communal identity to be defined by AIDS? Isn't the Castro more than a disease?

As I gazed down Castro Street, I realized that the new center would be an appropriate addition to the neighborhood. Sure it would make visible the continuing existence of illness and death among us, but AIDS was an ongoing fact of life, at least for now. The Castro district, with its half dozen gyms, various newsstands and magazine shops, florists and health food stores, could bear the weight of an AIDS-designated building. In fact, it felt to me as if this was an apt complement to the other venues in the area and served to complete our newly emerging communal identity. Yes, the gay community continued to struggle with AIDS, but we also had pizza, and crystals, and vitamins, and tit-rings. We had wheelchairs and Doc Marten's, latte and hip-hop music, performance art and freedom rings, kitty cats and flattops. If the neighborhood was dotted with churches, roommate services, clean and sober hangouts, and even a sex club, it certainly could sustain an AIDS service center, especially one which was called "The Life Center," which seemed to conceptualize AIDS as focused on life rather than death.

Tom turned my attention down Market Street, to the thick line of husky date palm trees which had been planted about a year and a half earlier. He remarked on their beauty and the function they seemed to serve defining the neighborhood and capturing the slightly quirky and flamboyant spirit of the gay ghetto. A few of them hadn't taken to their new locations and appeared to have died, their fronds dried and cracked, withering in the California sun. This seemed appropriate too, to place death and dying directly in the public eye without needing it to be hidden, denied, or ignored.

As we strolled past them, I thought that somehow these trees were the perfect symbol of contemporary gay life in America: bold, confrontational, and celebratory, while still struck by the powerful imprint of mortality. The landscape redefines itself; the neighborhood comes alive; the community regenerates.

CONCEPTUALIZING A COLLECTIVE FUTURE

What kind of future lies ahead for gay men in America? In twenty-five years, at the 50th anniversary of Stonewall, what will we think when we look back? What kinds of realistic possibilities exist for us?

There may or may not be a cure or a vaccine for HIV disease in the next quarter-century. In either case, gay men's lives have been irretrievably altered by the epidemic and we cannot change that. We cannot bring the dead back to life. The connection between male homosexuality and contagion in the public mind will remain for generations. Our relationship to pleasure and sexuality cannot return to what it was before the intervention of HIV. The gay male cultures we enjoyed in the 1970s will never return. We are different people now than we were a dozen years ago. I expect in another quarter century, we will be still more different.

Several portraits of life in old age come to my mind as I gaze ahead and consider possibilities for surviving gay men. Some will likely grow into bitter men, forever angry and resentful at the robbed potential of our generation. Others may remain mute, unable to discuss our lives because the overload of pain has permanently locked memories deep inside. These men will live out their years with closed hearts, capable of only a narrow range of emotions. Still other gay men will continuously revel in nostalgia, creating an ever-more-elaborate myth of the golden years which we shared with friends and lovers long gone.

Young people who survived Nazi death camps half a century ago, now in their old age appear to exhibit a wide range of characteristics: some are shut down and withdrawn while others are reflective and pensive; some are enraged and seek revenge while others appear remarkably forgiving. During a recent visit to Israel, I had several opportunities to speak with survivors; I also viewed films and videotapes in which others told their stories. Now in their seventies, eighties, and nineties, these men and women display a series of emotions and hold varied perspectives on the Holocaust. Some have never talked about what they experienced and witnessed during those years. Others have participated in efforts to confront history and preserve it for future generations. While some appear suspicious, distrustful, and easily angered, others are calm, warm, and open hearted. I was struck particularly by several who seem to have found ways to integrate the horror which occurred in their younger years and move forward.

Finding ways to regain mental health and perspective will be challenging, but gay men are not alone in these tasks. We are part of a large and increasing population of Americans who somehow manage to face the bizarre psychic deformations and powerful existential questions which arise in the wake of extreme events. We stand alongside political refugees from Eastern Europe, immigrants who had survived the Cultural Revolution in China or terrorism in Central America, combat veterans from World War II, Korea, Vietnam, and the Middle East. Our plight is shared by abused children and battered women, as well as people who live their entire lives victimized by poverty, gang violence, and drugs. We are not alone in our suffering.

Gay men who have lived through the decimation of AIDS face painful choices which will determine our individual and collective futures. We can proceed along paths of denial, shut down, and hysteria as our psyches continue to be pulverized by whatever horrors the coming years hold for us, or we can attempt an intervention which may offer hope.

I hope to live my middle-age years with the ability to be present and engaged by life in a way I haven't been able to be for most of the past decade. While I will never forget how this epidemic happened and the people who have died, I seek a life beyond AIDS and beyond suffering. I want to acknowledge the huge losses to my life and I want to move beyond rage and exhaustion. I hope to continue to contribute to the community's efforts against AIDS, but I don't want the disease to define me and be the central motivation of my existence.

When I enter old age, I hope I will be able to speak to people about the worlds in which I've lived and look back with a perspective that integrates anger and grief with appreciation and even humor. Like many, I am ambivalent about the thought of serving as a surviving witness to the disaster of these early years of the epidemic. I want the world never to forget what has occurred, but I feel conflicted about taking on the role of witness to decimation. This was not a role I ever wanted to play. In the multiplex theatre of life, I did not buy a ticket to this movie.

I think I will be most happy if I am able to see continuing evidence of the rebirth of a culture and communal life for gay men, which is informed by disease though not held captive by it. I believe this is possible, even before a cure is developed.

Hopeful signs of life already are appearing, particularly in newly evolving cultures and traditions of young gay men. These are not the same worlds which I inhabited when I came out in the 1970s and they will not be enriched by participation of significant numbers of men of my gay generation. I may be an observer or a visitor to these new worlds, but I will never be a citizen. Nevertheless this evidence of the continuing cycle of gay male life restores my hope and affirms my belief in the sacred nature of desire and my pride in human resilience.

To see men embrace and love each other in response to neither loss nor terror revives my dreams from a life long ago. To watch masses of men dance together, celebrating raw life-giving powers of music and desire forces me to acknowledge that the human spirit is not easily subdued. When once again two men can kiss hard on the mouth as neither victims nor survivors nor captives of stealth terror, then peace and order will settle over the tribe and life will again move forward.

Index